# Teachers Doing Research:
# Practical Possibilities

# Teachers Doing Research: Practical Possibilities

Edited by

**Gail Burnaford**
**Joseph Fischer**
**David Hobson**
*National-Louis University*

**LEA** LAWRENCE ERLBAUM ASSOCIATES, PUBLISHERS
1996 Mahwah, New Jersey

Lawrence Erlbaum Associates, Inc., Publishers
10 Industrial Avenue
Mahwah, New Jersey 07430-2262

Cover design by Gail Silverman

Pictures from THE INCREDIBLE PAINTING OF FELIX CLOUSSEAU by Jon Agee.
Copyright © 1988 by Jon Agee. Reprinted by permission of Farrar, Straus, & Giroux, Inc.

**Library of Congress Cataloging-in-Publication Data**

Teachers doing research : practical possibilities / edited by Gail
    Burnaford, Joseph Fischer, and David Hobson.
        p.    cm.
    Includes bibliographical references and index.
    ISBN 0-8058-2254-2 (pbk. : alk. paper)
    1. Action research in education—United States.  2. Teaching—
United States.  I. Burnaford, Gail E.  II. Fischer, Joseph, 1926–
III. Hobson, David.
LB1028.24.T4264   1996
370′.78—dc20                                        95-24866
                                                      CIP

Books published by Lawrence Erlbaum Associates are printed on acid-free paper,
and their bindings are chosen for strength and durability.

Printed in the United States of America
10  9  8  7  6  5  4  3  2  1

*We dedicate this book*
*to the hundreds of teachers we have known*
*in the Chicago area schools*
*who have become,*
*and continue to be,*
*teacher–researchers.*
*We have learned much from them and with them*
*about what it means to be lifelong learners.*

# CONTENTS

# PREFACE

*All the classes I've attended (and taught), all the curriculum guides I've followed,*
*all the lesson plans I've written, and all the texts I've read didn't mean anything*
*to me* personally *until I became a teacher-researcher.*

Mohr and McLean (1987, p. 55)

Several years ago, we attended a conference for educational researchers. During
that conference, we heard the story of a classroom teacher who had come to
the meetings with the hope of finding "research validation" for the wonderful
renewal and change that had been happening the last few years in her school
and classroom. She talked to many university professors and attended numerous
sessions at the conference concerning the latest research on effective schools,
restructuring schools, and classroom change. But, somehow, she couldn't find
the precise "validation" she was looking for. Although she learned much about
what was happening in schools and classrooms across the country, none of the
examples exactly expressed what she and her students were learning and doing.

Eventually, a teacher–researcher overheard this teacher discussing her dilemma and chimed in. "*You and your students* are the only real experts about
what's been occurring in your classroom and *you* can report what's been happening to other teachers. That's what we as teacher–researchers do!" This
comment changed the way that classroom teacher thought about educational
research. This story of a teacher who had been engaged in inquiry and change,
but who had not viewed herself as a researcher, helped us think about why this
book is important and who might enjoy reading it.

This book is intended for classroom and apprentice teachers who are interested in knowing more about ways to participate with students in classroom
research. We hasten to note that you will find no formulas or prescriptions for
this process because each group of students and teachers is different. The way

in which the research in a classroom unfolds and is documented is unique to that setting and that group of researchers. But we believe that you will find a repertoire of ideas to guide you in this journey. You will also find many examples of teachers' research in this text. The variety of their experiences and learnings reveals the possibilities for inquiry that are available to teachers who question and learn through their experiences.

Carol Avery, an elementary school teacher–researcher, claims that through research in her classroom, she finally discovered that "learning is a messy, mumbled, nonlinear, recursive, and sometimes unpredictable process" (Avery, in Olson, 1990, p. 43).[1] We know that the business of teacher research does not proceed smoothly and in an orderly fashion along a predetermined and immutable path. Rather, it unfolds as students and teachers discuss alternatives, plan for action, and evaluate what is happening. Throughout the research, all who are involved search for meaning in what they are doing. The making of meaning is the real learning, and it does not often occur neatly and easily. What attracts many teachers to inquiry about their field is the same thing that calls scientists and artists to theirs: Teachers want to know and to create; they are curious about their practice. Teachers hope that their research will inform that practice and lead to better teaching and learning.

We also maintain a deep belief that research is a collaborative process with students and teachers as co-researchers. As students become co-researchers, teachers can see themselves as co-learners. All take ownership of the exploration; students are no longer specimens to *be* researched. They *are* part of the research team. Classroom research is also collaborative in the sense that teachers can share in each other's inquiry. Teacher colleagues can provide a strong and reassuring sounding board for ideas; they can also raise questions and suggestions for continuing the conversation and the growth.

Research can be seen then as the search for practical possibilities—teachers and students searching themselves, their classrooms, and their worlds for educative meaning. Such meanings are contextual and often socially constructed. Research takes on new significance for those in schools as it becomes participatory and invitational.

We hope that this text will be useful to you as you engage in research. We invite you to continue the dialogue with other teachers and students on what you are doing and thinking as you participate in classroom inquiry. Sharing what we learn and what we know will strengthen our profession and validate what we do as informed and reflective teachers.

---

[1]Avery, C. S. (1990). Learning to research/Researching to learn. In M. W. Olson, (Ed.), *Opening the door to classroom research* (pp. 32–44). Newark, DE: International Reading Association.

# ACKNOWLEDGMENTS

Three years ago we sat down at the Bean Counter Cafe and began to discuss an idea for a book. It would be a book that would synthesize what we have learned with teachers about doing research in classrooms. It would be a book in which teachers and teacher–educators could explore the notion of teacher action research that is personally meaningful and engaging, and yet systematic and potentially helpful to the profession at large.

We were three university professors, working in a masters program in which intact groups of teachers remain with core instructors for a 2-year course of study. Teacher action research is a major course strand through this program. For the past 17 years, our institution had offered this graduate degree in which teachers have the rare opportunity to connect the theoretical to the practical through action research projects in their own classrooms. We, as facilitators of that process, felt that we had something to contribute to the knowledge base about classroom-based action research.

After just a few cups of coffee, we realized that this book could not be written solely by university professors who, although uniquely and intimately acquainted with teacher action research through the masters program, were nonetheless not the ones who engaged in that process with children. (We are, however, currently involved in action research on our *own* process of teaching at the university level.) We knew that this text would be most informative if it was a blend of the processes and contexts for such teacher action research—from the perspectives of both teacher–educators and classroom teachers who are engaging in research.

We would like to acknowledge the contributions of those teachers who are now published authors. Nancy Brankis, Vida Schaffel, Rick Moon, Marianne Newton, Doris Nash, Loleta Ruffin, Nancy Hubbard, Craig Hill, Kelli Visconti, Suzanne Goff, and Emmerich Koller encouraged us, informed us, and helped us look at teacher action research in thousands of ways. They helped us realize that we were writing about *many* processes, not just one prescribed method of inquiry.

We wish to thank Donna Midlowski for her hours on the computer. She worked with enthusiasm and intuition that saved us all. Thanks also to Naomi Silverman, our editor at Lawrence Erlbaum Associates, who widened our perspective to think about teacher action research and its impact upon the field of education.

Finally, we wish to acknowledge the powerful contributions of our colleagues in the Interdisciplinary Studies Department at National-Louis University. With peers such as James Beane, Smokey Daniels, Ethel Migra, and Janet Miller we could not fail to learn about what it means to be a learner and a teacher.

Since that first encounter in a coffee shop 3 years ago, we have had many sessions, over countless cups of coffee, thinking and rethinking, revising and rewriting, editing and advising. We have learned first hand what a collaboration entails and wish to thank each other for this opportunity.

*Gail Burnaford*
*Joseph Fischer*
*David Hobson*

# ABOUT THE CONTRIBUTORS

**Nancy Brankis** has been a classroom teacher for 15 years. She currently teaches elementary school in Lincolnshire, Illinois. She recently received a Fellowship in Gifted Education for her graduate work, which focused on the integration of Journaling Across the Curriculum. She has conducted staff developing workshops at her school concerning the Development of Reading Strategies, Odyssey of the Mind, and The Value of Journaling with Students.

**Gail Burnaford** is an associate professor in the Interdisciplinary Studies Department of National-Louis University in Evanston, Illinois, where she also teaches Literature for Children and Middle School Curriculum courses. She previously taught high school and middle school English/Language Arts and preschool. Dr. Burnaford also taught at Kennesaw State College and Georgia State University in Atlanta. Her research interests include teacher action research, curriculum integration, middle school curriculum, and children's literature. She has published articles in *The Middle School Journal, Music Educators Journal, Best Practice, Research in Middle Level Education,* and *Action in Teacher Education*. Her previous book, *Images of Schoolteachers in Twentieth-Century America,* coedited with Pamela Bolotin Joseph, is also published by Lawrence Erlbaum Associates.

**Joseph Fischer** is an associate professor and department chair in the Interdisciplinary Studies Department of National-Louis University in Evanston, Illinois. He is one of the funding instructors in the Graduate Field-Based Program in which teacher action research is a primary component of professional development. He has had a long relationship with the Chicago public schools and continues to be a constant involved with staff development and literature. He has lived and studied for many years in South America and Germany. His research interests include teacher action research, teacher centers, and comparative education.

**Suzanne Goff** teaches second grade in Wilmette, Illinois, a northern suburb of Chicago. As a 21-year veteran, her involvement in her profession has ranged from curriculum writing and parent/teacher networking to teacher association officer. Her masters' program, which featured an action research project, has stimulated her to continue research in the area of school culture and staff development through teacher-to-teacher support.

**Craig Hill** is currently an assistant dean and science teacher at Lake Forest Academy in Lake Forest, Illinois. He received his Masters in Education from National-Louis University and his BA from Lake Forest College. In 1995, he presented his teacher action research at the American Educational Researchers Association Annual Meeting in San Francisco.

**David Hobson** is a professor in the Interdisciplinary Studies Department of National-Louis University in Evanston, Illinois. He was a founder and long-time director of the Graduate Center for Human Development and Learning at Fairleigh Dickinson University. As a former middle and high school social studies teacher, he taught psychology and sociology to adolescents. Dr. Hobson has conducted numerous workshops throughout the country on journalkeeping and collaborative professional development. His research interests include teacher action research through collaboration, journals as tool for writing, and self study for teacher educators.

**Nancy Hubbard** has been involved in education for 13 years as a teacher and counselor. She received her BA from Carthage College and her Masters in Education from National-Louis University where she is presently pursuing a doctorate in Instructional Leadership. Currently, Ms. Hubbard is a third grade teacher in Batavia at McWayne Elementary School, a new concept school where multiple intelligences are the basis for learning.

**Susan Jungck** is an associate professor in Foundations and Research and Interdisciplinary Studies at National-Louis University in Evanston, Illinois. Her interests are focused on curriculum theory from foundational perspectives and interpretive and critical research. The opportunities she has had to work with teachers and college faculties conducting action research in both the U.S. and Thailand have contributed to her own understanding of the power of research for critical change. Dr. Jungck received her doctorate in Curriculum and Instruction from the University of Wisconsin-Madison.

**Emmerich Koller** teaches German at the Glenbrook High School in northern Illinois and at Northwestern University's Center for Talent Development. Mr.

Koller earned degrees in Philosophy, German, and education from New York State, Roosevelt, and National-Louis Universities, respectively. In 1989 he was the recipient of the Certificate of Merit from the Goethe House, N.Y. and the National German Teacher's Association for outstanding achievements in furthering and encouraging the study of the German language and culture in the United States. In 1993 he received the Distinguished Teacher Award from the White House Commission on Presidential Scholars.

**Richard Moon** is a physical education teacher for grades one through eight in Mundelein, Illinois. A 15-year veteran, Rick taught P.E. at the Diamond Lake Migrant School. He coaches boys and girls basketball, track and field, and boys volleyball. He completed a teacher research project focusing on gender relationships and competition/cooperation in physical fitness in 1992. His topic was especially of interest to him as he is the father of two girls, Amy, age four, and Kelsey, age two, who feature in his research project.

**Marianne Newton**, **Doris Nash**, and **Loleta Ruffin** teach at Beacon Hills School in Chicago Heights, Illinois. Nash teaches second grade children with special needs including behavioral disorders and learning disabilities. Newton is working with second graders with communication disorders. Ruffin is the inclusion multi-grades resource teacher working in several second grade classrooms.

**Vida Schaffel** (Cookie) has been teaching in Chicago since the early 1960s. She left the profession to raise her family and returned to the classroom in the mid-1980s after which she earned state certification in the field of English as a second language. She received her Masters in Education in Curriculum and Instruction in 1993 after conducting a teacher research project in her classroom involving literacy and language learning.

**Linda Tafel** is dean of the National College of Education of National-Louis University. She had previously served as a professor in the College of Education in Interdisciplinary Studies and Educational Leadership. She has been an active consultant in school reform initiatives in the Chicago area and teaches in the doctoral program in instructional leadership with particular interest in staff development and related issues. Dr. Tafel holds a doctorate in Curriculum and Supervision from Northern Illinois University.

**Kelli Visconti** is a fifth grade teacher in Skokie, Illinois, where she has been teaching for 5 years. Formerly, she taught for the Archdiocese of Chicago at the fourth grade level. In her research project she investigated attitudes of society toward teachers, coupling her analysis with an in-depth study of teachers' own feelings about the profession.

# 1

# BEGINNING WITH THE SELF: USING AUTOBIOGRAPHY AND JOURNAL WRITING IN TEACHER RESEARCH

David Hobson
National-Louis University

*The personal is most universal.*

—Carl Rogers (1961, p. 3)

## ONE STARTS WITH ONESELF

Researchers have been accustomed to distancing themselves from their work as if such separation would somehow render the work more plausible, credible, perhaps even more "scientific." We teachers often possess narrow notions about doing research from our university experiences where use of the word "I" was forbidden and we were taught that such expressions as "the researcher noted . . ." and "the investigator found . . ." were more appropriate. Happily, times have changed, and today the idea of "teacher-as-researcher" has gained greater value, not only in the educational research community, but also among classroom teachers who realize that investigations conceived, implemented, and evaluated by actual teachers in real classrooms among live schoolchildren promise to better stand the tests of practicality and personal relevance. This is research to be used by teachers, not merely displayed for purposes beyond the classroom.

Sometimes we are so close to a subject or an activity we can scarcely see it. One of the fundamental benefits of doing teacher research is the opportunity it affords us for perceiving our world a little more freshly. One of the purposes of the research process is to render the familiar a little strange. We want both things at once, to be close to the matter at hand, but also to develop the perspective that comes from a degree of distance. This is especially problematic in the world of the classroom teacher where what one *does* is so close to who one *is*.

Kurt Lewin (1948) asserted that the *person* stands at the center of his or her own life space, and that an understanding of that life can only be accomplished by beginning with the perspective of that individual. Lewin is also remembered for bringing the *action* into action research. Through action, teachers come to understand what is really happening in their classrooms. If you want to understand something, try to change it. This matter of change, of actually doing something even as one is studying it, is central to classroom-based teacher-conducted research. The teacher–researcher is not just standing back and observing some pristine phenomena from a distance. No, the teacher is in the midst of a group of children, and is doing: taking action, making things happen. Both of these ideas are central to teachers conceiving and implementing their own research among the students in their classrooms. One starts always with the person, student or teacher, exactly where he or she is, and tries to *do* something.

Many teachers are interested more in the doing than the saying. So much is said about good practice, but teachers tend to be very concerned with what is done. Argyris (1982) brought considerable attention to this seeming dichotomy when he described the differences between theories-espoused and theories-in-use. The first is comprised of what we think and say about what we do, whereas the latter must be constructed directly from observing our behavior, from what we actually do.

This kind of work is personally grounded in a teacher's own experience and is expressed in his or her own voice. Reflection is a process of making sense of one's experience and telling the story of one's journey. A teacher's current research possesses a history with stepping stones that have led to the present and constitute a path of inquiry that can bridge the gap between teaching and researching. In order to bring the two more closely together in the minds of teachers, teacher research needs to be thoughtful and intentional. Vida Schaffel feels it is important to situate her research in her own life. As a teacher who left the profession for a few years to raise children, she brings a real-life perspective to her research writing (see Vida Schaffel's Teacher Research). For Nancie Atwell, the shift toward greater reflection occurred when she began writing: "Writing fuels my best insight. It makes me understand things I did not know before I wrote," she explains (Atwell, in Patterson, Santa, Short, & Smith, 1993, p. ix). Our experience tells us, however, that finding the time to write is difficult during a typical school day and that it helps to match the rhythm of school life to the schedule of writing up one's research. As one teacher commented to us, "Writing up research is a summer job!" Some of the practical ways teachers have found to write even as they teach are described in this chapter. Writing is a valuable tool for reflection.

Schon (1983, 1987) carried this line of inquiry further and developed some ideas about reflective teaching, a concept that includes both *reflection-in-action* and *reflection-on-action*. The first of these is "reflection on one's spontaneous ways of thinking and acting, undertaken in the midst of action to guide further action" (1987, p. 22), whereas the second consists of reflection after the event, and includes a kind of metacognition, or thinking about the thoughts and reflections you were having during the action. A teacher who reflects *on action* after a lesson is over might consider: What kinds of decisions did I make during the lesson? What responses and reactions from the students affected those decisions? What was I thinking about and feeling during the lesson? That's what Schon refers to as *reflection-on-action*.

It is thought, of course, that reflection leads to better action (Schon, 1983) and that the reflective teacher is a more effective teacher (Grant & Zeichner, 1984). The point of all this is obvious, we teachers benefit from paying more careful attention both to what we say and do, and how these two elements work together. Teacher inquiry helps a teacher practice both *reflection-in-action* and *reflection-on-action*; both are really forms of research.

In his work on identifying the various intelligences, Gardner (1983) provided a framework for considering how human beings, including teachers and their students, learn and grow. He named five basic types of intelligence: logical–mathematical, linguistic, bodily–kinesthetic, musical, and spatial. Beyond these five, Gardner suggests two "higher intelligences," called "*inter*-personal" (the ability to notice and make distinctions among others, to look outward—see chapter 4 on creating a community for teacher research) and "*intra*personal" (relating with oneself, looking inward). These two forms of intelligence are intimately intermingled, neither able to develop without the other, and each dependent on the other. Gardner (1983) saw the sense of self as the balance struck by the individual between the promptings of inner feelings and the pressures of other persons. A developed sense of self is seen to be "the highest achievement of human beings, a crowning capacity which supersedes and presides over other more mundane and partial forms of intelligence" (pp. 242–243). These higher forms, put most simply, are "the capacity to know oneself and to know others" (p. 243). It is through use of these higher aspects of the self that we manage *how* we learn.

Here, of course, is an essential link with teaching and teacher research. Teachers are perfectly positioned at the intersection between these two domains, the inner and the outer. Teachers are very important factors in classrooms and much of what they know and think and do in their classrooms is dependent on their knowing of themselves, almost as, if you will, finely tuned and deeply resonating instruments. Each teacher brings a lifetime of experience, as teacher and student, in a variety of schooling environments, to the present situation. Even if new to the profession, teachers carry their experience of schooling to the present tasks. Teachers take in a multiplicity of stimuli continuously; they select and sort and make meaning all day long; they act on what they learn and "know" with those around themselves. Teachers are continually researching, working from the outside and the inside; looking outward and inward, perpetually moving back and forth between these two higher intelligences: the inter- and intrapersonal dimensions of human knowing.

It is especially important for a teacher to develop a deep understanding of how these dimensions develop because it is the teacher who has responsibility for facilitating such development in students. The teacher is a very visible model whom students watch carefully. A most obvious place to begin developing such an understanding is with oneself.

> The most meaningful image of action research derived from our teaching is a continuous, conscious attempt to seek increased meaning and direction in our lives with students, and in our own personal lives. (Schubert & Schubert, 1984, p. 5)

One of the primary teachings of Piaget was simply that knowledge is constructed by the learner and that new experience must be assimilated by the learner in ways that make sense to the learner. Teachers everywhere know this to be true, whether describing themselves or their students: One learns oneself. "All genuine learning is, in the last analysis, self-learning, self-discipline" (Cantor, 1953, p. 67). Knowledge must be constructed by the individual. Rogers (1961) put it this way: "The only learning which significantly influences behavior is self-discovered, self-appropriated learning" (p. 455). Allport (1955) suggested that it is the process of becoming that determines what is real for the person, and that self-awareness plays an important role in the drawing along of this becoming. Often, such self-awareness exists in the form of intuitive knowing, a sense of rightness and congruity, an emerging gestalt, or a growing sense of what "wants" to happen.

If we consider what this could mean with respect to teacher research, we might take a closer look at exactly how a research idea comes to mind. A teacher observes the classroom, the students, and himself or herself for a few weeks, asking the question: What wants to happen here?

Gail Burnaford tells a story about her early teaching days that demonstrates this notion of research based on observation. Sometimes, "what wants to happen" is unexpected and unplanned, as Burnaford's experience illustrates.

> I began teaching high school English in 1973. It was a time of student rights, choice and autonomy in curriculum, and attention to the interests of the individual child. Consequently, our department offered students a smorgasbord of possible electives which they could apply toward their English requirement. One such minicourse stands out in my mind.
>
> It was the last period of the day, and I was aware that those who would be sitting in my class for the course *Biography and Autobiography* would be the ones who had failed to sign up for any other course; they would be the students who attended school only sporadically and found little relevance in what was going on there for their own lives. Sure enough, when I walked into the room that day, I saw 37 adolescent bodies, all but four of whom were male, and most of whom could not comfortably fit into the chair-desks provided for them. There I was with my syllabus neatly typed and duplicated under my arm and a collection of biographies/autobiographes of famous people ready to roll. We would be reading about

people such as Benjamin Franklin, Thomas Jefferson, Clara Barton, and, yes, Florence Nightingale. After all, that's what the course outline prescribed and I was ready and willing!

When I looked out on that sea of faces, I can remember thinking, "Gail, you'd better think again." I asked the class if they knew what the terms "Biography" and "Autobiography" meant. A few hands passively went up in the air. Then, with a definite sense of trepidation, I seized the pile of carefully crafted syllabi, dropped them into the metal trash can beside the desk, and asked, "So, who do you want to learn about?"

With that, the room began to come a bit more alive. We brainstormed people they had heard something about during this turbulent time in their own history. They wanted to know what this guy Cesar Chavez was all about and what did he have to do with grapes? They wanted to learn more about Martin Luther King, Jr., Bobby Kennedy, and Malcolm X. They wanted to find out about Billie Jean King and what happened to Karen Carpenter. I asked them whether they thought they could write the story of their own lives so that they too would have an autobiography to add to the bookshelf and some hesitantly said, "Yea, that might be a good idea." With that, we were on our way. (Burnaford, personal communication, 1973)

One never learns it once and for all, as every teacher knows: "The discovery is never made; it is always making" (Dewey, 1929, p. 76). Working classroom teachers know that inquiries into practice are continuous and engage us in daily ways. It's especially important that preservice teachers realize that the discovery is never complete; we are constantly learning throughout our careers from our students, colleagues, and from our own experiences. Dewey (1929) counseled that the practical inquiry of teachers should be the *substance* of educational research. It is the "knowledge that enters into the heart, head, and hands of educators" that should be the material of our study, and that renders the educative process "more humane, more truly educational than it was before" (pp. 76–77). Today, as classroom research conducted by teachers in their own classrooms becomes more pervasive, Dewey's vision is even more compelling. His was "unmistakably a vision of the teacher continuously pursuing self-education in the course of the act of teaching" (Schubert & Schubert, 1984, p. 12). As Dewey (1929) put it, "each day of teaching ought to enable a teacher to revise and better in some respects the objectives aimed at in previous work. . . . Education is a mode of life, of *action.* [It] renders those who engage in the act more intelligent, more thoughtful, more aware of what they are about" (p. 74, 75–76, italics added).

Asserting one of the great ideas from the social sciences, field theorist Lewin (1948) found that decision is the link between motivation and action. Participation in the *decision* to take some action makes a difference in how invested one is in actually carrying the action through. To modern educators, this concept provides an essential linchpin to the practice of involving learners (including teacher–researchers) in the planning of their own learning.

Schubert (1992) told the story of how he got his first teaching job. He recalled his interview where, when asked how he would develop a program with a "multitext approach," he answered smoothly, despite the fact that he had never heard the term before. After securing the job, he did indeed use a multitext approach to teaching and became committed to multiple perspectives in his teaching—a commitment that was also shared by his young students. Schubert now describes his multitext approach as a form of teacher lore that he has to share with other teachers. Similarly, he has accumulated a wealth of teacher lore from other teachers he has known throughout his life who have influenced him.

Teacher lore, Schubert (1992) explained, "portrays and interprets ways in which teachers deliberate and reflect and it portrays teachers in action" (p. 9). He continued: "Teacher lore refers to knowledge, ideas, insights, feelings, and understandings of teachers as they reveal their guiding beliefs, share approaches, relate consequences of their teaching, offer aspects of their philosophy of teaching, and provide recommendations for educational policy makers" (p. 9). Schubert's story of his first job interview reveals one piece of the larger story of his view of learning and the practice of effective teaching. His story prompts other teachers to tell their stories about how they learned to do what they do.

## AUTOBIOGRAPHICAL NARRATIVE (TELLING STORIES)

Teachers can almost always be found sharing anecdotes about their experiences with children. This telling of stories can become a vital part of doing teacher research. According to Schubert (1992) it seems "that telling anecdotes . . . enables the teller to bring experience into language. In this way, we can come to terms, as teachers, with something significant, something worth telling, something important . . ." (p. 204).

The parallels between teacher stories and teacher action research seems clear from Schubert's explanation. As teachers share their beliefs and approaches and as they reflect and act upon their reflections, they are engaging in a form of teacher action research. Their actions may have influence and impact, not only upon students, but also on policy makers and others who study teaching praxis.

One way our mind makes sense of the world is through narrative. Our narratives include our insights, searches for meaning, and the connectedness we find in the world. We tell stories in order to see how others conceive of the world, and to share the journey of storytelling with others. Jalongo (1992) described a teacher story as a metaphor for change; teacher action research grasps that metaphor, brings it to life, then perhaps creates a new metaphor that enriches his or her teaching. Autobiographical narrative could be construed as the conceptual center of teacher action research. Narrative asks the question: What does this research have to do with me?

The telling of stories as a framework for teacher research also provides a context for viewing the teaching and learning that occurs in schools through a critical lens. One reason for conducting educational research is to "illuminate discrepancies or inequities or silences within aspects of teaching, curricular, and learning processes" (Miller, 1992, p. 166). Looking at our own autobiographies, reliving our own experiences with inequity, power, and authority in schools, offers us the opportunity to inform ourselves further and move forward to change situations in which today's students experience injustice. This aspect of educational research can be the work of teacher researchers who look at the world of teaching critically. Apple (1993) noted that "critical work needs to be done in an 'organic' way." He said, "the role of the 'unattached inteligentsia' seems a bit odd ..." (p. 7). Teachers are "attached" in the most immediate way to the real issues surrounding justice and pedagogy. Teachers can examine the lives they live in schools and the experiences children encounter each day in their classrooms in an "organic" way, stemming from their own histories and the histories of their students. Then, critical perspectives become more than theory. In a way, an autobiographical approach is a means of taking stock, of reassessing your knowledge and beliefs about the teaching of reading, for example. Action research becomes more than a means of adopting a teaching technique; it becomes "transforming," as Freire (1985) suggested. It becomes an avenue for constructive change which is personally meaningful and deeply felt.

Dan Lortie (1975), in *The Schoolteacher*, suggested autobiography as a way to increase awareness of one's views about teaching and "to expose them to personal examination" (p. 231). Grumet (1978) held that autobiography allows teachers to ask their own questions, articulate their own stories, explore their own memories, and strongly affirm the legitimacy of their own real experiences. Her way of going about teacher autobiography is close to the matter at hand: immediate, alive, fresh, and yet is simultaneously analytic, thoughtful, viewed from a distance. This storytelling is not without risk, however, and should be approached respectfully:

> And yet, even telling a story to a friend, is a risky business, the better the friend, the riskier the business. How many of you would like to get your own story back from a certain person? Do you remember how her eyes were glazed, how she didn't really listen, only waited for you to finish so her own turn to tell would come? Do you remember how she asked the wrong questions, appropriating only those parts of the story that she could use, ignoring the part that really mattered to you? (p. 321)

> So if telling a story requires giving oneself away, then we are obligated to devise a method of receiving stories that mediates between the self that tells, the self that is told, and the self that listens: A method that returns a story to the teller that is both hers and not hers, that contains her self in good company. (p. 323)

One way to open up fresh possibilities for storytelling is to shape the context so that the storyteller makes several passes at the telling, going at it from various vantage points, perhaps at different times.

Grumet (1987) asked for three separate narratives rather than for one longer, continuous account, having learned from Pinar's approach to educational autobiography that such a "triple telling" could usefully sort reflection into *past* experience, *present* situation, and *future* images. Multiple tellings, according to

Grumet (1987), "splinter the dogmatism of a single tale" and free the teller from "being captured by the reflection provided in a single narrative" (p. 324). This technique may be especially useful for pre-service teachers as they work to integrate coursework, classroom experiences, and reflections about who they will be in their own classrooms someday.

A K–8 physical education teacher and coach, Rick Moon, comes to mind as one whose teacher research had a very personal, autobiographical connection, and that was part recollecting the past, part examining the present, and part imagining the future (see Rick Moon's Teacher Research). He worked back and forth between these three perspectives, gaining much knowlege from perceiving his work from the different vantage points.

Moon's inquiry arrived with the birth of his daughter, Amy. Suddenly, this physical education teacher began to observe the girls and boys in his classes a little more closely. He noticed girls "holding back" because they were not "supposed to be so good." He discovered that not one girl thought herself more athletically skilled than *all* of the boys and not one boy rated *any* girl superior to himself, even though Moon was sure that several of the best athletes were in fact girls. When casting his net into the past, seeking the autobiographical connections that might inform his current research, Moon remembered his mostly male "methods" teachers in college having very firm beliefs about gender roles; beliefs to which he also subscribed, including the view that boys needed to learn combativeness "in order to prevent women and sissies from taking over society." A few years later he looked into the eyes of Amy, his newborn daughter and wondered what the future might hold for her. The possibilities, he thought, seemed limitless. As a teacher–researcher, he decided to study the matter of gender equity in his own classroom. "To be a man today and to be married, and to be a father, requires rethinking the images one holds."

Again and again in teacher research, we are confronted with the primacy of the teacher. It is the teacher who is at the center of action in the classroom; it is the teacher who is trying, in real life and real time, to understand what is going on in the classroom and to make a difference.

Ayers (1993) employed the metaphor of the highly personal, idiosyncratic journey:

> Much of what I know of teaching is tentative, contingent, and uncertain. I learned it by living it, by doing it, and so what I know is necessarily ragged and rough and unfinished. As with any journey, it can seem neat and certain, even painless, looking backward. On the road, looking forward, there is nothing easy or obvious about it. (p. xi)

Teachers can begin to connect their own autobiographies with classroom research by recalling elements of their own schooling and by thinking about their years as teachers. These "prompts" may help you get started:

- Discuss or write about the great (and not so great) teachers you have had in school. What were your experiences in those classrooms?

FIG. 1.1. "The things I could have written if I had a good pen!" Reprinted by permission of Joe Martin.

- Who were three of your "best" students? Why do you consider them "best"? What do your choices say about you as a teacher?
- What was one of your best moments as a teacher? As a student?
- What is a "good day" like for you?
- If you had a gift of 10 hours extra in school each week—just for you—how would you spend it?
- Describe yourself as a teacher. How would one of your average students describe you as a teacher?

Putting ourselves at the center of inquiry grounds the action in who we are; it relates the professional to the personal through teacher research (see Fig. 1.1).

## JOURNAL KEEPING

I am a long time journal keeper. I believe it to be a wonderfully rich and evocative teaching and learning tool. Keeping a journal has been a practice in both my teaching and my learning. As a way of developing a reflective ongoing relationship with oneself and one's work, a personal journal is hard to beat.

> The future enters into us, and transforms itself within us, long before it actually happens. (Rilke, 1934, pp. 64–65)

Teacher research represents a forming up of developmental reachings that have often been a long time in coming. A journal can be a means by which we bring into fuller awareness, both for the student and for ourselves as teachers, some of the deeper processes through which we make meaning. Sometimes we realize this when we reread the journal and realize that we've been working on something for a long time without knowing it. But once the lightbulb goes on, and we read our journal writings with the new insight in mind, we see Rilke's point come home; that the new development was there all the time, perhaps incubating, finding form, growing—what took us so long to see it? Our developmental reachings seem so obvious in hindsight. We see this very clearly in our students, but less quickly in ourselves. The journal can help to reveal the organic nature of development.

As part of her association with an ongoing group of teacher–researchers, Nancy Brankis realized how her own discoveries of learning seemed to be "connecting" and "weaving" together in the journal she kept (see Nancy Brankis' Teacher Research). Perhaps this is an illustration of Schubert's (1990) observation that journal writing can be helpful in developing the "organizing center of what it means to be a good teacher" (p. 218). Brankis also realized that she "had tapped an inner motivation and sense of connection from within." It was this experience that led her to wonder about possible implications for her own second-grade class and eventually to create a classroom research project collaborating with them.

Many teachers do this continually—use themselves and their own experiences as means for doing personal and practical research. The journal is a place where much of that very important research process can be described, drawn, reflected on, analyzed, and put back into use in the classroom. Each teacher's journal can become the textbook of emergent practice, ongoing research, and as such may be the most important book a teacher can fully write and read.

The experience of working with a journal, though, is far from cut and dried; it can require a considerable tolerance for ambiguity, uncertainty, and not knowing. I think of journal keeping as a form of active listening. Carl Rogers (1961) put it this way:

> It seems to mean letting my experience carry me on, in a direction which appears to be forward, toward goals that I can but dimly define, as I try to understand at least the current meaning of (my) experience. The sensation is that of floating with a complex stream of experience, with the fascinating possibility of trying to comprehend its ever changing complexity. (p. 275)

Fulwiler (1987b) conceived of journals as assignments given by teachers to their students and, having consulted with numerous such teachers, identified a number of common features that characterize such journals:

> They tend to be conversational, colloquial, first-person, informally punctuated, experimental, and expressed in the rhythms of everyday speech. They contain observations, questions, speculations, digressions, syntheses, revisions, and are full of information. They are self-aware. The entries tend to be frequent, long, self-spon-

sored, and chronological. These characteristics separate them from more formal assignments and make them especially fun to both write and read. (pp. 2–3)

Another kind of teacher journal, identified by Lytle and Cochran-Smith (1990), describes classroom life. Such journals are often kept by student teachers and are important means of dialoguing with cooperating teachers and university supervisors. In it, teachers describe their observations, make analyses of their experiences, reflect on their practices over a period of time, and make interpretations of what has transpired.

They intermingle description, record keeping, commentary, and analysis. Similar in some ways to ethnographic field notes, they capture the immediacy of teaching—teachers' evolving perceptions of what is happening with the students in their classrooms and what this means for their continued practice. (Lytle & Cochran-Smith, 1990, p. 86)

Such writing is especially helpful when it comes to reading the journals because the entries form a *written record of practice* over a period of time that teachers can use to evaluate their experiences. Such accounts provide a means by which teachers can construct and reconstruct interpretive understandings using data from their classrooms.

Teachers' journals can become repositories in which anecdotal records and chronological accounts of classroom activities are stored. Or, they may be more narrowly organized as very intentional and systematic inquiries, ones that can open up windows to show what teachers see going on in schools as perceived through their own eyes and written in their own voices. Such journals can also show how writing is used to illuminate and inform their work lives. Journals are the necessary link between action and reflection in a teacher-researcher's work.

After more than 30 years of experience of working with journals, I am sure of one thing: each person's journal is unique. The only real way to explore the experience of journal keeping is to give oneself the experience—to actually begin writing one's own. Each journal is a uniquely personal tool, which is best individually tailored to fit each person's special requirements. The most effective approach to understand journal keeping is simply trying it and discovering what works. Still, from watching myself and others experiment with creating our own forms of journal keeping, I have observed a few practices that seem to make the process more workable. You may want to try some of these to see how they fit you, and maybe rework or revise them to suit your needs.

## Formats

I use an 8½ × 11 page format, placed in a three-ring binder. This has the advantage of allowing you to remove pages, perhaps to show them to others, or to rearrange them in other sections. The page is large enough to tape or staple notes and jottings or photographs into your journal. The pages are easily printed from a computer or word processor on three-ring paper and slipped into the notebook.

A large notebook, though, can be somewhat unwieldy for carrying around, so some teachers prefer a smaller, 6 × 9 format. This kind of notebook can be slipped into a purse or carryall and is more easily transported. Some teachers advocate using a blank lesson plan book to make quick reminder notes for entries to be written later. Others keep a post-it note pad on the desk for easy access. John Edgcomb, a high school art teacher, asks his students to inspect their academic notebooks for doodles and then to expand upon them in art class. He and his students use a spiral-bound journal, which is printed with lines on only half the page, leaving some unencumbered space for drawings. In any case, it's important to use a format that is comfortable and convenient for you.

## Date Entries

This simple convention yields many dividends. It allows you to view developmental process over the continuity of time. The fact that the journal is sequential and chronological gives it the ability to provide material from which recurring patterns can be found, generalizations drawn, and hypotheses formed. Also, because entries can be moved around if you're using a loose-leaf format, the dates on the entries will allow you to reconstruct sequences if need be. It's a good idea to date and time your entries and to use a new page for each one.

## Time

Many teacher–researchers express frustration with the time constraints that seem to prevent them from keeping copious notes on the events in their classrooms. A teacher wonders, "I'll need to make my own journaling more a part of my life. But how?" Although there are no easy answers to this dilemma, there are solutions devised by teachers who realize the importance of capturing the data as it happens. Of course, tape recorders, video cameras, and invited observers can assist a teacher–researcher by gathering one kind of information that can be processed at a later time. Using post-it notes, index card files, and brief notes on a lesson plan book may be sufficient for in-class reminders of events and thoughts.

Eventually, though, it will be the teacher–researcher's task to debrief what has been collected in writing. One idea is to write while students are writing. Some teachers have discovered that an early morning hour is the best time to find a word processor and write freely without interruption. Researchers generally suggest that it is best to write about an event or a time period as soon as possible and before discussing it with anyone; oral expression appears to change what has occurred as the speaker shapes the conversation for its audience. Individual journal writing offers a teacher the time necessary to process it independently first.

Teacher–researchers who are desirous of specific and practical suggestions for using journals with their students would do well to look for the following books: Holly's (1989) *Writing To Grow* is a resource for adult journal-keepers. Fulwiler's (1987b) *Teaching with Writing* and (1987a) *The Journal Book* are indispensable. Zemelman and Daniels' (1988) book, *A Community of Writers* addresses journal writing with junior and senior high school students. Routman's (1991) *Invitations* and Isaacs and Brodine's (1994) *Journals in the Classroom* include helpful advice on journal writing in the primary grades.

## Descriptive Writing

With experience, many journal keepers come to value the usefulness of descriptive writing. Description is more than a transcription of reality. It is not just a tape recording. Rather, description recreates one's own perception of an event. Trying to describe a complex experience is very demanding. The act of describing an event makes one look more carefully, more discriminatingly, more thoroughly. Faithful description helps one to actually see more.

For example, I am doing classroom reseach on evaluation. I may want to write in my journal about seventh-grader Josh's conference with me about his progress report. Describing that interaction fully—in order for it to be significant for my research—I will want to include the following: My attitude toward Josh and his achievement, Josh's attitudes and feelings, my approach to the conference, how I heard and listened to Josh, how I believe he heard me, what was accomplished during the conference, and what was not. Direct quotes and an account of body postures and facial expressions would be valuable to a thorough, rich description as well. Later, when we want to read and work with our journal writing, we will want to read what is written there, to structure it in a variety of ways to reveal meaning, to reflect on it, to learn freshly from previously rendered experience. If, when the time comes for such a reading, all we have are a series of nondescript writings, there will be little information with which to work (i.e., "had progress report conference with Josh").

## Reflective Writing

Here is another kind of journal writing. Following a period of describing experience, journal writers often find themselves reflecting on the experience just described. Reflection is a standing back, a pausing to reread, to mull things over and search for connections, associations, significances, and possible meanings not noticed before. Reflective writing comes more from a distance; from a certain perspective. One moves from a description of experience to a sort of commentary on it. Perhaps you have a dim glimmering of a recurring pattern. Maybe you see a possible motivating dynamic and want to phrase a hypothesis. An association to another event bubbles up to consciousness. You're reminded of something you read last week. You're reminded of another student you had last year. When writing reflectively, the teacher–researcher's mind can be given free reign as it seeks to make meaning.

## Double-Entry Journal Writing

One way to make a more workable distinction between descriptive and reflective writing is to distinguish between them in the pages of the journal by using facing pages. On the right-hand page, write the descriptive account of a given experience, including its subjective aspects. On the left-hand facing page, reflect on that experience (see chapter 3 for a sample double-entry journal format).

## Daily Log

This is an attempt to describe the essence of a particular day: You woke up this morning, and then what happened? And then what happened? An accumulating collection of such entries can reveal, from a daily perspective, just what is occupying your mind, as well as be revealing of your activity. Done late in the evening or on the morning of the following day, an accumulation of daily logs can reveal what sorts of things absorb your attention, what continuing issues predominate, or what your priorities appear to be.

## Steppingstones

Developed by Progoff (1975), this technique is very helpful in discovering the continuity and exploring the meaning of remembered experiences a teacher brings to a particular subject or concern. Earlier, I mentioned the possibility of listing the great (and not so great) teachers you have known. Think about it this way: Name the first important teacher you knew. Write a few descriptors. Name the next important teacher in your life. And the next. And the next. You may come up with a dozen or so. Then, write a sentence or two about each of the teachers identified. These small descriptions can be viewed as forming the steppingstones by which you traveled to your present understanding of what it means to be a teacher. What do these persons have in common? From what contexts do they come? Which are role models you now use to shape your practice? Which of these remembered images do you wish to avoid? Identifying, and describing in writing, the steppingstones of one's experience is a powerful way of exploring and reflecting on one's development over time.

## Dialogue With a Person

Perhaps you realize from the previous exercise that one particular teacher had importance for you. Imagine yourself having a conversation with that person. Try to write down in your journal how the dialogue unfolds. Perhaps you will start with a question: What do you think of my teaching now? Then, as a playwright, you write down what that person says in your imagination. You reply. The other responds, and the written dialogue gradually unfolds. Such dialogues can be constructed with persons who have long ago passed away, people who are active in your life today but unapproachable, or people who are public or even fictional figures with whom you cannot interact directly.

## Underlinings

Everyday, all day long, our attention is drawn on by various objects. We are continually engaged in the activity of searching, scanning, noticing; our eyes are endlessly moving. It is very easy and often quite helpful to make an effort to consciously notice *what* has been drawing our attention, almost unaware. One obvious place to look is in the pages of what we've recently been reading. There is much to be discovered by searching a little more methodically for artifacts of "researching" that we have already been collecting and bringing the results of that investigation into the pages of one's journal. One needn't always start over from scratch; often we are ahead of ourselves, already producing evidences of an inquiry in progress.

## Journal of the Journals

A journal is not just for writing, of course; it is also for reading. If kept over a long enough period of time, a journal can be viewed as a repository for a teacher's observations, stories, insights, and wonderings. One way to help re-claim various renderings of such a story or a developing theme from journal material is to create what I call a "journal of the journals." The teacher–re-searcher reads a series of entries, seeking a theme, a recurring pattern, or a story often told. Once such a possibility is discovered, the author goes through the whole journal with a highlighter, emphasizing the material having to do with the particular theme or story. This strategy really opens up the substance of the material because the reading self perceives it from a perspective quite different from the writing self. And the editing self, looking at the collection of fragments from the journal, sees it in another way again.

A further elaboration of this technique is to invite a friend to read the lines that you have highlighted out loud. Hearing your own material read in another's voice, with different emphasis and varied style, allows hearing in yet another, often fresher, way. Application of this device allows more writing to flow as you begin to synthesize the various elements, or attempt to carry the story forward in another, perhaps novel way. The journal writer writes, reads, listens, and responds. Having worked with one such subject or topic or story, the teacher can make another pass, this time with another color of highlighter, bringing together the already written material having to do with a second aspect of the inquiry.

One of the great strengths of working with a journal is that it leads itself along. It suggests questions, identifies new areas to explore, reveals meaningful absences, and uncovers recurring patterns. As the teacher–researcher becomes more and more aware of the rich material contained in the journal, it becomes possible to use the journal itself to answer some of the questions, to gather the clues together, and to follow the paths to see where they may lead. The author of every journal gives the reader all that is needed to move the inquiry ahead. It is in the writing of the journal, of course, and it is also in the *reading*.

By thinking about research as a personal, as well as a professional endeavor, we can engage in classroom inquiry that is meaningful and really relevant in our own lives. We must constantly be reminded that classroom research is not just about children; it is also very much about the teacher. Long after this year's group of students move on to the next grade or the next teacher, you will still be there—learning about teaching and examining your practice. Your research about that process extends far beyond one class in one given year. It is about you and your profession in a much larger sense.

We have discussed two ways in which the personal can be brought to bear on teacher research: (a) calling upon your own autobiography as a means to reflect on your own style, attitudes, prior experience, and knowledge, and (b) using journal writing as a means to describe, reflect, and assess the study of your teaching and learning. Both autobiography and journal writing are tools for your use as you look at what your teaching is like. Both can also be tools for the students in your class to use as they engage in researching with you. What experiences have they had prior to this year that affect them as learners in your class? In what other ways have they encountered what you are teaching them now? What might be their views of effective teaching? Asking students to keep research journals during a study is a wonderful way to help young people learn to think about their own learning—and to become active in the classroom as teachers themselves.

You might ask students to keep journals of "exit slips" that they complete each day at the end of class. Exit slips might be reflections in which students think about what they learned that day, *how* they learned it, and what they anticipate tomorrow. The slips might be a place where they can record the most significant event of the day or the most surprising learning. Journals might be in the form of letters to the teacher, advising, suggesting, and contributing to the planning of learning for the next day or week.

These are tools not just for teacher research, but for learning. Research is meant to be *used* by teachers. Teacher research often begins with the individual but is shared with colleagues in a more public setting, as this book illustrates. When we start with ourselves and our students, however, we start with what is most meaningful and most useful. Then we move on from there.

## REFERENCES

Allport, G. (1955). *Becoming*. New Haven: Yale University Press.

Argyris, C. (1982). *Reasoning, learning, and action*. San Francisco: Jossey-Bass.

Apple, M. (1993). *Official knowledge: Democratic education in a conservative age*. New York: Routledge.

Atwell, N. (1993). Foreword. In L. Patterson, C. M. Santa, K. G. Short, & K. Smith (Eds.), *Teachers as researchers: Reflection and action* (pp. VII–X). Newark, DE: International Reading Association.

Ayers, W. (1993). *To teach: The journey of a teacher*. New York: Teachers College Press.

Cantor, N. (1953). *The teaching-learning process*. New York: Dryden Press.

Dewey, J. (1922). *Human nature and conduct*. New York: Holt.

Dewey, J. (1929). *Sources of a science education*. New York: Liverisht.

Freire, P. (1985). *Politics of education*. South Hadley, MA: Bergin and Garvey.

Fulwiler, T. (1987a). (Ed.). *The journal book*. Portsmouth, NH: Heinemann.

Fulwiler, T. (1987b). *Teaching with writing*. Portsmouth, NH: Heinemann.

Gardner, H. (1983). *Frames of mind: The theory of multiple intelligences*. New York: Basic Books.

Grant, C., & Zeichner, K. (1984). On becoming a reflective teacher. In C. Grant (Ed.), *Preparing for reflective teaching* (pp. 1–18). Boston: Allyn and Bacon.

Grumet, M. (1978). Curriculum as theatre: Merely players. *Curriculum Inquiry, 8*, 37–62.

Grumet, M. (1987). The politics of personal knowledge. *Curriculum Inquiry, 17*(3), 319–329.

Holly, M. L. (1989). *Writing to grow: Keeping a personal-professional journal*. Portsmouth, NH: Heinemann.

Isaacs, J. A., & Brodine, J. S. (1994). *Journals in the classroom*. Winnipeg, Manitoba, Canada: Pequis Publishers.

Jalongo, M. R. (1992). Teachers' stories: Our ways of knowing. *Educational Leadership, 49*(7), 68–73.

Lewin, K. (1948). *Resolving social conflicts*. New York: Harper.

Lortie, D. (1975). *The schoolteacher*. Chicago: University of Chicago Press.

Lytle, S., & Cochran-Smith, M. (1990). Learning from teacher research: A working typology. *Teachers College Record, 92*(1).

Miller, J. (1992). Exploring power and authority issues in a collaborative research project. *Theory Into Practice, 31*(2), 165–172.

Progoff, I. (1975). *At a journal workshop*. New York: Dialogue House Library.

Rilke, R. M. (1934). *Letters to a young poet: Letter #8* (pp. 64–65). M. D. Herter Norton (Trans.). New York: W. W. Norton and Company, Inc.

Rogers, C. (1961). *On becoming a person*. Boston: Houghton-Mifflin.

Routman, R. (1991). *Invitations*. Portsmouth, NH: Heinemann.

Schon, D. (1983). *The reflective practitioner*. New York: Basic Books.

Schon, D. (1987). *Educating the reflective practitioner*. San Francisco: Jossey-Bass.

Schubert, W. (1992). Personal theorizing about teacher personal theorizing. In E. Ross, J. Cornett, & G. McCutcheon (Eds.), *Teacher personal theorizing* (pp. 257–272). Albany, NY: State University of New York Press.

Schubert, W., & Schubert, A. (1984, April). *Sources of a theory of action research in progressive education*. Paper presented at the annual meeting of the American Educational Research Association, New Orleans, LA.

Zemelman, S., & Daniels, H. (1988). *A community of writers: Teaching writing in the junior and senior high school*. Portsmouth, NH: Heinemann.

# DISCOVERING THE REAL LEARNER WITHIN: JOURNALKEEPING WITH CHILDREN

Nancy Brankis
Lincolnshire/Prairie View Schools

In my practice as a second-grade teacher, "burn-out" hadn't yet arrived, but the idea of returning each day to the same classroom with the prescribed curriculum had lost its luster. Certainly, I explored through staff-development sessions and educational texts the ideals of integrated curriculum, thematic approaches, process writing, whole language philosophy, and all the other up-to-date suggested practices. Yet the comfortable, real implementation of these approaches to learning was not truly finding its way into my classroom in any cohesive form.

In the midst of trying desperately to actualize my teaching practice, I entered a graduate program and began the life of an adult student. Parallels existed between my adult classroom learning situation and the environment of my second-grade students. Both groups were in self-contained situations, both had curricula and certain texts with requirements, and all of us shared the trepidations of school life.

Part of the requirement in my graduate program was to keep a daily journal of my own thoughts, questions, experiences, and practices as an educator. The idea of having to maintain a response journal on a daily basis without boundaries was foreign and unsettling to me. I really didn't understand its purpose or reward. Busywork did not appeal to me, yet I had the expectation that all children should be motivated to accomplish my prescribed tasks, so why shouldn't that same expectation apply to me as a student? I decided to give it my best shot and started writing. After a time, I found a pattern emerging in my journal entries. My teaching seemed to be a series of wonderfully crafted units, themes, and projects, yet they were all defined by *me*. I felt glory in the products that resulted. Yet I began to question, "Where is the child?" in the scheme of the learning.

Through the process of keeping a journal, I recognized how I had gone through my teaching life seeing it as a series of lesson plans; I had not been highly reflective, and seemed to move from one year to the next without really looking at why I was doing things. Sullivan (1989) referred to a journal as the "Lost and Found" of the self. I began to take notice of my own revitalized desire to learn and wondered about the power of response journaling and its implications for use in my own second-grade setting.

No journaling experiences existed for my students and I began to envision its potential impact. Journal writing, I imagined, could be a means of providing wholeness to a curriculum. I felt it could be used as a timeline of student growth and an eventual table of contents. It could be a place where one's life and learning had a place to authentically unfold.

## RESEARCHING AND IMPLEMENTING JOURNALS IN CLASSROOMS

Research begins when one starts to question, wonder, and seek answers. Journal writing is quite a personal method of learning and one that I theorized could accommodate any student at any level of functioning. I had questions that needed answers. In what ways would students' critical thinking skills evolve? How would students use journal writing as a place to capture thought, organize and clarify thinking, reflect, and grow as learners? In what ways can journaling stimulate questioning and self-learning? How does journal writing provide connections, coherence, and a framework for learning? Are students becoming more empowered in their learning as a result of personal journals? I certainly had an agenda in tackling the topic of journal writing across the curriculum. I wanted to capture with my own group of students the impact that journaling was having on changing myself from a passive learner to a very active, passionate participant.

I had developed a focus for researching journal writing, but it was time to move from speculation to the actual collection of data. I shared my intent to research journal writing with my graduate peers and principal, as well as with other teachers in my school. There were several of us who had similar interests and we formed an informal research "buddy group." As a group of researchers, we linked up and developed a network of sharing data. My topic seemed infectious! Teachers fed me helpful articles and wanted to know how to implement journals in their classrooms, as soon as I figured it all out. My principal anxiously awaited a future time when I could share what I was doing with the staff. Re-familiarizing myself with the university library was accomplished and many searches for materials were completed. At last with a roomful of books, journal articles, people to interview, my own personal research journal, and the computer turned on, I was ready to begin.

Research Plan Entry: Finally, I'm starting my project. I've assembled numerous books and articles and don't know where to begin. What is it that I'm really trying to do? How many articles will be needed? How to assemble all this knowledge by "experts" into some pattern. Am I excited? Hmmm. I'm starting with *Active Voice* by James Moffett. I like some of his chapter headings.

(Four days later) Sitting at dining room table trying to figure out where to begin. Find out what experts in the field have found to be true for them. Now how to figure out exactly how to put all info together. I think I'll read, jot down ideas and see if groups of knowledge emerge.

(Twenty days later) I am struggling. I have no motivation to begin this project. I guess I don't have a plan and it's disturbing me. I don't know how to fit this together. In bed the other night, some ideas did come to me.

Good journals, according to Fulwiler (1987), have common features regardless of subject and age level. The journal is written in the first person. It focuses on the "I" and demonstrates what the writer thinks as opposed to what others think. Journals are ongoing debates with the writer and his or her several selves. Language is natural and experimentation with style is a feature. Journalers have more questions than they have answers. They speculate and wonder aloud on paper about meaning, events, issues, facts, readings, and find it a free place to experiment without fear of condemnation.

"The importance of a responsive audience is confirmed by research showing that children invent more interest and energy in journal writing when their teacher writes back to them" (Calkins, 1986, p. 101). Students are able to communicate freely at a more complex level. Inventive spelling is encouraged and language mechanics are determined by the student's own level of written language functioning. By responding directly to students' journals, the teacher is able to model conventional spelling, syntax, and mechanics, and elaborate on the students' earlier entries. An indirect editing process takes place.

D'Arcy (1987) explored the student–writer situation. She felt that teachers of writing look at the words on a page rather than through the words to the meaning. Teachers who concern themselves more with grammar, spelling, and mechanics tend to view writing as a code. She found that students come to form an impression of themselves as successful writers if they are able to encode. Students who struggle with this ability see themselves as failed writers. As a result of D'Arcy using journals in her classroom, she felt her students were freed to catch thoughts as they came, their own voices were heard, and they were given space for rehearsal and reflection in their journals. The students demonstrated their knowledge and gained confidence as learner–writers.

At first I felt compelled to read everything that even remotely related to the topic of using journals in a classroom. However, after some experience, I became more selfish and discriminating. I was drawn to those pieces of research that were done by teachers. There was such a personal element to their writings.

Their investment in searching to make a difference for their students was so clear and inspiring. I found a camaraderie with those authors. These researchers all seemed to have a story to tell. Their motivation to change their teaching and involve students intimately in the learning process was evident. My research began with the reading and writing educators and later expanded to include math, science, and political science areas as well.

I chose the beginning of a new school year to begin my study. My new group came noisily flooding into the room with supplies bursting from their backpacks. I wanted us to capture this first day and so I pulled out a large stack of blank books. I started out by introducing the book as their own "Feelings Journal." Their very own book was a place in which they had the freedom to write about anything. The children had pencils, crayons, markers, and were busily creating their covers. As I watched, I noticed that different colors and themes reflected different children. Monsters, frogs, turtles, and rainbows all adorned their covers (see Fig. 1.2).

> Research Journal Entry: I'm sure I'll quickly get to know their books, not by name but by cover. I just overheard, "You know, school isn't so bad."

Use of the "Feelings Journal" continued. There seemed to be an immediate acceptance and I wondered if the children had experienced using them before. Wonderful conversations were shared with many children desiring to know as much about me as I wished to know about them (see Fig. 1.3 for samples of these conversations).

Feeling such success, I decided to introduce the "Learning Journal." I explained that this was the journal that would have topics given to them in which they would be asked to respond in their own way about ideas learned in class. With the first topic given, questions were numerous. "Can we make a list?" "How much do I have to write?" Some children immediately made excuses to go to the bathroom and others needed to sharpen their pencils. I answered as best I could, but really with no experience to support my replies.

> Research Journal Entry: Struggle. They aren't turned on by this. Only the third entry—maybe it will grow on them . . . like mold.

FIG. 1.2. Children's journal covers.

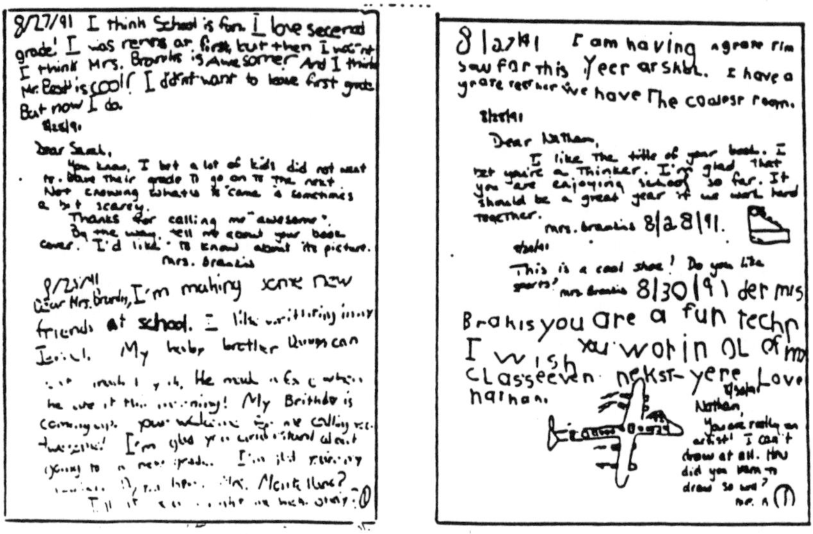

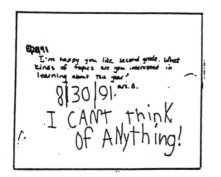

FIG. 1.3. "Feelings journal" conversations.

"Ahhhh" (yawn), says Matt. "Matt, I don't see anything in your journal." "I can't think of anything," he replies (see Fig. 1.4).

Research Journal Entry: Alison continues to sharpen pencil. Four more pencil sharpenings. Ah, the quest to avoid journaling spreads. Many are not on task. They write one thing and say they're done. The extensions of thought, the build-up of critical thinking is not showing itself. Humming, whispering. It's started to rain; this distracts them. Oh great, now thunder!

We continued forward using our journals and started sharing our responses. I noticed that as they sat listening to others' ideas, they became quite passive. I realized the richness of conversations that were present, and needed a way for children to capture this exchange of ideas. I suggested that when they hear

FIG. 1.4. "I can't think of anything."

an idea that appealed to them, they should write that down in their journal. "Isn't that cheating?" asked one. It became apparent that the ethic of worksheets is to do one's own work. Therefore, the idea of cheating had already been instilled in them. It would be a hard task to challenge that idea in these very young, literal minds. "Oh, no!" I replied. "Sharing ideas and learning from each other is the way scientists have made great discoveries. As a matter of fact, I think that every time you would like to accept someone else's idea, you should put a star next to it. That will show me that you are a star learner, a person able to learn from others."

> Research Journal Entry: I enjoy keeping my research journal and already find that I'm far more intimate with my class at this point in time as a result of these journals.

I found that as I continued to work with the journals the handling of them seemed to fall in place. I experimented and fine-tuned the process as we moved along. The beauty of the journal was that it allowed each child the decision to shape his or her learning. So many times in the past I had dictated what was to be learned. We shape children's learning through our questions and answers. This avenue for the collection of thought gave each child the freedom to outline, expand, and react to thoughts.

> Research Journal Entry: I'm letting the journals just be a part of their daily lives. The children know I don't collect them all the time, I don't edit or grade or really challenge them. It's funny—they don't seem to be writing less, trying to get out of work or appear unmotivated—they keep getting better and I'm doing less!
> Yes! I'm doing less. This might be the *key*. The ideas, thoughts, expressions come from them—not me—No control—No absolute answers. They own their journals. Maybe they *feel* because it is their journal, *truly theirs*—not mine that it is a free, honest, safe place to learn. No public arena to be embarrassed, wrong, just a SAFE place to think.

I had realized that the journals allowed each child to be heard in his or her own voice. Each child was unique and expressive. Prior to discussing my journaling research with fellow staff members, I asked each student to write a letter in his or her journal about their likes and dislikes of its use. I felt if they had an audience other than myself, they might be inspired to write and share their perceptions honestly.

Figure 1.5 shows one child's comment to teachers about journaling.

Through the use of my own detailed research journal and my current journal, I realize that even when not writing, my mind mentally writes as a researcher. I capture details, look for patterns, and am much more intimately involved in the process of learning than in its product. I believe that research is valid and vital if change is to occur. It was not the integration of journals in the classroom that has made such a profound impact on learning with my students. It was my

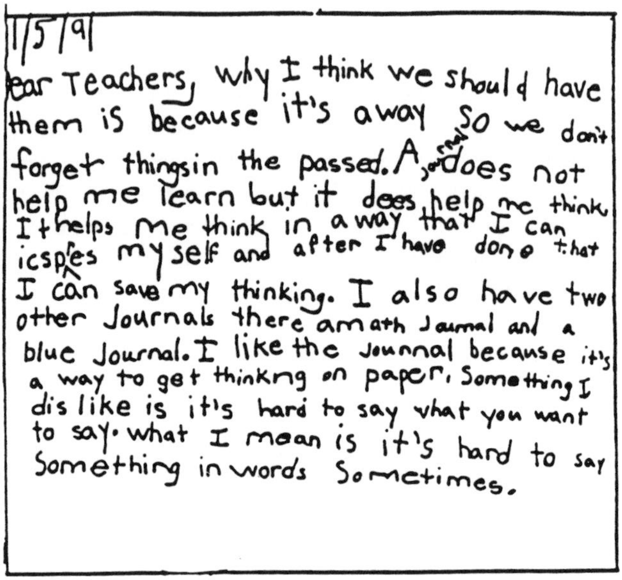

FIG. 1.5. A child's view of journal writing.

personal discovery that I am more comfortable orchestrating learning than controlling it. Authentic teaching is a misnomer. It is the process of authentic learning that is powerful and lifelong. I am no longer the teacher in the classroom, but rather the learner. I share in the process with my students and adult peers. We take responsibility in our learning and the creation of our own text. We reflect on our thoughts and self-evaluate. Research is discovery, but what I really discovered was myself.

## REFERENCES

Calkins, L. (1986). *The art of teaching writing*. Portsmouth: Heinemann Educational Books.

D'Arcy, P. (1987). Writing to learn. In T. Fulwiler (Ed.), *The Journal Book* (pp. 41–46). Portsmouth: Boynton/Cook.

Fulwiler, T. (1987). *The Journal Book*. Portsmouth: Boynton/Cook.

Sullivan, A. (1989). Liberating the urge to write: From classroom journals to lifelong writing. *English Journal, 78*, 55–61.

# SHIFTING GEARS: AN URBAN TEACHER RETHINKS HER PRACTICE

Vida Schaffel
Chicago Public Schools

I began teaching in Chicago in the 1960s, took time out to raise a family, and then returned some 15 years later. In my K–1 classroom, I had a couple of students who were pulled out for English as a Second Language (ESL). This area was new to me. I found it most intriguing because I, too, learned ESL. A position opened up in ESL and because I had the certification, I was given the job. I worked with students from the kindergarten to the eighth-grade level. I liked working with mixed ethnic groups; I enjoyed their diversity. After a few years, my school became more populated with Hispanic and Polish students and more bilingual classes were created. The demographics were such that there were fewer students in the category of "other," so there was no longer a need for two ESL teachers and I began teaching reading in a pull-out program.

After my 15-year hiatus, I found it hard to believe that so little had changed. The basal was still there, the vocabulary was still contrived, and the stories were not very interesting. There was, however, a new twist in that the new series of basals did reflect an ethnic mix of society, at least in the pictures.

The school was bursting; there were students everywhere. Every classroom and every closet was occupied. A place had to be found where my students in the pull-out program could meet. It was finally decided that the best available space was a vestibule off the back entrance of the balcony of the assembly hall. No one went back there and we wouldn't be disturbed by anyone. If the noise from the music class got too loud, we could just close the door and try to ignore it. The space there was able to accommodate a table, some chairs, a few posters on the wall, a chalkboard, and a teacher's desk. What could be bad? What could be wrong with a place like this, away from everything and everybody, a place where no one could bother you because no one could find you? Most people were unaware of the existence of such a place. My students and I were truly isolated from the rest of the building.

In this new pull-out reading program, I was once again faced with the teacher's guide that told me what to do and how to do it, along with the basal text of mostly uninteresting stories and the accompanying skill-based workbook. I found the basal reading program stifling and the teacher's guide an insult to my intelligence. The stories I liked best in the basal were the folk tales and the fables. Those were the stories the students liked too.

According to Bettelheim and Zelan (1982), the children who teach themselves to read before coming to school read from texts that are of interest to them. So why not read stories in school that are also of interest to the students? I began reading aloud to my students every day. This was a new experience for me. In the past, I read to my students but it was never on a regular basis. The books we shared were predictable stories, patterned stories, and stories rich in language and story content. The students drew pictures about the stories, read words from the stories, and made up their own stories following the pattern set from the book. There was excitement and enthusiasm, and the students looked forward to our time together.

One day, one of the groups came upon what the text referred to as "a book." This was a page that contained pictures with some dialogue that the students were to cut out and staple together to replicate a book. Michelle was first to have her book in order, so I asked her to read it. She began reading her book. She knew all the words. The entire book had a vocabulary of six words. She finished reading the book, looked up at me and said, "This is a book?" How can this possibly be compared to the interesting story content and rich language of the stories she had been exposed to? Is this what reading is all about? More and more I became convinced that to instill a love for reading one must go beyond the basal.

As I began to read the research that had been done in the field, I was surprised to find that I was not alone in my thinking and that there were many educators who also questioned the old basal skill and drill methodology that still prevails in the schools. When teachers complain that it is getting harder and harder to teach reading and the methods that worked years ago are not working now, we have to look to see what we can do to change the tide to achieve better results.

I felt I had to change the way I approached the area of literacy, specifically the teaching of reading. In my research, I was surprised to find that there was a natural connection between the reading and the writing process. I never really connected the two areas before, but now this idea made so much sense to me. Of course the two are connected. I became excited with the prospect of trying out this new approach. Connecting reading and writing in a meaningful, real-life way became the focus of some action research. How does one go about changing one's way of teaching? Can I be a pioneer and try to work it out for myself?

When the requests for the next year's assignments came out, I requested to be put back into a classroom. The pull-out reading program that I was involved in was both fragmented and isolated from the rest of the school program. There was no connection, no continuity with the rest of the day. Something was awry. Reading should be the whole day's program and not a separate piece of it, and writing should be the other component part. It is writing that gives expression to the knowledge that children possess and it is writing that leaves evidence of what they don't know or do not understand (Graves & Stuart, 1985). Writing gives children a vehicle through which to explore the meaning of their past experiences (Cramer, 1978). Goodman and Goodman (1983) affirmed that "people not only learn to read by reading and write by writing, but they also learn to read by writing and write by reading" (p. 592). It would seem that the reading and writing combination is quite strong and would reinforce each other in literacy development.

I was given a second- and third-grade split class. I like the idea of multi-age grouping where there can be a helpful give-and-take in the classroom. I saw this as a positive with definite benefits for both groups of students. Because I intended to individualize the reading program, it really did not matter what grade the students were in, for they would all read on their own level and at their own pace. I might add that my colleagues could not understand why I did not object to this split. A split is not looked upon as a favorable placement. My only objection was that there were 36 students in the class. The large number of children is what made the job difficult, not the split.

The students in this class were mainly from urban working-class families. There were students from single-parent homes as well as intact family homes, foster homes, divorced and shared-custody homes. There were homes that took an interest in their child's work and homes where no one was able to assist the child in learning. There were homes where a variety of books could be found and others where there was no printed material at all.

Initially, I wanted to use trade books as the text for reading, but I found that I did not have the fingertip familiarity with enough books at each of the different student levels. I didn't know what to recommend to everyone and many of the students seemed to be floundering, unable to make choices and in need of direction. I observed some students reading books well below their level and others reading books that were far too difficult for them. I became concerned at the prospect of the students not progressing. I was also getting looks from the other teachers, my colleagues. When they would ask me what basal I was using and what story I was on, I would answer that I wasn't using a basal. I got lots of surprised looks, as if to say, "What are you doing, lady?" I had no one in the school to collaborate with, although I was able to discuss some thoughts and ideas while riding to school with one of my colleagues who taught the fifth grade.

Teachers in the primary grades are usually given some basal readers, accompanying workbooks, phonics workbooks, science texts, and social studies texts along with all the accompanying teacher's manuals. How one uses these materials is not mandated, but most of the teachers use the texts in the most traditional way. At this time, my school was slowly switching from one set of basals to another. I stayed with the old basal because I was more familiar with this series and I was already anticipating making major changes in my teaching. I felt this would make my life a little easier.

I became insecure about what I was doing and began using the basal during reading workshop. I rationalized to myself that maybe it was okay to use the basal as long as they were reading other books in class and trade books during independent reading time and their free class time.

The children were reading from six different basals. Only one reading group existed and that was because they needed to learn some reading strategies before they could read on their own. I was not fond of reading groups because I felt the students did not spend enough time actually reading. The good readers were held back and the slower readers usually had difficulty keeping up. In my plan, the students would be able to go at their own pace; those who needed to go slowly could do so and those who could go faster would not be held back.

Due to the number of students, I found that I was not able to monitor their reading as much as I had hoped. For the group that still needed more help, I tried to initiate peer tutoring from the students in the classroom, but I found that it took too much time away from their own reading to ask them to do it on a regular basis, so I matched these children up with students in the highest-level self-contained learning disabled (LD) class. The tutoring was a success; the students were able to go at their own rate and they did more reading than they would have done had they been in a group setting. The other students were more independent and read by themselves or in pairs. Periodically, they read a story together as a group. Some enjoyed working with another student on a worksheet pertaining to the story better than working alone whereas some preferred to do their work by themselves.

As a recipient of the Rochelle Lee Grant that provides trade book libraries in the classroom, I knew how important it was for children to have an acquaintanceship with books. I also knew the benefits of "read aloud" to the students. The general feeling among most of the teachers is that read aloud is fine for a fill-in, but how can you take time from the regular subjects and read out loud? Read aloud took place twice a day. In the morning, I read a short trade book and in the afternoon I would read a chapter book. I wanted them to try to stretch their thinking and be able to carry over a thought from one day to the next. The books I read served as a stimulus for the students to re-read the books on their own. Some students followed along in the chapter books as I read. These students were able to visibly see the modeling of reading with inflection and the use of punctuation.

Is there a natural connection between reading and writing, and is there an effect that each of these disciplines has upon the other? "... All language processes develop concurrently in an unrelated manner. Each process informs and supports the other ..." (Strickland & Morrow, 1988, p. 70). Graves and Stuart (1985) supported this same idea. They said, "as children become better writers, they also improve their reading skill" (p. 116). Goodman and Goodman (1983) said that it is not necessary for readers to write during reading, but writers must read and re-read during writing. In my own mind I became more and more convinced of the connection and saw that connection made in my action research. Writing is powerful. Through writing, it is possible to know what students are aware of in their reading as well as to know what they have learned. Here, their knowledge of the letter-sound relationship, which is applicable to reading is evident. Students write what they know; that is why writing is so revealing.

One of the most important parts of my action research was the journal writing that took place first thing in the morning. This activity turned out to be a most profound experience for me. Students were given free expression in whatever they wrote; I continued to reassure them that this would not be graded and they should write without being burdened by formal constraints. I even encouraged them to begin by drawing and then add some words to tell about their drawing and what came to mind. What struck me about this whole process of journaling was that the thoughts were all coming from them and they were writing from the heart. Each piece of writing had its own "voice." They chose their own words to convey the uniqueness of an experience, thus giving meaning to the words and personality to the writing (Graves & Stuart, 1985).

The writing was, in a sense, cathartic for them and so revealing to me. Neither show and tell, nor being given subjects to write about in a composition, nor prompts could possibly have evoked such natural, flowing thoughts. I provided them with the permission, in a sense, and they took off. I wrote back to the students providing them with a dialogue; I wanted them to know that someone was listening but not judging. Sometimes their classmates became their audience and asked them questions about their piece. As they gained trust in me and the other students, the juices began flowing and the thoughts, words, and feelings began to pour out on the pages. Their feelings could now be expressed knowing that they will be accepted and not evaluated. After all, feelings are neither right nor wrong; they just are.

Their progress in writing was readily visible by the documentation of the date on each piece of writing. There was no formula to the order of progress. Each child progressed in his or her own way and at his or her own rate. I was in awe of the whole process. The content of their pieces gave a glimpse into the things that were on their minds. When children are given carte blanche to write, they reveal their real feelings and concerns, hopes and wishes, likes and dislikes.

I was surprised to find that the children who have difficulty reading texts generally do not have difficulty reading their own writing. It seems that what they write they can read, but what comes in print is more difficult for them, unless they are familiar with the storyline and can use context clues or other reading strategies. For some children, their best reading is their journal reading.

Little Marisa was going through a most difficult time in her life when she came into my class. She and her family had just come from Romania and within a year her mother died, leaving her and five other siblings alone with their father. Marisa did not talk much in class, she kept to herself. She first mentioned her mother and father in her journal about mid-September. From the end of September until the end of November the subject of her mother's death was repeated over and over and over again. "My mother died when I was asleep," is what she kept writing. That sentence kept appearing in her writing. Almost every day, that sentence was found somewhere in her journal writing. Once she wrote "I don't have a birthday after mother died." From the end of November until February she moved on to talk about her family, her brothers and sisters and what she liked to do. Then in February she began to allow herself to write about and seek the friendship of others. After that, she was ready to reach out and accept the friendship of her classmates.

Journal writing has been one of the most positive experiences for me and for the children. It is hard to believe the kind of growth that takes place through this very simple media. I feel badly that I was not able to keep up a dialogue with the students. Most of the time I used my preparation time to write back to the students. As much as I wanted to do it every day, and I had the best of intentions, the logistics of it never seemed to work out. Being alone in the classroom with 36 students made it much too difficult to do.

It is difficult to be the only one in the workplace trying out new ideas. Even though I felt what I was doing was right, it still didn't make the task any easier. What did keep me going was the support and encouragement of a group of teacher–researchers from the suburbs that I met with once a month. Many of these teachers had new ideas and were also trying out different methods in their teaching, and they too were confronted by the traditional teachers who fought change. Being able to share my feelings of frustration and receive support from other colleagues was most important for me. Another important factor for me was the reinforcement I received from attending workshops. At workshops, one usually finds like-minded teachers and that gave me encouragement. The workshops confirmed to me that I was on the right track and that my frustration was just a matter of working out the logistics.

Without learning there can be no growth, and without growth there can be no change. This holds true for both the student and the teacher. I see myself more now as a facilitator rather than the purveyor of knowledge. I am constantly collecting data in my classroom while I analyze my own teaching and learning. I view children in a more holistic and developmental way than I did previously. I am more conscious of "process" and see "product" as being multidimensional and multifaceted. I am not the same as I was before.

Change is not easy. It is lonely being a majority of one and it is hard working against the grain. The need to connect with other educators is essential for me, and unfortunately there is no time in the school day to talk to colleagues. (Twenty minutes of lunchtime does not allow for any exchange of ideas!) It is difficult not to do what I believe; for to do otherwise, I would not be true to myself. I look forward to more growth and new challenges as a teacher–researcher in the future.

## REFERENCES

Bettelheim, B., & Zelan, B. (1982). *On learning to read: The child's fascination with meaning*. New York: Alfred A. Knopf.

Cramer, R. L. (1978). *Children's writing and language growth*. Columbus, OH: Charles E. Merrill Publishing Company.

Goodman, K., & Goodman, Y. (1983). Reading and writing relationship: Pragmatic functions. *Language Arts, 60*(5), 590–599.

Graves, D., & Stuart, V. (1985). *Write from the start: Tapping your child's natural writing ability*. New York: New American Library.

Strickland, D. S., & Morrow, L. M. (1988). Emerging readers and writers: New perspectives on young children learning to read and write. *The Reading Teacher, 42*(1), 70–72.

# TOPICS AND THEMES
# FOR FURTHER DISCUSSION

1. Write about how the personal and the professional were related in the research that Nancy Brankis and Vida Schaffel did. In what ways do their experiences as students *and* teachers influence their research?

2. Describe how your professional career is influenced by who you are as a person. What are your research interests in which both dimensions are present?

3. Write a letter to one of the teacher-researchers who has written her/his story for this book. Think of the letter as a beginning of a conversation. What are you interested in asking that teacher-researcher? What common experiences do you have to discuss? Send it.

4. Begin to keep a teacher research journal in which you maintain a "written record of practice." After writing daily for a week or two, try writing a "journal of the journals," as Hobson describes in his chapter. What themes or recurring patterns occur, if any? How does the journal inform you about what is happening in the classroom?

5. Write your teaching autobiography and share it with a few peers.

6. Write your autobiography as a learner. Discuss how your experiences relate to your career as a teacher.

CHAPTER

# 2

# OPEN TO IDEAS: DEVELOPING A FRAMEWORK FOR YOUR RESEARCH

Joseph C. Fischer
National-Louis University

*. . . I like to try to find ways into a subject that will catch everybody's interests; . . . I like to see the most productive of questions get born out of laughter, and the most frustrating of brick walls give way to an idea that has been there all along.*

—Eleanor Duckworth (1986, p. 481)

## INTRODUCTION

This chapter rests on the belief that action research is a natural part of teaching. Central to both teaching and action research are instructional decisions informed by personal values, trial and error, reflection on experience, and conversations with colleagues. To be a teacher means to observe students and study classroom interactions, to explore a variety of effective ways of teaching and learning, and to build conceptual frameworks that can guide one's work. This is a personal as well as a professional quest, a journey toward making sense out of and finding satisfaction in one's teaching. It is the work of teacher-researchers.

I have found that when teachers view research as being quite separate from teaching and mainly the purview of specialists, they have difficulty seeing themselves as researchers (or finding time for research). I also have discovered that when teachers are invited to discuss their work in supportive settings, they express a rich variety of questions, wonderments, and ideas they wish to explore further.

Our task in this chapter is to examine a variety of paths teachers take as they begin to inquire and reflect upon their work. Specifically, the aims are to: (a) discuss how reflections on teaching, and the ways teachers think about teaching, constitute a vital and important foundation for doing research, (b) describe how teachers sort out and identify their research interests, formulate research questions, and develop frameworks that can serve as practical guidelines for their research, and (c) consider how perceptions of the potential role of research are linked to each teacher's hopes for teaching, goals for professional development, and beliefs about how knowledge is constructed.

The chapter draws on experiences of teachers who are doing or who have recently completed research studies. The experience and insights of these teachers have been gathered from their research writings, journals, interviews, and discussions. The chapter is divided into the following sections, conceived to help you begin to develop a framework as you think about your research.

Reflections on Teaching as a Basis for Research: An important and practical guide for research is your own knowledge of teaching, gained through experience and reflection on how you arrived at this knowledge. Such reflection can help you view your work from a critical perspective and provide valuable insights on how you think about teaching—core ingredients of teacher research.

Beginning With Observations and Interests: Many teacher–researchers begin their inquiry with observations, interests, and ideas they might want to pursue more systematically. Usually, they begin by trying out some idea or strategy to see how it might work with their students. Studying the students' responses leads to further elaboration of their ideas and research interests.

Suggestions for Developing Research Topics: Research topics emerge in many ways, evolve over time, are short term and long term, and vary in breadth and depth. Suggestions on how to consider and sort out topics for research are given.

Types of Research Topics and Questions: There are many ways of categorizing teacher research topics. To help you develop a framework for your research and examine the nature of your questions, three types are offered: (a) setting and context, (b) teaching strategies and content, and (c) visions and hopes for teaching.

Looking for Patterns, Themes, and Meanings: Research topics tend to reflect teaching beliefs and feelings, and hopes and visions for schools. These suggest important reasons why teachers pursue research interests and can serve as helpful guides in implementing the research itself. A main goal of teacher research is to identify patterns, themes, and meanings that emerge throughout their work of research. These become evident as teachers reflect on their thoughts and feelings about what is happening in their classrooms.

Teacher Research As an Unfolding Dynamic Process: Teacher research is a reflective process that unfolds and generally is connected to your teaching year. Classroom observations begin early in the research journey and questions continue to emerge during the year. New teaching strategies are tried out as the need arises, and student involvement is an integral part of the research process. Readings and discussions with colleagues are ongoing and viewed as enriching your inquiry ideas and your understanding of teaching. This unfolding dynamic also can be seen as a narrative inquiry that is intimately connected to your own teaching career and how you see yourself as a teacher.

## REFLECTIONS ON TEACHING AS A BASIS FOR RESEARCH

Duckworth (1986) told us that what she enjoys about teaching is knowing "that teachers are as interested as I am in how people learn, so the dialogue is deeply felt." She continued, "I always learn . . . when I see the endless variations on how they use what they learn in their own teaching." Her teaching is based on the belief that "people must construct their own knowledge and must assimilate new experiences in ways that make sense to them" (p. 481). She views her teaching as a form of research.

Eisner (1994) noted that teachers have a unique and central role to play in creating knowledge about teaching: "One must have a great deal of experience with classroom practice to be able to distinguish what is significant about one set of practices or another. . . ." He believes that this requires not only a "sensitivity to the emerging qualities of classroom life, but also a set of ideas, theories, or models that enable one to distinguish the significant from the trivial" (pp. 220–223).

In supportive settings among trusted colleagues, teachers are able to express the concerns and issues they face in their work and celebrate the insights realized through self-examination and reflection on their teaching practice. To facilitate such discussions and reflection, I have found the following questions useful:

- As you think about your teaching, how do you know when something really went well? What do you feel you are good at? How did you get good at it? As you think about your work, what stands out? Briefly, how would you describe yourself as a teacher?
- What role do your feelings and intuition play in the way you think about teaching? What intrigues you about teaching, learning, students? What are you working on now?

Gordon Will, a high school biology teacher, describes how self-reflection came to play a central role in his teaching. Throughout his teaching career of more than 30 years, he has found that new questions are always unfolding, and new knowledge is built on previous knowledge—but not without struggle and hard work.

Fifteen years ago I found myself covering the content, and did not find ownership in my teaching. It was a struggle before I began to realize that I did not need to give lectures revealing my wisdom. I learned to be more introspective. Today, I am more consciously aware of what I am doing, of what makes things work. I am beginning my 30th year of teaching and still ask, "What is it that I do?" My classes are my research. The students give me clues for what to do.

Early in my teaching career, I often did activities because I thought that the students would enjoy doing them. They sometimes fit into a particular unit, but often did not. Gradually I gathered them into one unit—a kind of "science methods" or "scientific inquiry" unit that we did during the first weeks of school. I wanted students to experience science, to lay a foundation, to set a tone for the year. I wanted that "first" unit to say something, to illustrate what I thought was important, what I valued. Most importantly, it was meant to get students engaged, excited and curious about science.

Jan De Stefano thought about the role that reflection played in the way she taught high school mathematics. Thinking about ways to make geometry more relevant and satisfying for her 10th graders, De Stefano decided to try out more discovery and collaborative learning strategies in her class. She hoped to find ways to help students learn geometry through more of an inductive than a deductive approach. Her research about these new ideas of teaching eventually revealed how students can discover an underlying mathematical system through class discussions and reflection. Her observations on the first day of trying out this new approach illustrates how students began to talk about their learning.

> I walked between the two rows trying to observe what they were writing. Believe me, it was nothing that made any sense. I then suggested that we discuss the problem. "Let's start with what kind of diagram we have up there. Does anyone know what that's called?" Well, finally we started talking.

> We discussed segments, angles, rays, symbols, etc. . . . I never wrote one definition on the board. We never did solve the problem, at least not that day. I was feeling great about the experience. It was new, it was different, but mostly it worked. We conversed in our new language. . . .

De Stefano was providing her students with an underlying structure through the kinds of problems she selected. There was constant reflection and discussion of what they were learning. After a month of not looking at their texts, she asked the students to compare their definitions with those in their books:

> Their facial expressions and responses were enjoyable for me. Apparently their definitions weren't so different from the ones in their book. We discussed the words—their meanings and the book's meanings. How many words on our list are not found in the first chapter? Many! How many words in this first chapter were not on our list? Few! I now explained that we were building a mathematical system, composed of definitions and statements that we would use throughout the course of geometry. The words are just the start of that system.

> . . . the class was able to see different methods of solving the same proof. This is when the class really became interesting for me. This group was solving problems that I

would never have used with this class level before. What is even more interesting is that I learned different ways to prove these problems than I had ever thought possible. I might add, even ways that were less complicated than I would have anticipated.

Significantly, the strategy included class meetings to evaluate what was happening in their mathematical thinking. De Stefano was tapping what was making sense to them and what meanings they were finding in their work. She thought carefully about what questions might guide these reflection sessions with her students. Some examples: "What suggestions do you have to make our classroom a place where learning can be more enjoyable for you? How do you like to learn best? Let's have a round, and everyone name one thing they know about triangles: No repeats. What did you do in the last month that really worked for you? Where have we come in the last 4 months? How do you feel about the class?"

As a result of her decision to change her teaching strategy, De Stefano discovered that lesson planning and decision making had to be shared responsibilities. The basis of the decisions rested partially with the students. But, something more was happening. The students were discovering that the mathematical system they were creating had an internal logic. Decisions about what worked and what did not were embedded in the structure of the mathematics itself. The students' own words and dialogue were the threshold to that logic.

De Stefano's initial research concern was to use more discovery-based, inductive, and collaborative-learning strategies in teaching geometry. Eventually, she found that her research questions contained more elaborate and basic issues:

> After eighteen plus years of teaching mathematics, I am finally zeroing in on the meaning of learning and the meaning of educating my students. Too often, I have seen teachers obsessed with the notion of teaching a particular subject, forgetting that what we are teaching is not as important as to whom we are teaching and for what purpose in mind.

> Somewhere toward the end of September or the beginning of October, this group became 'my class.' I felt a closeness with them, probably because we were really students together. They were learning geometry, and I was learning how to teach geometry in a new way. I would try to sit with each group and listen to how they attacked each proof. I found this fascinating.

> One thing I've learned is that students have a lot of thoughts, and they need the opportunity to express them. They also need to be able to express their negative feelings as well as their positive ones without being reprimanded or be made to feel guilty.

> . . . We use our intellect as well as our feelings to develop true meaning and real learning. Good teachers, who are good learners, must realize the importance of interacting with their students and generating feelings of warmth and acceptance. . . . Real teaching is not the subject you are teaching, but the people you are teaching.

Jan De Stefano demonstrates an important trait of teacher–researchers who invite discussions with their students about how they came to learn what they have learned. These class discussions and reflections are a powerful instructional strategy and a valuable way to collect rich information for understanding the nature and extent of learning. Some of the most frequent questions used by teacher–researchers to foster such dialogue and reflective thinking are:

- What do we see here?
- What do you think is happening?
- What makes for a good day in this class?
- What have we learned together?
- How did you go about doing it?
- What worked for you? What didn't?
- What did you find most useful, most enjoyable?
- What could we do differently?
- What might be our next step?

As teachers ask their students to think about their work, they come to realize more deeply that these reflection questions serve both instructional and research purposes. They come to understand that reflection and discussion are essential to learning and to understanding what happens in class. The questions generate important information as teachers and students try to sort out what works and what makes sense. Such reflective questioning illustrates the integral part research plays in teaching.

## BEGINNING WITH OBSERVATIONS AND INTERESTS

John Dewey (1897) in *My Pedagogic Creed*, reminded us that learning begins with interests, with what we feel passionate about, with what motivates and attracts our attention:

> I believe that interests are signs and symptoms of growing power. I believe that they represent dawning capacities. Accordingly the constant and careful observation of interests is of the utmost importance for the educator (quoted in Dworkin, 1959, p. 29).

That teachers' research interests can be considered "dawning capacities" is a very attractive concept. Ultimately, in studying our research interests, we are tapping hard-earned insights, understandings, and meanings we have gained from our teaching. Such interests represent what teachers value in their work, what they are committed to, and what they have learned through observation and self-appraisal. They also often reveal issues and concerns that still must be pursued, and hence can be seen as "symptoms of growing power." Thus, reflection on teaching interests (on their origins and how they evolve) can be particularly useful as teachers seek guidelines for their inquiry.

Classroom events, student interactions, unexpected surprises—all that transpires in school—have potential for research about teaching and learning. Teachers' and students' emotional responses to these events, reflections and thoughts about experiences, and attitudes and motives about learning, make research possibilities varied and extensive. How to sort out the possibilities is one of the chief struggles for teacher-researchers. How does one prioritize, make choices, and also focus on certain observations and interests?

One helpful way to begin is to study the research interests of other teachers, examine their reasons for wanting to pursue a particular topic, and categorize these under general groupings. Possible categories include: (a) an interest in knowing more about how students learn, (b) wanting to try something new, to innovate in a curriculum area, (c) a desire for change in one's teaching, and (d) a search for connections and meanings in one's work.

## An Interest in Knowing How Students Learn

An interest in knowing students: how they learn, how they think about their learning, and ways they make meaning, is one of the main reasons and motives why teachers engage in research. Observing students is central to teaching and forms an equally critical foundation for teacher research. When teachers see learning as constructing knowledge, and students as active in this construction, their ideas for research tend to emerge from this framework.

A desire to know how students become active learners became a research concern for Sue Hahn. Writing in her research journal, she described how she tries to begin her day with her third graders, hinting at an idea for her research. "I'm anxious to see the children, listen to whatever they want to tell me, and get them ready for the day, hopefully filled with many new beginnings for them. A new day of school is a chance to try a new approach. I think teachers are unique in that they don't give up easily and will try over and over again until they succeed in getting through to their children."

Chuck Sentell remembered his third graders asking him, "Mr. Sentell, are we going to get a chance to read?" He had been using a mastery learning skill program during reading with his class. The students' question caused him to pause. "The children helped me ease up on my role of complete structure, and of blindly following the district's curriculum mandates with little regard for the students' needs and interests," he said. "Good teachers know what kids can do. You can forget what is going on. But the students bring you back. You must continue to try to know their perspective. Over the years I've learned to be good at kid-watching."

Mary Ann Stocking's research study focused on how her class of sixth graders learned to communicate, developed more effective social skills, and how they began class discussions on their learning progress. After teaching in a large urban school system for more than 26 years, she wrote in her research journal about how her students began to work together. Her teaching skills benefit from her keen observation skills and her empathic understanding of students.

We are separate islands yet. We've started our journals and will soon move into groups. I'll have reading centers with extra library books instead of text books. The journals have helped me know what they are interested in, and the students tell me what they know about me. We are taking wobbly steps. We can talk now. As I look at these students, I think about when I was 15 and my Mom felt it was time to visit her aging mother in Poland. She wanted me to go along. Going over on the boat I read *Anna and The King of Siam*. Little did I know that years later I would return to that book to teach the pain and anxiety that people suffer through as traditions and customs are changed. My sixth-grade class and I share stories of poverty. We talk about games and the rules each game is played by. Then, I tell them the story of *Kim*, by Rudyard Kipling and how he learned the game of life. Our conversations in class lead to an openness and a willingness to participate in the game called school.

## Interests in Curriculum Innovation

A frequent source of ideas for research stems from a desire to try out something new, to "be updated" in a content area, or to work on some area of curriculum development. Some teachers even view research as an opportunity to construct the curriculum with their students, as Georgia Vidmont did with her first graders: "The children have ideas about first grade: 'We're going to learn how to read.' Still, this group is anxious to experiment, afraid to try out. They've set limits for themselves. I try to build the curriculum around them, their likes and interests, who's talkative, who's quiet."

Jurate Harris told me how she began constructing the curriculum with her students early in her career, and how reflection and class discussions helped shape and reshape what they did.

All I had my first year of teaching was a stack of books, the kids, and me. That's it. No curriculum objectives, no teacher's guide, no resource materials, just an empty room. I was responsible for teaching language arts to junior high school students. What made me think that I could undertake this? My thought was, if I really knew the students well I could teach them. I had to believe that. I thought, too, that with an intuitive response to the curriculum things would work out. That empty room helped make me an exploring teacher always looking for materials, trying to get to know the students, and creating opportunities for them to inquire and interact. From that first year of teaching I realized that I could never just cover the content, page by page, unit by unit, chapter by chapter. I wanted to put me into it, and I wanted to build it with the students. I was always trying to keep in mind the big picture. "What is this for?" "Why are we doing this?" I always wanted the students' world and the things we did in school to connect.

## A Desire for Change in One's Teaching

For many teachers, the desire for change is a main reason behind their interest in doing research. Cynthia Moore, teaching in an urban school, reflected on her teaching and how doing research with a group of teachers might be useful for her: "As I look and listen to the various people, it is as if we are all crying out to be heard for the first time. It is as if each of us is looking for support and help. I feel at times I can change everything that is wrong, but then I look for strength to get from one day to the other. If there were more people like us, we would begin to make a difference, we would begin to start that long hard change in the school system."

Sonja Groves wrote frankly about being discouraged in teaching and her hopes for change. As she reflected on her work, several possible research ideas could be found. "Each school year I start out with these great plans about all the wonderful things I would like to do with my children. I'm all excited in September and by December everything that I'd thought about doing is just thrown out. There is no time for it. Over the past few years I've become more of a disciplinarian than a teacher. I would be much more satisfied with the children being in control of themselves rather than to only cooperate or behave because of me standing there."

In thinking about her teaching, Lynette Emmons described her students' daily struggle for survival. She is not clear what role research might play in helping her face the overwhelming realities of her teaching, but she is exploring where she might begin and how the group of teachers she is working with might help her. "Every day I see students who have little or no hope for their future. I felt cheated in my undergraduate degree. They didn't tell us about the children we would meet. What about TJ who witnessed her mother's murder? Or DL who fears women since his mother deserted him? Or FS who wants to die because his future looks awful? We need to talk about the reality of the children. I come home so stressed out, I want to scream. It is as if no one is listening to me or the children. I have been accused of caring too much. Is that possible? I try to make my classroom atmosphere one of creativity and ease. We validate each other's feelings and all feel like part of a family. They respond positively to a teacher who can joke with them or break out in song and dance. . . ."

## A Search for Connections and Meanings

As they explore possible topics for research, teachers often begin to examine the beliefs that guide their teaching, as Pamela Flewelling did: "I feel it is so important to constantly reflect on what is happening around you and to allow your students to do the same. What am I doing that is in line with my philosophy? What am I doing that can be changed to meet my beliefs?" Elizabeth Chase agreed that exploring one's philosophy is important, and might even suggest a topic for further study: "I really believe that a person's philosophy about life very much affects their teaching philosophy. I am very interested in learning more about group dynamics. How can I further develop students' sense of responsibility when working in a small group without me? Even though I strove to play a facilitative role last year, I was still a very central (annoyingly at times) figure." Chase began to compare the image she had of herself as a teacher with what she felt she was actually doing in class. Her research was being conceived within a vision (framework) she had of herself as a teacher.

In discussing their teaching, other teachers express a desire to find connections in their work. Many teachers find ideas for research from their reading, as was the case for Mary Ban: "I really got into reading Carl Rogers. Not only did I find it interesting at an academic level but I also found it to be extremely uplifting mentally. I feel like something amazing is going to happen with the way that I teach this year and I feel like I am on the brink of discovering things about me that I haven't been pushed to discover yet."

In summary, to explore ideas for research, teachers must feel supported and valued in revealing their experiences and feelings about teaching. They need to feel comfortable about expressing themselves when opportunities for listening are created. By sharing their observations and interests among trusted colleagues, they help each other sort out the many potential ideas for research that might address their needs, concerns, and hopes for teaching. Ultimately, teachers must feel free to innovate and make key instructional decisions, feel supported in changing their teaching, be willing and encouraged to take risks, and be receptive to comparing their teaching beliefs with what they do each day in their teaching.

## DEVELOPING RESEARCH QUESTIONS

What might be some useful ways to help frame research ideas and to formulate research questions? Our task here is to present a variety of strategies that might help clarify areas of research interests, questions, and ideas. Another goal is to help you identify structures and frameworks behind your questions, which can help you pursue your inquiry interests. The hope is that the following approaches and activities will liberate your thinking rather than confine you to simple formulas or mechanical methods.

One of the greatest benefits of teachers working together on research is the potential for sorting out, clarifying, and elaborating their possible research questions. Tentative ideas and questions can become working ideas and guiding questions as teachers discuss each other's research interests. Multiple perspectives enrich these seeds of ideas and explorings for inquiry. Group support and discussion can stimulate the vaguest beginnings of an idea, and help make sense out of the multifaceted realities teachers face in their work.

Brainstorming is one of the most useful ways that teachers can help each other map out research interests and ideas. As teachers brainstorm ideas, the goal is to both generate many ideas and perspectives and find connections and natural guidelines that can help the research journey. Brainstorming serves another equally useful function by helping teachers relax and feel more comfortable about the seemingly heavy and serious work of research. In working with teachers, Burnaford offers the following questions that can help in brainstorming research interests.

- What keeps going around in your head as you look at yourself and the students in your classroom? What about your classroom or teaching intrigues you?
- What about your classroom or teaching challenges you or is a problem sometimes for you? What do you definitely want to know more about when it comes to teaching your grade level or subject area?

I have found the following questions helpful in elaborating further this brainstorming activity:

- What are possible ways we could look at this idea, topic, or question?
- What are some things we already know about this idea, topic, or question?
- How might these ideas be interconnected?
- What are some unifying themes and patterns in this topic?

Formulating research questions and deciding on a research topic can become an all-absorbing preoccupation. Most teachers find, however, that once they decide on an idea, the work of research tends to take on a life of its own. This probably happens because the working idea suggests an inherent structure that helps guide the research. Our intuitive feelings about our teaching usually suggest insights and, thus, a potential structure and focus for research. The challenge is to look for patterns and themes as you explore these feelings and brainstorm ideas. In developing your framework for research, what seems prudent is to keep research possibilities open, but also to take note that ideas might have a structure, a kind of network of associations.

Another way to help consider research ideas is to formulate "what if" type sentences. What this activity does is elicit images of what could be, of visions about what teaching could become. Such images often reveal the beliefs and philosophical stance that teachers hold for their work. Gathering "what if" sentences can reveal how one's hopes for teaching correspond to teaching realities and practice. This might be a sobering exercise, but it could also keep the direction one wants to head in focus. Again, we turn to Burnaford to illustrate some "what if" type sentences.

- What if art and music were integral parts of the social studies curriculum?
- What if we had no ability groups for reading/language arts?
- What if kids wrote for 5–10 minutes in each subject area?
- What if kids in 5th grade spent time each week with those in 1st grade?
- What if students generated their own tests?
- What if business leaders were in the classroom on a regular basis?

Murray (1993), held that writing is a discovery process and that we are often surprised at what we learn as our writing unfolds. To gather thoughts and ideas for writing, Murray suggested keeping a journal. Such a journal can help you sort out your research interests and let you keep in touch with your thinking and learning. Writing in a journal is useful in helping teachers see that the task of research is manageable, has boundaries, and it relates to their teaching in a natural way. Moreover, it is a practical way of getting started. Inquiry does not have to wait until a full-fledged research plan of action (with readings, methodology, and conceptual frameworks) is designed. Step by step, teachers can begin their inquiry and make it a part of their teaching. Eventually, through their journal, teachers may discover that the parts fit into a unifying structure, a holistic approach that has larger meanings for their teaching.

## Types of Research Topics and Questions

Although research questions overlap and interconnect, we can identify three areas or groupings they tend to fall under. These are offered to illustrate possible areas of research interest, but it should be emphasized that research questions tend to encompass elements of each area. The purpose of creating this typology is to help you get started in focusing on your research and perhaps formulate some guiding questions.

*Settings and Context.* Research questions can originate from concerns about contextual issues, for example, school and classroom settings and creating climates and opportunities for learning and teaching. Examples of questions of this type include the following.

What rewards for teaching and learning are present in this school? What norms and values about teaching and learning do the faculty hold? What makes for an effective school culture for learning and for teaching?

What roles do parents play in the life of this school and in the learning of their children? What voice do students have in setting the goals of this school? What voice do teachers have?

How do students view their life in this school over the years they are here? How do their attitudes change year by year? How do they feel connected to this school, to each other, and to the teachers? How does this school provide opportunities for students to take charge of their learning?

Is there a real community of learners in this school? How could one be created? How should we deal with conflict, antisocial behavior, abuse, and neglect? How should we build on the strengths and gifts of all students? Of all faculty members?

What are some ways to build a climate for learning in my classroom? What makes for a good day—for me and for the students? How can I help students reflect on their work, assess their learning, and feel good about their accomplishments? How can positive relationships, interactions, and communication be fostered in my classroom? How might internal and self-discipline replace external and teacher directed norming?

***Teaching Strategies and Content.*** Research questions in this area deal with teachers' concern with instructional strategies, ideas for teaching content, and ways teachers and students together might build the curriculum. The following examples of possible research questions, are based on Burnaford's work.

How can I stimulate more class discussion that is productive and enhances learning in my subject area? How can I use writing to help students learn to be critical thinkers and problem solvers? How can I use a literature-based language arts approach in my teaching?

How can I introduce a more hands-on and inquiry-based approach in my social studies and science curriculum? What are some practical ways I can help students construct learning opportunities in my class? What role can students play in curriculum development? What role can I take in developing curriculum in my teaching?

What are the ways that I can investigate how much talking I do in class and how much talking the students do? What kinds of teacher questioning produce optimal learning? How can I help students generate questions to help them learn and be researchers?

How can I help the parents of my students understand what goes on in my class? How can the teachers on my team or on my grade level work together to educate parents on "best practice" at our grade level?

What are the ways in which I can utilize a variety of assessment measures in my class (writing samples, portfolios, exhibitions, journals, student-generated tests, self evaluation)? How can I help students learn to monitor and evaluate their own learning?

***Visions and Hopes for Teaching.*** These types of research questions include exploring professional development interests, visions for teaching, and hopes of what schools can be. One effective way of tapping this area is for teachers to reflect on their teaching career and the main learnings and knowledge they have already constructed. Embedded in their career history are evolving beliefs about teaching and learning. (The preceding "what if" sentences listed are one way of tapping the visions and hopes of teachers.)

> What motivated me to enter teaching, and what keeps me in the teaching field? Who were my mentors? Who influenced and still influences my learning and teaching? As I look back over my career, what stands out? How have I evolved as a teacher? What would I change?

> When do I feel good about my work? When do I feel I have the "touch" in my work? Do I still have what it takes? Do I have a personal style of teaching? What image do I have of my teaching? What image do students have? How do I reconcile my teaching image with the public images?

## Looking For Patterns, Themes, and Meanings

Teachers find that their ideas and questions continue to evolve during their work of research. Gradually, their initial questions become more complex, unearthing more basic issues and concerns. As they continue their inquiry, teacher–researchers frequently find themselves asking: Does this make sense? What does this mean? How might I see this differently? They become more aware that their central research questions ultimately are interpretive ones addressing the issues of meaning and value. Behind teachers' research interests are particular perspectives, belief systems, and visions for teaching. The task is to explore the underlying structures embedded in their questions and wonderments about their work. There are layers of meanings present in classrooms that can be explored through particular kinds of questions that teachers ask. Good questioning techniques, suspended judgement, and attentive listening by teachers are necessary in order to probe for deeper understandings and meanings.

How we see reality is the starting point of the questions we ask about our work. In turn, our questions are a way of uncovering the narratives and meanings in our classrooms. What attracts many teachers to inquiry about their field is the same that calls scientists and artists to theirs: teachers are curious about ideas, want to be creative, and hope their research will lead to a better understanding of and fulfillment in teaching. Behind teachers' research interests and questions are hopes and images of teaching and the kinds of schools they want for students and for themselves.

Teacher–researchers are finding that as they try out new ideas and reflect on their work, they begin to see themselves as creators of meaning and theory-builders in their own right. They become more aware that they are interpreting their practice through the lens of their unique perspectives, searches for meaning, and conceptual frameworks constructed throughout their career.

Looking for meaning starts from the very beginning of inquiry when teachers explore possible topics for research. It is at the basis for reflection on one's teaching, constructing the curriculum with students, identifying and analyzing related research literature, sharing one's research with colleagues, and writing a research report. Constructing meanings also rests on the visions and beliefs teachers hold about teaching and learning.

In her research, Paley (1986) used a tape recorder to capture her kindergartners' discussions. As she listened to their conversations, she looked for patterns and analyzed them in terms of her own organizing frameworks and her ideas about what is meaningful.

> As I transcribe the daily tapes, several phenomena emerged. Whenever the discussion touched on fantasy, fairness, or friendship ("the three Fs" I began to call them), participation zoomed upward. If the topic concerned, for example, what to do when all the blocks are used up before you can build something or when your best friend won't let you play in her spaceship, attention would be riveted on this and other related problems. . . . These were urgent questions, and passion made the children eloquent. They reached to the outer limits of their verbal and mental abilities in order to argue, explain, and persuade. No one moved to end the discussion until Justice and Reason prevailed. (p. 124)

Paley's constructs of *fantasy, fairness,* and *friendship,* are part of her larger view of what is happening in her classroom, of what the classroom interactions might mean. We all invent such conceptual frameworks in order to make sense out of what is happening in our teaching. A purpose of research is to help us become more aware of the perspectives, belief systems, and searches for meaning that underlie our work. Our challenge in studying the work of teachers who pursue research is to understand the particular conceptual frameworks that might guide their teaching. Our hope is to compare their meanings with those we have discovered.

Research experiences are illuminated by the meanings we attach to them, by how we interpret them, *and* by the messages our colleagues find in them. Discussions with colleagues and other teacher–researchers can help identify what stands out in our research, what we are trying to accomplish, and what connections we are making. Importantly, such dialogue helps us put into words the complex experiences we are trying to understand. Maxine Greene wrote about this: "The realities we construct mean what they mean because we have internalized common ways of thinking about them and talking about them. But, at the same time, each of us looks upon the common world from a particular standpoint" (in Lieberman and Miller, 1991, p. 4).

Each of us creates our personal reality of what our teaching and research mean. When we describe and write about this knowledge for other teachers, we add our voice to the literature of teacher research, and acquire a greater awareness and appreciation of our work as teachers and as researchers. Greene considers teacher inquiry as a way to understand teaching realities, and holds that it is both a social and an autobiographical process. She sees teacher research as a language that helps us describe and clarify what captures our attention: "We live in continuing transactions with the natural and human world around us . . . Only as we begin moving into the life of language, thematizing, symbolizing, making sense, do we begin to single out certain profiles, certain aspects of the flux of things to attend to and to name" (in Lieberman and Miller, 1991, p. 4).

## Teacher Research As an Unfolding Dynamic Process

As you become involved in research, you may find that there is a cycle or rhythm to research, as there is to all learning. Carr and Kemmis (1986), in studying the work of teacher research, referred to this as a "self-reflective spiral," suggesting that teachers ". . . used the self-reflective spiral of action research to make initial observations and analyze their current teaching practices, then planned ways they wanted to change and observed the problems and effects of the changes they introduced, then reflected on their observations to decide how next to act in the process of improving their practice" (p. 168).

Another way of describing teacher research is to see it as an unfolding dynamic process. This unfolding can be described as follows:

- During the early explorations of a topic for research, we reflect on our teaching experiences, observe students, think about what is taking place, and consider what is working and what might need change. Our purpose is to continue to build on our teaching experiences, reflect on what is happening and, where necessary, make changes.
- As we reflect on our observations we look for patterns and connections in our teaching. This includes noticing themes in the ways students approach learning and in the class discussions about what is working and what sense it is making.
- Gradually, our introspection and inquiry include an examination of our teaching beliefs, values, and frames of reference that might guide our work.
- How we describe what is taking place becomes more elaborate, and builds on previous understandings, insights and meanings. Sharing our understandings and questions with others is a reoccurring theme all during our inquiry journey.

Whitehead (1967) in his much quoted work, *The Aims Of Education*, proposed that all learning has rhythms that alternate between freedom and discipline. The first stage he called *romance*—a time of freedom to explore and discover, the next he saw as *precision*—a time of discipline, organizing, structuring one's ideas, and the last stage he called *generalization*—characterized by freedom when connections, patterns, and meanings are constructed. I find this a useful construct in my work with teachers who look for guidance in doing their inquiry.

Teachers have found that these stages of romance, precision, and generalization occur throughout their research journey.

The propensity of storytelling among teachers suggests another potential framework to both guide research plans and to describe understandings gained through research. Multiple insights are embedded in teacher stories and can serve as a rich basis for continued reflection and inquiry. Connelly and Clandinin (1990) held that "The main claim for the use of narrative in educational research is that humans are storytelling organisms who, individually and socially, lead storied lives. The study of narrative, therefore, is the study of the ways humans experience the world. . . . Narrative names the structured quality of experience to be studied, and it names the patterns of inquiry for its study" (p. 2). As in all good stories, narrative inquiry is no mere telling of experiences or classroom events. Memorable stories aim to find meanings suggested in experiences and are constructed through reflection, interpretation, self awareness, and a concern for audience. Our challenge is to recognize and study the messages conveyed in our stories and those of our colleagues.

Michael Polanyi's (1962) pioneering work, *Personal Knowledge: Towards a Post-Critical Philosophy*, has inspired a dramatic shift in our thinking about how we build knowledge, how we know what we know, and how we tell others of our understanding (e.g., through narration and dialogue). Polanyi believes that central to constructing knowledge is what each person brings to it, and calls this thought-provoking idea, *personal knowledge*. His thesis has profound implications for understanding the work of scientists, artists, teachers, and students. "I have shown that into every act of knowing there enters a passionate contribution of the person knowing what is being known, and that this coefficient is no mere imperfection but a vital component of his knowledge" (p. viii).

As teachers engage in action research, one of the most satisfying aspects of their experience is the personal mark they put on their inquiry—their own voice that emerges in their writings and conversations. From somewhat tentative beginnings, their ideas and research questions evolve in unique and significant ways. And, as they discuss their work with their colleagues, they find pleasure in the meanings they discover in telling their research stories.

## REFERENCES

Carr, W., & Kemmis, S. (1986). *Becoming critical*. Philadelphia: The Falmer Press.

Connelly, F. M., & Clandinin, D. J. (1990). Stories of experience and narrative inquiry. *Educational Researcher, 19*(5), 2–14.

Dewey, J. (1897). *My pedagogic creed*. In M. S. Dworkin (Ed.), *Dewey on education: Selections*. New York: Teachers College Press.

Duckworth, E. (1986). Teaching as research. *Harvard Educational Review, 56*(4), 481–495.

Eisner, E. W. (1994). *The educational imagination: On the design and evaluation of school programs* (4th ed). New York: Macmillan.

Greene, M. (1991). Teaching, the question of personal reality. In A. Lieberman & L. Miller (Eds.), *Staff development for education in the '90s: New demands, new realities, new perspectives*. New York: Teachers College Press.

Lieberman, A., & Miller, L. (Eds.). (1991). *Staff development for education in the '90s: New demands, new realities, new perspectives*. New York: Teachers College Press.

Murray, D. M. (1993). *Write to learn*. New York: Harcourt Brace Jovanovich College Publishers.

Paley, V. (1986). On listening to what the children say. *Harvard Educational Review, 56*(2), 122–131.

Polanyi, M. (1962). *Personal knowledge: Towards a post-critical philosophy*. Chicago: The University of Chicago Press.

Whitehead, A. N. (1967). *The aims of education, and other essays*. New York: The Free Press.

# THE PERSONAL AND THE PROFESSIONAL: LEARNING ABOUT GENDER IN PHYSICAL EDUCATION

Rick Moon
Mundelein Schools

## THE REASONS FOR MY RESEARCH

I am a K–8 physical education teacher and coach at Fremont School in Mundelein, IL. My wife and I are parents of two preschool girls, Amy and Kelsey. In this chapter, I will try to relate what happened in my life as a teacher, coach, and father during my two-year research project that focused on gender stereotypes.

I believe that my interest in this topic, particularly as it relates to athletics and physical education (PE), can be directly traced to the birth of my daughters. Prior to that point in my life, I concentrated solely on male athletics. I coached all the boys sports programs at Fremont since 1979 and, though I helped score or officiate some of the girls' athletic competitions, I realize now that I did not have much respect for them. Regretfully, I was among those who felt "it's just a girl's game."

I learned most of what I know about teaching from experience and most of that experience came from teaching physical education to boys. Looking back, I see that my undergraduate physical education teachers were almost all males who had very firm beliefs about gender roles. The following is an excerpt from a notebook I turned in to one of those college PE teachers in 1976:

> Our society is being taken over by women who won't allow their children to play any rough sports and condemn any fighting. By doing this, the young boys of our society are becoming sissies. It is our job as PE teachers to teach combativeness, roughness, and physical contact to students, without causing serious injury, in order to prevent women and sissies from taking over our society. My teacher responded to this with the words: "And don't ever forget it!"

**51**

The fact that my first-born child was a daughter was clearly the impetus to change this perspective. I immediately became more observant of the girls in my physical education classes and I helped out at the girls' basketball games more during that first year after Amy was born than I ever had before. In fact, it was then that I decided to coach a girls' basketball team. During my research, I have listened to girls and boys, regardless of age, saying that boys are all stronger, faster and more highly skilled than girls, and that teams are unfair if one has more boys than the other. I have observed highly skilled girls hold back and not perform up to their capabilities for fear of what others might think or say about them because they are not "supposed" to be good. I have seen less skilled boys find ways not to play so they could avoid the negative comments from others for not performing at a "boys level" of play. Through my research, I sought to explore these attitudes and experiment with methods in physical education that could challenge them to rethink these gender stereotypes.

My teacher action research project was also my way of examining my own perceptions and beliefs about girls and athletics. In addition though, it was a way to experiment with different methods and approaches to teaching physical education. I decided to focus on the elements of competition and cooperation, as they relate to gender in physical education. Ultimately, I discovered that the more attentive I was to my own attitudes about gender in my classes, the more responsive the students were. Also, I learned that a physical education curriculum that is balanced between competition and cooperation is one that allows for the active participation of everyone, not just the athletically talented.

When young children ranked a list of desirable school behaviors, girls identified "to be nice" and "to be smart" as the most important, whereas boys identified "to be a leader" and "to be good in sports" (Caplan & Kinsbourne, 1974). Children tend to define sports as more masculine than feminine (Stein, 1971). Boys learn very quickly that demonstrations of athletic skill earn the praise and attention of adults, especially from fathers who show more emotion and enthusiasm for sports than anything else (Lever, 1978).

> From a sixth-grade girl, during a flag football skill drill: "Do we have to play football? Can't we play tea party or something?"

"Have we conveniently allowed lesser skilled females to congregate in the game room and flee the playing fields?" (Greendorfer, 1980). Much research indicates that females often exhibit less self-confidence in achievement situations than males (Sadker & Sadker, 1986; Feather & Simon, 1973; Maccoby & Jacklin, 1980). Because competition is an achievement situation, women may demonstrate some lack of self-confidence when they face competitive sports activities. Lower self-confidence in turn affects their performance and success in physical education classes, which are highly competitive in focus.

"If our goal in physical education is physical development and not development in becoming competitive, it would appear that a physical education program that emphasizes sports, rather than other forms of physical activities, discriminates against women" (Nicholson, 1983, p. 280). It is often true that poor execution of sports skills by some females can be attributed to incomplete learning and not enough practice rather than a consequence of lack of ability. Positive reinforcement from others and positive personal expectations are important ingredients in the sports socialization process. I intended to investigate how to instill both of these factors more consistently in all students in my physical education classes during my research.

## TAKING ACTION

> My classes were practicing throwing and catching when the head of maintenance came into the gym. I told him I was trying to eliminate the bad habit some kids have of throwing off the wrong foot. He said, "Oh, you mean they throw like girls?"

Throughout my 13 years of teaching, I have shared the gym with a female physical education teacher. Typically, she was the "girls' gym teacher" and I was the "boys' gym teacher." I shudder to think about it now, but what we had was a female teaching girls to "play like girls" and a male teaching boys to "play like boys." Is it any wonder that the competitions we had, pitting the boys against the girls, were often rather unpleasant situations? I remember a basketball unit when the girls' teacher did not allow the girls to steal the ball or block shots. She thought the games would get too sloppy and rough. She believed that she was providing the appropriate playing environment in which the girls could develop their basketball skills without becoming overly preoccupied with winning. I, however, was busy in the next gym teaching the boys to play an aggressive, winner-takes-all basketball game!

Greendorfer (1980) pointed out that boys and girls define appropriateness and importance of activities differently. Girls tend to emphasize effort whereas boys tend to emphasize ability in their play. Boys stress winning, play more competitive games, and highly value sports activities. Girls tend not to be rewarded for participating in physical activity and do not highly value competition or master of skill in sport; rather, girls play less goal-oriented games that involve less complex rules and fewer number of players or participants (Lever, 1978; Greendorfer, 1980).

The first change I made through my action research was to bring the boys and girls back together again for coeducational classes in grades 1–5. (The middle school program was already coeducational.) The change eventually met with great success. Our students were learning skills in a cooperative atmosphere where active participation by all students was stressed. In past years, I would readily allow girls to "slack off" during activities, believing I was doing them a favor. I have now come to the realization that allowing them to do so was a great disservice. Last year, when I began my research project, I did not tolerate lack of effort from any students. I started the school year with constant encouragement towards active participation in activities where skills were being learned and improved. This directly and positively carried over into competitive activities. Once the students had developed and practiced skills, they were much more eager to display them in a competitive activity.

> From one eighth-grade girl who chose not to play in a coed game one day: "We must make a great play every time or we get ridiculed by the boys."

I have also tried to make sure that the competitions are fair. I have had absolutely no boys versus girls competitions. Insisting on active participation from everyone has also resulted in fewer complaints from the boys about having too many girls on their teams or in their groups. I believe that those kinds of complaints were more about the lack of effort, actual or perceived, than because their teammates were boys or girls.

Another change I made in my curriculum was to change from the Presidential Physical Fitness Test to the American Association of Health, Physical Education, Recreation, and Dance Fitness Program (AAHPERD). After analyzing both, I became aware that the Presidential test uses different standards for girls and boys on all five of the tests through all ages, 6 through 17. Girls were, in other words, required to do less to achieve the same awards as the boys. More important, students got the idea that what was considered physically fit for girls was far less demanding than for boys. The AAHPERD program bases the students' fitness levels on five tests. Before the age of nine, the standards are exactly the same for boys and girls on four of the five tests.

## FURTHER REFLECTIONS

As I was collecting data during my observations of physical education classes, which were coeducational and noncompetitive along gender lines, I occasionally noted an interesting phenomenon. Consider this story from my research journal:

> I play a game with fourth graders called "Elimination." The game involves throwing and catching skills as players try to eliminate other players by either throwing the ball and hitting them with it or catching the ball when they throw it to you. The first time we played, the game was very individualized. Everyone had opportunities to throw, catch, run, and dodge.

> Soon however, an interesting change occurred. Two of the higher skilled boys teamed up to try to eliminate everyone else. The next "level" of boys then teamed up to try to survive and would occasionally win too. The girls never tried to form their own teams but did eventually try to team up with the two boys' teams. They would usually stay in the game until the other team was eliminated and the boys with whom they had joined turned on them. The girls would then scatter and be systematically eliminated by the rather sophisticated teamwork of the boys. Another group of girls simply ran from the action, choosing to escape being hit by the ball over the chance to throw it.

All the students were very active, yet the observations I collected from this game, as well as from others during my research, offer some interesting reflections into gender differences in physical education. It seems that the boys in my classes are more comfortable with organizing themselves into teams that then allow them a greater opportunity to win. The girls do not display that willingness to organize themselves quickly and efficiently into teams nearly as often. Is it because more boys have experiences outside of school with team sports and are thus accustomed to this approach? Is it because parents train their boys to play as team members even in casual outdoor play at home? As I continue being a teacher-researcher, this is a subject I would like to explore in greater detail.

## FINAL THOUGHTS

My research on competition, cooperation, and gender role stereotypes changed my role as a teacher by helping me to become more observant than ever before in my classes. Instead of just teaching my students, I became much more aware of my *learning from them*. Things had begun to get fairly routine and there were some things I felt were in need of change. My research gave me a reason to make a few of these changes.

Note: All throughout her last pregnancy, my wife claimed she was going to have a boy. "Only a boy would cause this much trouble" were her exact words. Perhaps Kelsey Lynn was getting a head start on shattering gender stereotypes. Anyway, she looks great in the *blue* sweater her Grandma knit for her!

## REFERENCES

Caplan, P. J., & Kinsbourne, M. (1974). Sex differences in response to school failure. *Journal of Learning Disabilities, 7*(4), 232–235.

Feather, N., & Simon, J. (1973). Causal attributions for success and failure at university examinations. *Journal of Educational Psychology, 64*(1), 46–56.

Greendorfer, S. (1980). Gender differences in physical activity. *Motor Skills: Theory Into Practice, 4*(2), 83–90.

Lever, J. (1978). Sex differences in the complexity of children's play. *American Sociological Review, 43*, 471–483.

Maccoby, E., & Jacklin, C. (1980). Sex differences in aggression: A rejoinder and reprise. *Child Development, 51*(4), 964–980.

Nicholson, L. (1983). The ethics of gender discrimination. In B. Postow (Ed.), *Women, Philosophy, and Sport*. Trenton, NJ: The Scarecrow Press.

Sadker, M., & Sadker, D. (1986). Sexism in the classroom: From grade school to graduate school. *Phi Delta Kappan, 67*(7), 512–515.

Stein, A. (1971). The influence of masculine, feminine, and neutral tasks on children's achievement behavior, expectancies of success, and attainment values. *Child Development, 42*(1), 195–207.

# TOPICS AND THEMES
# FOR FURTHER DISCUSSION

1. Think about the mentors you've had in your life. In what ways have they influenced you, your philosophy of life, your way of learning, the way you teach? Write a letter telling a mentor how she/he has influenced you.

2. Interview a teacher and talk about your mutual interests and questions about teaching. Compare the influences on your teaching. What helped your teaching? What did not?

3. Think about your early writing experiences. What made it pleasant and useful; what was difficult, even painful? What lessons about writing have you gained from these experiences? Talk to someone who had a different writing experience. What made for the difference?

4. Develop one or two research topics which are of interest to you. Write a *focus statement* for each. Try to characterize your topic(s) as Fischer describes in chapter 1: a) focus on knowing more about how students learn; b) focus on curriculum innovation; c) focus on change in teaching; d) focus on connections and making meaning in one's work. Talk with peers on the steps to take to get started.

5. Fischer describes how Jan De Stefano invited discussions with her students about her classroom research. Moon also included students as co-researchers. How might such a process shape your research topic?

# 3

# A Life of Its Own:
# Teacher Research and
# Transforming the Curriculum

### Gail Burnaford
National-Louis University

*It is not enough that teachers' work
should be studied;
they need to study it themselves.*

—Stenhouse, 1975

## INTRODUCTION

Often the curricular reality of schooling is invented somewhere other than the classroom. Curriculum mandates, teacher-proof textbooks, and system-wide objectives often preclude the task of creating curriculum that is personal, immediate, and in fact, alive. Elliot Eisner viewed teaching as an art and we can extend his metaphor by saying that creating and reshaping curriculum through teacher research is an artistic act (Eisner, 1994). Entering one's own classroom as a researcher may be likened to entering a work of art. It is an act of creating, of personalizing, of inventing the reality that works for those children at that time.

Bissex and Bullock (1987) told us that "classroom-based research presents a serious challenge to current and traditional education and to the public's definition of what teachers are and do" (p. xi). A teacher research approach to curriculum not only alters the way in which we think of teachers and their roles; it also suggests a new way to think about students and the ways in which they learn. During the last decade, teachers have been urged to promote critical thinking in their students. Critical thinking involves questioning, trying possibilities, interpreting, justifying, and evaluating. Yet, quite often, the curriculum teachers feel obligated to address attempts to cover vast amounts of information rather than to deepen thought in selected, integrated subject areas.

Viewing the construction of curriculum as a collaborative action research process affords both teachers and students the opportunity to engage in critical thinking. "People are not recorders of information but builders of knowledge structures" (Resnick & Klopfer, 1989, p. 4). In a classroom where teacher research is occurring, there are many opportunities to become builders of knowledge. In fact, that is the main activity! When teachers see themselves as helping to construct knowledge as it is lived daily with children, children may begin to understand that curriculum is developed in and through their own learning as they participate in researching their classroom.

## TEACHER–RESEARCHERS:
## A VOICE IN THE CURRICULUM

Carol Santa, a curriculum director for a large district wrote: "I have chosen not to spend my time in my office, writing fat curriculum guides. In fact, our entire district curriculum fits neatly in one slim folder. Teachers found our previous curriculum manuals cumbersome—more useful for pressing flowers than for guiding instruction" (Santa, in Olson, 1990, p. 65). Curriculum, for teacher action researchers, is something that is *lived*; it is what and how we teach and learn in school buildings and playgrounds. It is what children experience. Instead of relying solely on curriculum guides to make instructional decisions, teachers note that they inform themselves each day by watching and listening to their students—judging when it is time to move on and when more time is needed for individualized attention, choosing one kind of activity over another based on the attitudes and abilities of a given class of children. Few teachers follow the exact same curriculum each year simply because, as one teacher commented, "The children are different each year! How can I teach the very same thing in the same way?"

J. Harste described the teacher research movement as a parallel to the "whole language" initiative in literacy education. He says that a whole language approach to literacy gives a voice to children; it encourages them to write about what they know, read about what they are interested in, and connect what they are learning every day to their own lives (Harste, in Olson, 1990). Similarly, teacher research gives teachers a voice in their own professional development (see chapters 5 and 6, this volume). It affords them a chance to shape what happens in their classrooms and relate what they believe with what they practice.

If we view the predictable, though weighty, curriculum guides as informational tools rather than as strategic mandates—and if we reduce the district curriculum to Santa's one slim folder—then what happens to the role of the teacher and the students? How does the curriculum come to reflect what each brings to the shared experience? What happens to the subjects being taught?

## ACTION RESEARCH STRATEGIES IN THE CURRICULUM: A DEEPER UNDERSTANDING OF CONTENT

Our goal is to develop a deeper understanding of the relationship between the strategies for teaching, the acknowledged structure and organization of a subject, and the real-world experiences of children. To that end, I sat down with a group of teacher–researchers and brainstormed ways in which classroom research might help us to establish a connection between methods of teaching, the content of the lesson, and the needs of children. Here are a few of our ideas for shaping a teacher research project with special attention to the *who, where,* and *when* of the curriculum. These ideas may be especially helpful for preservice teachers who are interested in connecting what they are learning in methods classes with what they are studying about specific content fields and child development. Often the classes in these areas are separate. Teacher research can help to bring the elements of curriculum together in a meaningful way. These ideas are starting places that will help teacher–researchers rethink their own voice in the curriculum.

"It's the starting place which is in question ... it's different when it begins with *me* and *my students* than when it begins with a content area," one teacher–researcher explained. The strategies do not drive the inquiry; rather, the inquiry reveals the strategies that the classroom researchers collaboratively design. In this classroom, at this time, with this group of people, a variety of choices and decisions can be made that will enrich each person's learning and allow each to take responsibility for growth.

*Ideas for Classroom Research in Curriculum*

1. Look at the textbooks and other resource materials for use in a content area. What kinds of knowledge are emphasized? Whose knowledge is it? Where did the concepts come from and how are they expressed? What topics are missing from the texts? Whose stories are missing? What other sources of knowledge are available to students beyond the textbook? Ask students to discuss these questions with you. Tape the discussion and analyze it with them.

2. Look at methods textbooks that preservice teachers use to learn about a content field. What kinds of information do these texts present? What's missing? How would you have written such a methods text differently? What kind of preparation do you feel is most beneficial for a teacher in that content field?

3. Try to come up with a definition/description of a content field. For example, what exactly **is** social studies? Where did the term come from? What do *you* think is important in social studies? What has been most present in your teaching and learning of social studies? What has been absent? Ask your students to define or describe a subject area. How do they describe the field of mathematics? How might their description guide your teaching practice?

4. Examine what you are *not* knowledgeable about in a content field. What is your felt puzzlement in science, for example? What's bothering you about what you are doing? What do you know too little about? One teacher–researcher explained, "Some of the things I was trying in my music class weren't working and I didn't know why. I was afraid to ask anyone; I was *supposed* to know this stuff!" Teacher research is the opportunity to explore what we *don't* know. Another teacher wrote, "I don't feel particularly comfortable with this . . . that's why I chose to study it."

5. Find out what the students know and don't know about a content field. Ogle's KWL method is an excellent one to examine what children bring to a learning experience (see Fig. 3.1). Teachers may wish to adapt the first column to read "What Children *Think* They Know," allowing for the misconceptions that children have which guide their curiosity and eventual discovery. These naive understandings held by children may be the starting places for teacher research. How do children move from misconception to understanding? What is the role of the teacher in that process?

6. Investigate an interest in a specific strategy or philosophy of teaching; perhaps this topic emerges from a district initiative or perhaps it's something you've read about in the professional literature. I leave this option for last because it seems common to look for strategies or methods as an *initial* thrust. Only after looking more closely do we see that more philosophical questions emerge whenever any teaching activity is adopted unilaterally within a district or school building. For example, what is the source of the literature-based approach to reading that the district is supporting? Can we find anything similar in past teaching practices? Whose interest is best served by this approach? How does it fit into your own beliefs about teaching and learning? How is it compatible with the experiences of students?

# K-W-L STRATEGY

FIG. 3.1. KWL: A strategy for student inquiry.

## RELATING TO THE RESEARCH "OUT THERE": WHAT ARE OTHER TEACHERS DOING?

As teachers begin to sharpen the focus for their research project, they often begin a process of exploration that connects them with others who are curious about what we can learn from looking into classrooms. Tapping into the experiences and knowledge of others through a variety of means of gathering information, then scaffolding what we have learned and incorporating what we are doing in our own classrooms, is a way of making meaning of a wealth of experiences.

Teachers, as a matter of course, are often on the lookout for ideas to use in their teaching. They share ideas through conversation, order materials through workshops and teacher centers, and search available journals for the newest methods and materials. Learning about what other teachers are doing in a subject area or research focus is a natural activity for an inquiring teacher. Such an exploration may be viewed as a means of enhancing one's understanding of a theme, topic, or research question to be investigated in the classroom. Teacher action research, in a sense, makes that inquiry more systematic in order for teachers to preserve what they are learning and build on it.

*Must* one delve into books and journal articles in order to do classroom research? Some would argue that such a venture impedes the work of a teacher who comes to the process with a felt need that is context-specific and real. A few might say that reading the literature of a content area or educational topic deters teachers from devising their own solutions to problems and using their own "educational imagination" to make decisions (Eisner, 1994). One fifth-grade teacher had read none of the literature concerning literature circles, for example, but designed her research around an idea that she and her fifth-grade students invented together called Reading Teams. In effect, she and her class had developed their own curricular strategy, for which there might be parallels in other classrooms, but it is uniquely their own. I would guess that group of fifth graders assumed much greater ownership of that endeavor than they would have with a similar version of literature circles imported by their teacher. The process that fifth-grade teacher used is something like what Hyde and Bizar (1989) described as "giving the students the chance to be thinkers" (p. 3).

And yet the profession is a community of learners; we cannot ignore the experiences present in the writings of other researchers that can be beneficial to teachers in the process of their own research. Reading with a teacher-researcher's eye means trying to understand others' research with special attention to one's own practice. Looking at the writings of teacher-authors or other educational researchers does not imply a comparison to one's own practice, but rather suggests that we might learn from a careful response to others' work, based on our own grounded experience. Nixon (1987) described the knowledge gained not as a literature of our findings, but rather as an accumulation of stories, of histories, in order to inform ourselves.

Reading research literature is often a new experience for teacher–researchers; one that deserves discussion in a teacher research collaborative setting.

It may be useful for teacher research groups to analyze the ways to approach the research literature in journals and books. Zeuli's (1992) questions for response to research are helpful for discussion and/or journaling:

1. What is the main thing the author seems to be saying and how does he or she convince the reader? What does the author do to make you believe the article?
2. Is there anything in the article you have trouble understanding?
3. What conclusions, if any, would you draw from the article for your teaching, and why these conclusions?
4. Did you enjoy any article more than the others? Why or why not?
5. In light of how you think research should help teachers, does any article succeed more than any other? Why or why not?
6. Did the authors use similar kinds of evidence in each article to support their views? Was any evidence more or less convincing? (pp. 7–8)

Migra (1992) suggested that teachers think about these reflective questions while they read the literature about teaching:

What experiences do you bring with you to this activity?

Do these writers or speakers seem to be speaking to *you*?

Have they sufficiently convinced you that they are in touch with the realities and complexities of the classroom?

Do these ideas inspire, bore, enlighten, anger, educate, or confuse you?

Figure 3.2 shows a double-entry journal format that may be useful to teacher–researchers. The columns are an effective way to write what seems interesting in

| RESPONSE | SOURCE |
| --- | --- |
|  |  |

FIG. 3.2. Double-entry journal. The idea here is to deliberately separate the source material from one's response to it, thus keeping the "voices" identifiably separate. Make note of the complete bibliographic citation for the source your are using and make note of the date of this writing

the reading in the right column and immediately respond to that passage, describing impressions, connections, and personal related ideas in the left column.

There are subtle dangers in relying solely on the literature rather than viewing it through the perspectives gained from practical experiences. Hattrup and Bickel (1993) described a teacher research collaboration project involving university researchers and classroom teachers called *Thinking Mathematics*. The goal of the project was to combine the clinical insights of teachers, the recent research on mathematics, and the National Council of Teachers of Mathematics (NCTM) standards in order to construct a meaningful math curriculum for a school district. They began the project by asking the teachers to spend time reading other people's research, after which they would gather and discuss that reading with the university participants. What resulted from this approach was that the teachers became increasingly reluctant to share their classroom knowledge with each other or the university researchers. They became quite concerned with what the products of this collaborative effort should look like, including what was required and when. The goal of the research—to connect to teachers' own practice—was subsumed by a preoccupation with the research and teachers' own voices became lost. Fortunately, the group soon realized what was occurring and the teachers' own experiential knowledge became essential to the success of the curriculum project.

The *Thinking Mathematics* project offers some insight for teacher–researchers, whether they are working collaboratively or individually within their own classrooms. It's probably not necessary to be consumers of vast amounts of research in the field; the goal of accessing information is to turn attention to what knowledge can continue to be generated and consciously documented in the classroom. "To be generative, knowledge must become the object of thought and interpretation, called upon over and over again as a way to link, interpret, and explain new information that students encounter" (Resnick & Klopfer, 1989, p. 209). Even as we read about the work that others have done, we can be consciously linking, interpreting, and explaining, using our own voices as teachers.

Some teachers have found it beneficial to refrain from immediate judgment of the applicability of the ideas inherent in a book, article, or workshop presentation. One teacher described the process as "responding to what jumps out, then letting it incubate for awhile." Likewise, teacher–researchers may want to read and listen for a while without trying to determine where or how this material will be used or written about. Kelsay (1991) called this "meandering through the research process" (p. 18), during which teachers sample the smorgasbord available without evaluating its immediate usefulness in the classroom. Instead, they seek understanding and a deeper knowledge about what other teachers think and feel. The essence of the question is the opening up, and keeping open, of possibilities (Van Manen, 1990). Such is the nature of effective exploration of what is out there. If we consider what we do with students as a curriculum of possibilities, we are opening ourselves to learning beyond our own experiences.

Reading the literature also has tremendous implications for curriculum. Often, teachers are unaware of the kinds of ideas being traded in the field and the ways in which other teachers in other school systems throughout the country are teaching and learning. Teachers often feel isolated in their own classrooms. Access to professional organizations related to subject areas they teach may assist teachers as they extend the dialogue beyond their own classrooms or schools.

Many teachers are unaware of the journals being published each month that pertain to their teaching grade level, content area specialization, or to the profession as a whole. These journals seem readily available to teacher educators, but are not always present in the lives of classroom teachers. Even though many schools provide a professional library for teachers, teachers seldom have enough time or the incentive to delve into its holdings. A teacher research project invites teachers to look at what is available; the project provides real motivation for the search because what is learned applies directly to their own classrooms. Readings are often surprisingly accessible and timely and teachers are often amazed to see what others have done and shared (see Fig. 3.3 for a partial listing of journals that are helpful to teacher–researchers).

---

### SELECTED JOURNALS FOR TEACHER–RESEARCHERS

American Educational Research Journal
American Journal of Education
Art Education
Arts and Activities
Arts Education Policy Review
Arts Magazine
Action in Teacher Education
Best Practice
Center for Children's Books Bulletin
Child Development
Child Study Journal
Children Today
Children's Literature in Education
Chronicle of Higher Education
Classroom Computer Learning
Cognition and Instruction
Computers in the Schools
Curriculum Inquiry
Curriculum Review
Democracy in Education
Early Education and Development
Education
Education Week
Educational Action Research
Educational Computing and Technology

---

FIG. 3.3.  *(Continued)*

Educational Foundations
Educational Horizons
Educational Leadership
Elementary School Journal
English Journal
Equity and Excellence
Exceptional Child
Exceptional Child Education Resources
Feminist Teacher
Focus on Exceptional Children
Foreign Language Annals
Gifted Child Today
Health Education
Illinois Reading Council Journal
Instructor
Journal of Curriculum Theorizing (JCT): An Interdisciplinary Journal of Curriculum Studies
Journal of Health, Physical Education and Recreation
Journal for Research in Mathematics Education
Journal of Computer Based Instruction
Journal of Curriculum and Supervision
Journal of Curriculum Studies
Journal of Research in Science Teaching
Journal of Research on Computing in Education
Journal of Special Education
Journal of Staff Development
Journal of Teaching Writing
Journal of Youth and Adolescence
Language Arts
Learning
Learning Disabilities Quarterly
Lion and the Unicorn
Mathematics Teacher
Middle Ground
Middle School Journal
Middle School Voices
Music Educators Journal
National Education Association (NEA) Journal
Phi Delta Kappan
Physical Educator
Primary Voices
Reading and Writing Quarterly
Reading Research Quarterly
Reading Teacher
Research Quarterly
Rethinking Schools
Review of Educational Research
School Arts
School Library Journal
School Science and Mathematics

FIG. 3.3. *(Continued)*

Schools in the Middle: Theory Into Practice
Science
Science and Children
Science Education
Science Teacher
Social Studies
Social Studies Review
Teaching and Change
Teaching Pre K–8
Theory Into Practice
Today's Education
Writing Teacher
Young Children

FIG. 3.3.   Selected Journals for Teacher–Researchers

If we think of the process of reading other teachers' research as an accumulation of stories in order to inform ourselves, then *what* we do with what we read is really up to us! Ownership of the process of learning through reading about what other teachers have found helpful is critically important. If our writing is a compilation of relating and responding personally, we remove it from the guise of objective, distanced research and place it in the realm of writing that can be useful to other teachers in turn. The review of what one finds "out there" then becomes both personally relevant and professionally sound.

A few teacher–researchers comment:

> Through this process of research, I have been able to define what my idea of good teaching is. As a new teacher, I had been more involved with and worried about the mechanics of it all. But now I am starting to look more at the meaning of it all.

> After reading articles on improving relationships with others and conflict resolution in the classroom, I noticed myself more and how I interact. I've found things I do that I really didn't know I did—some good and some bad. I can really see benefits coming from this knowledge and this will improve my teaching.

> Through this process of research, I have reconfirmed my beliefs—it's a validation of sorts!

## TRANSFORMING THE CURRICULUM: THE "ACTION" IN TEACHER ACTION RESEARCH

One teacher recently exclaimed, "You can't just read, you have to experiment!" Absolutely! As the curriculum of possibilities becomes more of a reality for teachers, the potential for experimentation becomes unleashed and the willingness to take risks becomes more evident. Research becomes more than *informing*; it is in fact *transforming*. The curriculum comes alive as teachers decide what kinds of activities they will try and how they will collect the data about what happens. It is this aspect of teacher research—the part we call "the action" or implementation—that is at the heart of curricular innovation and change.

Action research suggests a process in the classroom that may include trying something different. It may also mean the careful and systematic observation of phenomena that are not new in the classroom, but that in some sense demand a closer look by the teacher–researcher. During the observation of the "action", the teacher–researcher devises some means to capture the occurrences for reflection, perhaps through journal writing, student responses, or feedback from colleagues. In turn, a theme for teacher research can spring from the activity that occurs regularly each day in the classroom. Action can lead to reflection, followed by observation, which in turn may reveal more action to be taken.

In my attempt to describe what happens in a teacher–researcher's classroom, I run the risk of appearing to outline structures that may be perceived as criteria for "good teacher research." In trying to describe what teacher research looks like, feels like, and smells like, I risk implying that I know what *is* "good teacher research." My intent is to share the practice of teacher research, not to establish norms or standards. Hopefully, teachers will critically and thoughtfully examine what is offered here, using what seems to make sense for them and their students.

What happens to the curriculum when these elements of reflection, action, and observation occur intentionally and somewhat systematically in a class-room? How is the curriculum in some way *transformed* by this classroom research? Dewey (1943) reminded us that for many educators, attention is fixed on the importance of the subject matter of the curriculum rather than the child's own experience. This focus on subjects has resulted in the delineation of separate content areas in the curriculum, which "fractionizes" the world of the child (1902/1990, p. 184). The curricular discussion becomes one that dichotomizes the child *versus* the curriculum rather than centering on the child *and* the curriculum. In most school subject matter, Dewey continued, curriculum "furnishes the end, and it determines the method" (p. 186).

Dewey also insisted that the two are not in opposition. Instead, a teacher's true challenge is to discover how the subject matter can be drawn from the experience of the child. The subject areas, such as math, science, or history, "are themselves experience . . . reflectively formulated" as teachers and children explore them together (p. 190). This is precisely what can happen when a classroom becomes the environment for teacher research. The subject areas in the curriculum are transformed as they reflect the real experiential framework of children who are the learners. Through teacher research, the subjects become more than sets of external facts, logically ordered and sequenced; they become authentic experiences.

Dewey (1943) used the analogy of the map as the curriculum for a subject area, absent the involvement of the learners (1902/1990). The map is not the experience of the journey; it's in fact only a map . . . a piece of paper—and cannot substitute for the experience itself. Similarly, "the logically formulated material of a science or branch of learning, of a study, is no substitute for the having of individual experiences" (p. 198).

## EMERGING PATTERNS IN THE TRANSFORMING CURRICULUM

What happens to life in classrooms when action research is going on? How exactly might the curriculum be "transformed" by this process of collaborative research? Although there are clearly no definitive answers to those questions, there do seem to be three patterns that occur when teachers and students examine curriculum through research in their classrooms. As teachers begin to do classroom research, they: (a) see the connections and relationships across content areas, (b) pay more attention to the affective aspects of teaching and learning, and (c) recognize the need for students to participate knowingly and actively in the process.

When the curricular discussion concentrates on the child *and* the curriculum together, (reminiscent of Dewey's conception), teachers may begin to recognize the connections across content areas. As we look more closely, we can see the relationships between the processes in teacher action research and those utilized in integrating curriculum (Burnaford, Beane, & Brodhagen, 1994). Teacher action research is drawn from the experiences of all the participants in the classroom context. In teacher action research, one begins with the questions and issues raised in the classroom; that starting place is also ideal when designing integrative curriculum. Teacher action researchers work with students as co-researchers; in an integrative curriculum, students are active participants in shaping and planning curriculum.

Therefore, when teachers actively examine their classrooms through the lens of action research, their teaching may "borrow" from other subjects, in terms of methods and strategies, as they see the usefulness of these techniques. Studying the use of a strategy in one content area opens the door to exploring applications elsewhere. Cooperative grouping is adaptable to lab sciences, social studies projects, and math problem solving. Similarly, the content used in one subject area may be applied in other areas. There is much in the literature that describes the power of integrative curriculum in which children's literature is applied to mathematics and science, fine arts is used as an integral part of a language arts or foreign language curriculum, or mathematical concepts are reinforced through fiction (Beane, 1990; Burnaford, Beane, & Brodhagen, 1994; Jacobs, 1989; Pappas, Kiefer, & Levstik, 1994; Stevenson & Carr, 1993; Whitin & Wilde, 1992). As teachers observe children, record what is happening in their classes, and reflect on what they have experienced, they often begin to see that what occurs is not specific to just one area. Connections across disciplines often are perceived and more readily accepted by teachers as they take the time to look more closely at their own practice through research. Focus is often shifted from the parameters of a subject's content to questions about how children learn.

Brodhagen's eighth-grade class members became her co-researchers as they explored the alternatives to traditional assessment in their class. They experimented with several different progress report and report card designs throughout the year, which were more compatible with their integrative curriculum (Brodhagen, 1994). Although the teacher began with a research question, "How can progress be reported and grades given in a teaching–learning situation when using an integrative curriculum approach?", she immediately recognized that the question would change over time, particularly as students assumed more of the ownership of the investigation (p. 240). That is an important point to consider; when we invite students to take part, we invite some sharing of the control of what students learn and how they learn it; such input most assuredly changes the research focus when it occurs.

A second pattern that also relates to Dewey's comments on the child and the curriculum is that of increased attention to the affective aspects of learning, that is, how students and teachers feel about what and how they are learning. One teacher conducted a study on the use of manipulatives in mathematics with learning disabled students. Although she was pleased to have discovered some wonderful tools to use with the children, she was much more interested in how this new strategy *made her students feel*. She began to sense that the more positive feelings they held about math and their ability to "do math" had perhaps more to do with their success than any other single thing. A first-grade teacher admitted to the influence of her viewing her young charges "as writers". Her students realized that she was watching very closely as they learned to express themselves on paper—at first through scribbles and drawings with dictated captions, and eventually blossoming into elaborate stories using invented spelling. This teacher reported that the more she watched, the more "writing" the young scribes did! The affective dimension of the action research project definitely impacted on the cognitive gains of these kindergarten children.

This affective dimension of learning about a subject often becomes the primary focus of the research for teachers. A project might begin with an attention to a content field and develop into a study of self-esteem and its implications for classroom pedagogy. A seventh-grade social studies teacher designed a research project on this basis, after realizing, "I don't really teach content, I teach self-esteem. This is an important revelation for me as a junior high teacher."

The theme of attending to the affective aspects of teaching and learning, then observing the influence on the curriculum, extends to the self-perceptions of teacher–researchers as well. A sixth-grade teacher who did some classroom research on science stated: "This project forced me to do something about my weakness. I learned that there really is a little scientist running around in each of us—even me!" The methods and materials she discovered in her classroom research reshaped the curriculum from one that was textbook-defined to one that was experiential and problem solving in orientation. Shumsky (1958) claimed that "rarely has the emphasis been on the impact of researching on the researcher" (p. 3). In fact, the learning that teachers carry away from action research, which is *about themselves*, may be the most influential, most central, and most important outcome of such activity.

A teacher–researcher in first grade wondered, "What can you learn from applesauce?" (Clark, 1990). She experimented one day making applesauce with her first-grade students. The teacher listed the learnings from this experience, dividing them into those that were intended and anticipated by her and those that were surprises and/or "subtle side effects" (Clark, 1990, p. 328). These side effects included what the teacher learned about herself and about teaching. We often resist or even forget to talk about this. During her "applesauce day," this first-grade teacher learned more about her own necessity for detailed planning; she became more aware of the gender roles in the class and their impact on the experience, and she realized her own low tolerance for risk involving young children and sharp knives!

A final pattern appears as teachers examine the relationship between the child and the curriculum. When teachers engage in classroom research, they realize as they proceed that they desperately *need* the active involvement, support, and feedback from their students in this endeavor. This feedback is more than just the surveying of a class on the success or failure of a lesson or an approach. Rather, this involvement of students in the research process is a valuable opportunity for the learners to also be the teachers, and for their needs, experiences, and interests to be at the heart of the curriculum decision-making process. Much to teachers' exasperation sometimes, students often ask, "Why are we doing this anyway?" An action research approach to curriculum invites this question—both in the asking and the answering. No one has *the* answer, but the class can come up with many answers as students participate in the decisions about how to learn in their own classrooms. Stevenson (1986) noted that "when we inquire, we ask others to teach us—to help us close the gap between our understanding of a topic and theirs" (p. 5). If those "others" are our students, the research process becomes collaborative and the curriculum comes alive. It is probably wise to find out what students think early in the process about the focus of the research or the research question, if it involves them immediately and directly. Their early feedback could shape the eventual design and planning. Similarly, the results of the research project are shared with those who provided that original information, namely students, parents, community, and teacher colleagues who have shared in the inquiry. Craig Hill, in his research focusing on high school chemistry, invited continuous responses from his students as he tried a new approach to learning in his classroom (see Craig Hill's Teacher Research). He claims that he surely learned as much from his students that year as they did from him!

What kinds of curricular decision making can result when the students are active curriculum planners with a teacher? What would happen if we conceived of teacher research as a means of curriculum development with *students as co-researchers and observers in the research process* rather than as subjects of a laboratory experiment? The potential for such study is inherent in teacher research. Van Manen (1990) reminded us that current educational research tends toward abstraction, thereby losing touch with "the lifeworld of living with children" (p. 135). If we consider the students as co-researchers in classroom study, curriculum planning and the resulting content becomes incontrovertibly transformed.

A junior high physical education teacher was interested in pursuing a study about how to motivate her female students to do well in PE classes. She proceeded to read extensively about motivation. She analyzed works dealing with early adolescent females, and she looked at the latest writings about middle-level education. Finally, one of her colleagues offhandedly suggested, "If you want to know why the girls aren't motivated in PE, *why don't you ask them?*" How many times do we make educational decisions without ever thinking of asking the students what they think, how they believe they learn best, and what it is that would encourage them to continue to learn and improve? This PE teacher went back to her school the next day and proceeded to listen—to large groups of girls, to small groups, and to individuals through indepth interviews. She gave them surveys, she invited them to keep PE journals, and, in the end, she realized that this listening was a new form of teaching for her—one that was in and of itself motivating for these junior high girls.

These three patterns, namely, the seeing of connections across content areas, the realization of the affective dimensions of curriculum, and the involvement of students in decisionmaking, all transform the lived curriculum in a teacher–researcher's classroom. The transformed curriculum is contextual; it has in fact been shaped by research. Viewing action research *as* curriculum, rather than something being done *to* curriculum is a shift in definition which is transformative.

## "I WISH I KNEW EXACTLY WHAT I WAS LOOKING FOR!" DATA COLLECTION IN TEACHER ACTION RESEARCH

This process of gathering information, sometimes called *data collection*, is one that is shaped and reshaped as action research continues. There are, however, some kinds of procedures and types of data that may be useful as guidelines for classroom teachers. According to Bogden and Biklen (1982), *data* are "the rough materials researchers collect from the world they are studying" (p. 73). Data are both the evidence and the clues in this adventure; they are what supports the reflections and the analysis and they are what is used to make meaning for future researching in a classroom.

Figure 3.4 lists some of the means of data collection that teachers have found useful. For more detail on these approaches in action research, see James McKernan's (1992) *Curriculum Action Research* text. When selecting data collection techniques, it's important that a teacher evaluate *why* a particular approach would be valuable and whether that technique actually addresses his or her need in the research. Nixon (1981) reminded us: "There is no single way of doing research in the classroom" (p. 13). The question is, what works for me?

For a teacher–researcher, one of the most important sources of information is the collection of *fieldnotes* kept during the research. Fieldnotes are "the written account of what the researcher hears, sees, experiences, and thinks in the collecting and reflecting on the data" (Bogdan & Biklen, 1982, p. 74). Fieldnotes help the researcher reconstruct dialogue using language that is as close as possible to that which was heard in the classroom. They help describe the specifics of setting and interaction in an environment. Collecting data essentially means experimenting with a slightly different role in a classroom, one in which a teacher "juggles the green roll book in one hand with the tape recorder in the other" (Johnston, 1988, p. 17).

Many teachers find it useful to keep a *research log* or *journal* in which various kinds of data can be stored. Research journals can be a valuable means of recording anecdotes and personal recollections each day during a teacher re-search process that can be elaborated on at a later, more convenient time. One teacher–researcher called these notes "word pictures". A high school teacher commented, "I write in my journal every day. I find it necessary to track all the currents in the room."

Researchers generally suggest that it is best to write about an event or a time period as soon as possible before you discuss it with anyone; verbal language appears to change what has occurred as the speaker shapes the conversation. Individual journal writing offers a teacher time to process it independently first. Chapter 1 describes data collection through journal writing in greater detail.

In teacher action research, McKernan (1991) reminded us that the aim of the data collection "is description and interpretation from the inside rather than strict measurement and predication of variables using a quantitative approach" (p. 59). The purposes "do not include the illusion of proof" (Stevenson, 1986, p. 7). Findings from teacher action research are not intended to be statistically generalizable, although their insights and results can inform other teachers immeasurably. Nonetheless, teachers engage in this research using their own personal and professional lenses of experience. What they choose to study and what kind of data they gather reflect that personal experiential base from which they build their research. Even as we collect information about what is happening, we are already *transforming* curriculum in the classroom (Van Manen, 1990).

By the very fact that we collect specific anecdotes, select certain pieces of a discussion, or directly quote a particular student, we have attached meanings to those episodes, thereby transforming them and declaring them to be part of

*Observational Techniques*

1. Checklists
2. Rating scales
3. Anecdotal notes (includes nonverbal behavior, room environment description, exact language in an interaction—it's often useful to jot these on index cards and keep them in a file)
4. Case study (a detailed description involving a single person or a specific type of event—case studies are essentially stories; they enable the teacher researcher to view students as individuals in the research process after a period of intensive observation, writing, and reflection focused on that individual)
5. Diaries and journals (kept by participants in the research)
6. Fieldnotes
7. Shadow studies
8. Photographs, videotapes
9. Taped recordings
10. Interview notes

*Nonobservational Techniques*

1. Attitude scales
2. Questionnaires
3. Interviews (Interviewing can be a complex venture and deserves much thought. The degree of structure, the relationship between interviewer and interviewee, and the implicit and explicit purposes for the interview are all critical considerations. For more discussion, see Van Manen, M. *Researching Lived Experience*, 1990)
4. Life history accounts
5. Letters (to one's class, to a colleague, to an administrator)
6. Art/other demonstrations of student learning or creativity

*Evaluative Techniques*

1. Triangulation (a method for documenting multiple points of view, i.e., events from the perspective of a student, a teacher, and an administrator. This term also refers to the use of multiple methods, i.e., survey, interview, and participant observation, for the purposes of comparing and contrasting. For more information, see McKernan or Nixon (1981) *A Teacher's Guide to Action Research: Evaluation, Enquiry and Development in the Classroom*)
2. Peer coaching
3. Student evaluation
4. Curriculum criticism (see Eisner's (1994) *The Educational Imagination*)

FIG. 3.4. Data collection strategies.

our research. After much data have been collected by students and teachers, the co-researchers can begin to look for the *themes* that emerge from the data, with the awareness that whatever surfaces has already been transformed by our own interaction with that material. The curriculum of lived experience is one that is contingent on interactions, exchanges, and the prior experiences of students and teachers.

Data collection, then, is not a process for finding definitive answers. The teacher who exclaimed, "I wish I knew exactly what I was looking for!" has expressed the frustration, perhaps, but also the compelling appeal of teacher action research. Keeping one's eyes open for what may happen, being aware of the issues and dilemmas that occur in the midst of one's research, and being able to shift attention to themes when they appear may be the reason teachers who become researchers in their classrooms remain that way after their first research effort is complete. This constructive ambiguity may be unsettling, but it is what motivates us to generate new questions and take new risks.

## ACTIVE REFLECTION: SEEKING MEANING IN THE DATA

"My research has many facets. Which is most important?"

"I am wondering if my research will show anything conclusive."

"I have mounds of data. I always wanted to write a novel, but I never had anything to write about. Now ... I have enough material for a couple of novels!"

What do we do with the data that have been collected during teacher action research? In most traditional research, teachers or their students are " 'studied', not 'studiers', and have little or no control over the research, what is reported and how it is disseminated" (McCutcheon, in Nixon, 1981, p. 187). Teacher–researchers and their students have the control and the experience to communicate what they have learned in a manner and format that is compatible with their own style.

Most teacher–researchers learn to write their stories with authority, using the first person, discovering and amplifying their own voices. They synthesize the mounds of data, looking for patterns perhaps, writing about their own learning, and eventually, generating new research directions or questions. Such synthesis does require some active analysis, not to mention organization. Figure 3.5 lists some suggestions for looking at the data collected, with the cautious reminder that although these methods of organization and analysis have been useful for other teacher researchers, each teacher must find the approach that is personally meaningful.

Van Manen (1990) noted that our texts "need to be oriented, strong, rich, and deep" (p. 151). The teacher research texts are oriented in the world of personal

1. Gather all the data in one place and spread it out. (Dining room tables and living room floors are popular for this.) Try to determine the kind of information that appears to surface: themes, common statements, patterns of behavior, points of frustration, general structural pieces of the project. Then use colored dots (available in stationery stores) to color code the themes or patterns discovered in the data. For example, purple dots might be attached to anecdotes and journal entries focusing on student behavior, yellow dots may be used for description of curricular activities, and green dots may be for personal reflections and feeling statements.
2. Draw a picture, chart, or diagram of the information, thinking about lines that connect, arrows that indicate direction, or circles which overlap.
3. After looking through the data, begin analysis with brainstorming sentence completions, such as "I think ...", "I believe ...", "The children in my class are learning ...", "The climate in my class ...", "They need ...", "I need ..." Then examine the data for evidence to support your responses.
4. Rank order the kinds of data you have accumulated. Are student journals most important? Are surveys what should be addressed first? Why?
5. Compare the nature of information you gather in different ways. How are survey data different from checklists? How are questionnaires different from journalwriting?
6. Examine the anecdotes of classroom life. Could any be used as organizers? What patterns are evident in them?
7. Explore the data with the particular intention of examining your own role in it. Who were you? Where were you? Did you sense personal and/or professional change through the process? Who are you now?
8. Look through the data for surprises or unintended learnings.
9. Look through the data for specific improvements and/or positive changes.
10. Look through the data for specific challenges or setbacks.
11. Invite a teacher–researcher colleague to look at some of the data. What does he/she see? What is communicated to an informed, but nonparticipating observer?
12. Invite the students to look at some of the data. What do they see? How do they interpret what they see?

FIG. 3.5. Data analysis/organization ideas.

engagement and practical experience. They are strong and rich because they illustrate the power of first-hand exploration, which is generative and multidimensional, providing examples of what students bring, what parents contribute, and what other teachers may have shared. They are deep in that they transform the lived curriculum in classrooms.

## TEACHER–RESEARCHERS AS AUTHORS: CONTINUING THE DIALOGUE

Teacher–researchers often find that they are anxious to share what they are learning and doing with an audience other than themselves. The very presence of an audience shapes how we begin to write about what we are doing and what we are thinking. How and what we think is often shaped by the audience that is held in our own minds. How will I be discussing my research with my students? Who will be listening to the story of my teacher research? Will I be sharing what I am learning with parents? With my administration? With other teachers? Zemelman and Daniels (1988) gave this perfect example of how one's sense of audience can shape what one writes:

> The effect of a real audience is as crucial for adults as for teenage students. In the Illinois Writing Project, we've enjoyed over the years the sure-fire shock that comes when we ask a group of teachers to write a letter to the trusted friend about a student who has frustrated them and then to revise the letter so it can be sent to the child's **parents**. (p. 179)

One of the primary purposes a teacher serves by conducting teacher research is that of improving his or her own practice in the classroom so, in that sense, the primary audience for the research is the teacher involved. A collegial research group can become a wonderful audience as well, and a greatly experienced one at that. A research group is much more than just an audience though; it is an interactive context in which many of the aspects of the teacher research process can be conducted. It is a place where teacher researchers can listen and respond to and really help each other get the work of the research done. Thinking about other audiences for research can be a valuable use of time for the teacher research study group. Participants might ask, who else would be interested in what we are doing? Who else needs to know about our research?

Sharing the dynamics of teacher research can take many forms. Some teachers discuss their work in their own teams or departments either in a formal or informal presentation. Schools who view teacher research as professional development in which teachers plan for their own growth and learning have experimented with a variety of ways that teachers can share what they have been studying in their classrooms (see chapter 6). Certainly a clear focus on such a mechanism for sharing is a necessity in a school setting where collaborative research and informed investigation are high priorities.

Those who feel comfortable with writing and wish to seek publication for their efforts can look to a growing number of journals that welcome teachers' work. The Teachers and Writers Collaborative publishes a newsletter and books about teaching and writing that may be useful to teacher-authors (Reissman, 1993). Some teachers have started a newsletter in their district to communicate research efforts across buildings and grade levels. Journals such as *Teaching and Change, Primary Voices, Middle School Voices, Best Practice,* and *Rethinking Schools* actively seek articles by classroom teachers who have conducted research. There is a special interest group affiliated with the American Educational Research Association (AERA) called *Teacher-As-Researcher,* which welcomes membership and presentations by classroom teachers at their annual meetings. There are also several list serves on the Internet for teacher researchers.

Carol Avery writes of finishing a year-long teacher research project in her elementary classroom. As she gathered with her colleagues in their research study group, the facilitator began with, "So, what are you researching next year?" (Avery, in Olson, 1990). For a moment, she was taken aback. And then, she realized that after watching, listening, and noting what occurs in a classroom in a reflective, inquiring way, it would seem difficult *not* to keep doing so. The focus may change; the interest may shift, but the transforming continues.

## POSTSCRIPT

There is a children's picture book written by Jon Agee (1988) called *The Incredible Painting of Felix Clousseau*, which captured my attention as I was writing this chapter about teacher research and curriculum. Agee's story seems to be a wonderful symbol for the art of teacher researching.

Agee's book tells the story of a painter named Felix Clousseau who creates incredible paintings that have some living element to them. If he paints a duck, the duck quacks and eventually strolls off the canvas. A portrait of a volcano actually erupts and fills the museum with smoke. A waterfall on painted canvas spills out all over the floor! Incredible, yes, and unsettling too! In fact, as Agee announced, "Wherever there was a Clousseau canvas, there was chaos" (see Fig. 3.6).

In Agee's book, the magical painter Clousseau is punished for his amazing art and is sent to prison. Eventually though, he is released after one of his paintings of a watchdog performs a heroic duty and prevents a burglary from happening. When Clousseau leaves prison, where do you suppose he goes? He finds his way back to one of his paintings, steps into the canvas, and proceeds on his way. The scene comes to life as Clousseau steps into it and the painting is forever changed (see Fig. 3.7).

If we view teaching as an art, then the imagery in this picture book is clearly an invitation to think more deeply about teacher research. Clousseau enters his own work of art in the same way that a teacher is invited to enter into the daily acts of learning in the classroom and change them through the process of teacher research. Although the new perspectives may at first be disquieting, just as Clousseau's paintings were disquieting when they suddenly came "alive", that learning becomes part of the process of change and development for both teacher and students. In order for curricular change to occur in a meaningful way and at a personal level, it may be necessary to take the risks and feel the discomfort. The reward is in the experienced curriculum, which in fact, comes alive through the process.

Teacher–researchers have used this imagery as they described their research process. Their words evoke the symbolism of Clousseau's amazing artwork:

I'm still on the outside looking in—I am not yet a part of my research.

The research should speak for itself, and yet it should also be a portrait of ourselves.

My research is an invention created by me. If you will, a unique expression of my classroom story. In many ways, it has a life of its own.

In fact, wherever there was
a Clousseau canvas, there was chaos.

FIG. 3.6. "Living" paintings of Felix Clousseau.

Clousseau was a hero.
He was awarded the Medal of Honor.
Released from prison,
he went back to his studio...

and returned to his painting.

FIG. 3.7. Clousseau steps into his own artwork.

# REFERENCES

Agee, J. (1988). *The incredible painting of Felix Clousseau.* London: Farrar, Straus, and Giroux.

Avery, C. S. (1990). Learning to research/Researching to learn. In M. W. Olson (Ed.), *Opening the door to classroom research* (pp. 32–44). Newark, DE: International Reading Association.

Beane, J. A. (1990). *A middle school curriculum: From rhetoric to reality.* Columbus: National Middle School Association.

Bissex, G. L., & Bullock, R. H. (1987). *Seeing for ourselves: Case-study research by teachers of writing.* Portsmouth, NH: Heinemann.

Bogdan, R. C., & Biklen, S. K. (1982). *Qualitative research for education: An introduction to theory and methods.* Boston: Allyn and Bacon, Inc.

Brodhagen, B. L. (1994). Assessing and reporting student progress in an integrative curriculum. *Teaching and Change, 1*(3), 238–254.

Burnaford, G., Beane, J., & Brodhagen, B. (1994). Teacher action research: Inside an integrative curriculum. *Middle School Journal, 25*(3), 5–13.

Clark, C. M. (1990). What you can learn from applesauce: A case of qualitative inquiry in use. In E. W. Eisner & A. Peshkin (Eds.), *Qualitative inquiry in education* (pp. 327–338). New York: Teachers College Press.

Dewey, J. (1990). *The child and the curriculum.* Chicago: University of Chicago Press. Original work published in 1902.

Eisner, E. W. (1994). *The educational imagination* (3rd ed.). New York: Macmillan.

Harste, J. C. (1990). Foreword. In M. W. Olson (Ed.), *Opening the door to classroom research* (pp. v–viii). Newark, DE: International Reading Association.

Hattrup, R. A., & Bickel, W. E. (1993). Teacher-researcher collaborations: Resolving the tensions. *Educational Leadership, 50*(6), 38–40.

Hyde, A. A., & Bizar, M. (1989). *Thinking in context: Teaching cognitive processes across the elementary school curriculum.* New York: Longman.

Jacobs, H. H. (1989). *Interdisciplinary curriculum: Design and implementation.* Alexandria, VA: Association for Supervision and Curriculum Development.

Johnston, P. (1988). *Looking from the inside: A teacher-researcher's view of theory and practice.* A paper presented at the Ethnography Forum, Philadelphia, PA.

Kelsay, K. L. (1991). When experience is the best teacher: The teacher as researcher. *Action in Teacher Education, 13*(1), 14–21.

McCutcheon, G. (1981). The impact of the insider. In J. Nixon (Ed.), *A teacher's guide to action research: Evaluation, enquiry and development in the classroom* (pp. 186–193). London: Grant McIntyre, Ltd.

McKernan, J. (1991). *Curriculum action research: A handbook of methods and resources for the reflective practitioner.* New York: St. Martin's Press.

Migra, E. (1992). *Teachers' classroom inquiry.* Evanston, IL: National-Louis University.

Nixon, J. (1981). *A teacher's guide to action research: Evaluation, enquiry and development in the classroom.* London: Grant McIntyre, Ltd.

Nixon, J. (1987). Contradictions and continuities. *Peabody Journal of Education,* Winter, 20–32.

Olson, M. W. (Ed.). (1990). *Opening the door to classroom research.* Newark, DE: International Reading Association.

Pappas, C., Kiefer, B. Z., & Levstik, L. S. *An integrated language perspective in the elementary school: Theory into action.* New York: Longman.

Reissman, R. (1993). Becoming a teacher-author. *Instructor,* May/June, 54–55.

Resnick, L. B., & Klopfer, L. E. (1989). *Toward the thinking curriculum: Current cognitive research.* Alexandria, VA: Association for Supervision and Curriculum Development.

Santa, C. M. (1990). Teaching as research. In M. W. Olson (Ed.), *Opening the door to classroom research.* Newark, DE: International Reading Association.

Shumsky, A. (1958). *The action research way of learning.* New York: Teachers College Press.

Stenhouse, L. (1975). *An introduction to curriculum research and development.* London: Heinemann.

Stevenson, C. (1986). *Teachers as inquirers: Strategies for learning with and about early adolescents.* Columbus, OH: National Middle School Association.

Stevenson, C., & Carr, J. F. (1993). *Integrated studies in the middle grades: Dancing through walls.* New York: Teachers College Press.

Van Manen, M. (1990). *Researching lived experience: Human science for an action sensitive pedagogy.* Albany: State University of New York Press.

Whitin, D. J., & Wilde, G. (1992). *Living and learning mathematics: Stories and strategies for supporting mathematical literacy.* Portsmouth, NH: Heinemann.

Zemelman, S., & Daniels, H. (1988). *A community of writers: Teaching writing in the junior and senior high school.* Portsmouth, NH: Heinemann.

Zeuli, J. S. (1992). *How do teachers understand research when they read it?* East Lansing: National Center for Research on Teacher Learning.

# A WHOLE LANGUAGE TRILOGY:
# THE COVERED BRIDGE CONNECTION

Marianne Newton
Doris Nash
Loleta Ruffin
Beacon Hill School

*Covered bridges of Brown County*
*Link the countryside as well as a people*
*Weaving the history of the past*
*Encouraging the weary traveler.*

*Approaching these lonely bridges of life*
*Heart beating wildly at the thought of new challenges*
*Hesitation, uncertainty lurking in the souls of those who dared to cross*
*Looking back with doubt and skepticism.*

*What lies ahead?*
*These narrow passages to roads not fully traveled*
*Choices to become, to experience anew, the possibilities of a lifetime.*
　　　　　　　　　　　　　　　　　　　　　　—Marianne Newton

## Covered Bridges of Brown County ...

It seems by chance we have come to reflect on covered bridges in respect to our research, but on closer look, their connection seems clear—their connection to learning in general, and especially to whole language.

## Link the Countryside as Well as a People ...

Covered bridges were built to last. Built with a plan, skilled hands, sturdy materials, and experience, they stand as a framework of support. Whole language is all of these things too. Whole language is a framework of language theory in

FIG. 3.8.  The covered bridge connection.

practice (Edelsky, Altwerger, & Flores, 1991, p. 7). The roads leading to the bridge symbolize the approaches many of our predecessors have taken in their discovery of whole language.

## Weaving the History of the Past . . .

The three roads leading up to the covered bridge represent the forerunners of whole language: progressive education, language experience, and open education. No way of teaching or learning exists in a vacuum. Whole language owes a debt to its predecessors; we have learned much today from studying what they have contributed to literacy learning.

## Encouraging the Weary Traveler . . .

Old bridges can feel shaky, having weathered time and abuse. Investigating the foundations of whole language became an unsettling exploration into our own philosophies of education. When those philosophies seemed shaken, we searched for cover, a cover that was already there for us, but which we did not recognize. Through our readings from those who ventured before us in whole language, we discovered that our hesitancies and uncertainties were a natural part of our learning. We began to realize that there were natural *connections* between the research that others had done and what we were trying to do with

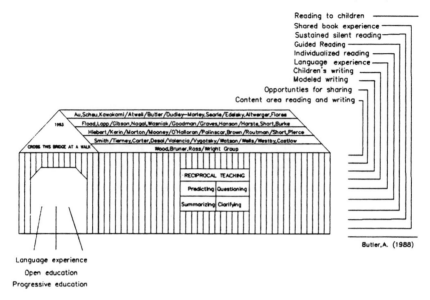

FIG. 3.9. The covered bridge connection.

the children in our classrooms. Our conversations led to the construction of our own covered bridge, in which we represented those connections between what they call theory and what we call practice (see Fig. 3.9).

## Approaching the Lonely Bridges of Life . . .

Why were the bridges built so that only one carriage could pass at a time? As we began this journey, all three of us wrote with one voice. We discovered though that we could not pass through the whole language connection as one person. We came to terms with our own individual speaking voices, just as the children would do.

Why were the bridges totally enclosed? Covered bridges provide protection from above, but also from the sides. As travelers in whole language, we looked up to the gurus, such as Goodman, Edelsky, Routman, Atwell, and others; their ideas protected us from above, their inner voices coaxing us on all sides.

Why was there usually a window situated halfway across the bridge? How dark the passage would be without the window, the window of reciprocal teaching, where predicting, questioning, summarizing, and clarifying were integral in our collaboration (Palinscar & Brown, 1986).

Above the entranceway of a covered bridge is written, "Cross this bridge at a walk." Single travelers on horseback surely were tempted to race through the bridge, but we could not hurry this process. Change takes time. Crossing at a walk slowed us down, allowing time for conversation and reflection.

All of these issues were links to our discovery of whole language as we traveled through the bridge.

## We Dared to Cross . . .

It was not an easy decision to cross this bridge together. Goodman (1986) stated that "whole language learning builds around whole learners learning whole language in whole situations" (p. 40). As we made the commitment to cross together, we knew that we all would reach our own individual destinations.

## Looking Back With Doubt and Skepticism . . .

We all made the decision to attend a reading conference in March, 1993 in order to hear Regie Routman, the keynote speaker. The room was filled to capacity; we could barely see her form, but we could hear her message.

Back in the hotel room that evening, we listened to the tape Doris had made of Routman. We discussed her ideas and explored ways to incorporate this experience into our classrooms. It was two o'clock in the morning and without realizing it, we had developed an "intimate literacy club" (Smith, 1988, p. 11). There was no looking back now. After all, turning around on a covered bridge is virtually unthinkable!

## What Lies Ahead? These Narrow Passages
## to Roads Not Fully Traveled . . .

As we learned more about whole language, we realized that the steps we as individual teachers took would indeed be specific to our own classrooms and the children in them. No one else would have the very same experiences, no one else would have traveled the very same road. In one sense, we were carving out new paths. Taking these first baby steps was a teetering experience. Like small babies, we continued to cling to the experiences and knowledge of those who had come before us to keep us balanced, upright, focused, and encouraged. But actually, these steps would have to be our own.

## Choices to Become . . .

"Becoming" flirts with the notion of growth, but with a hint of apprehension that one will never really "arrive". We felt a hesitancy when we were tempted to just keep on gathering more information through our readings without ever really *doing* anything with that information in our classrooms. Jumping in would further the risk of making mistakes. But our biggest concern, making mistakes, became one of our biggest discoveries. You cannot really make mistakes in whole language. Everything you do, even the mistakes, in some way connects.

## To Experience Anew . . .

Wells (1992) discussed the importance of certain conditions in order for teachers to be able to collaborate: (a) the topic must be one which the teachers themselves choose, (b) participation must be voluntary, (c) time must be allotted for participants to get to know each other and for the activities to be implemented, and (d) all involved must have a willingness to learn. We have witnessed the importance of all of the conditions. We realized that, through this collaboration, we would be experiencing teaching as if for the first time. The privilege of collaboration hurled us into an "intellectual apprenticeship" (p. 173), which took each of us out of the traditional teacher-as-expert role.

## Possibilities of a Lifetime . . .

Coincidence or fate? Life offers many opportunities to grow. Often, adversities and struggles lead to adventures and challenges. A school burning to the ground set up a chain of events that led us to this collaborative research. The year was 1990 and this particular fall day would be forever etched in our memories. When the blaze subsided, teachers walked among the rubble, devastated. What happened after that fire changed our district. Grade reorganization and faculty relocation occurred throughout the school system. The changes brought the three of us together. We began to explore other means of change, new possibilities in our new classrooms.

We focused on three aspects of whole language for our teacher research: social interaction, portfolios, and guided reading. Here is what we did.

## MARIANNE NEWTON

Presently, I teach second grade in an open classroom with Doris Nash and another teacher. Each teacher has approximately twenty-four students, who are from diverse cultures, social classes, and family structures.

Doris and I enrolled in a graduate class in which we collaborated on a presentation on friendship and cooperative learning. When the project was completed, we both sat back and marveled at how much we had learned about learning together. I was continually learning while I was sharing my thoughts and ideas with Doris. Then, I realized that I did not see what I had experienced happening with my own second-grade classroom. Children were not given the same opportunity to discuss and share their learning as I had. *Social interaction* was at the heart of meaningful learning, and it is a central element of whole language, but I did not see that connection at first. I had found a theme for action research. I would explore social interaction through whole language with my students.

I did not have to wait long to feel the need to begin. October, Book-It Month at our school, was a perfect opportunity to improve student involvement in reading. To enrich the experience, I facilitated a weekly book sharing in which four students individually shared simple book reports with each other. After each group's presentations, the students returned to their desks for a brief discussion concerning their performance. This simple, verbal self-evaluation corrected problems that seemed to occur within any group. Through a whole language literacy event, which provided students choices in their reading selections, an opportunity for social interaction, and time for reflection, children took ownership for their learning with greater understanding of what they had read and greater effort on their book reports.

One of my greatest learnings through my action research was the initiation of "The Author's Luncheon." Briefly, the idea was that children would eat lunch together in small groups in the classroom while sharing literature. There would be an "Author's Chair" for the reader of the day and a bulletin board for posting titles of books for lunchtime reading and "Notes to Authors," which was used by students who wished to communicate with other authors in the classroom. My project sounded so exciting, well-planned, and predictable, I was sure that it would be successful.

Was I surprised! Not only did the children misbehave, they showed a total lack of respect and cooperation to those children who were brave enough to participate as authors. Six weeks were spent solving the social dilemmas: How do we choose fairly who eats with whom? How do we eat with a partner? How do we read to a large or small group? Social interaction is quite unpredictable, a significant discovery on my part.

But through the sometimes tedious brainstorming to solve our problems, the children did gain a new respect for one another and began to understand the true meaning of cooperation and community in the real world. Giving children the time and space to evaluate their book sharing groups and decide on solutions to try resulted in major changes in how they saw themselves as learners.

To add focus to our literature sharing, I introduced the reciprocal teaching strategy of summarizing to the children. Students who were previously finding it difficult to listen to another child read were remaining attentive in hopes of being chosen to summarize the literature when the author had finished reading. Journal writing at the conclusion of each luncheon provided time for reflection and metacognition, learning about our learning together. Children completed simple rating scales and wrote statements concerning their participation in the luncheon as "good readers" and "good listeners."

The end of the year was approaching when the children stumbled across "The Song of the Swallows," by Leo Politi. Their interest in this mystery led us to explore all of Leo Politi's books. The underlying theme, festivals, was a connection in his own life as well as in the stories that he wrote. Before I knew what was happening, the children and I were planning an Author's Festival, focusing on the works of Leo Politi. The festival was to feature my students as authors, reading to other children in the school. They chose their reading selections, wrote invitations to the students to whom they wanted to read, and at the assigned time, on the day of the festival, picked up their friends at their classrooms. Four author's chairs, decorated and arranged in various places in the hallway, were visited and revisited by many students all morning long. The activity of sharing literature was further enhanced by their displays of their accomplishments on 5 foot author strips, which included each student's picture, author's interviews, summaries of their lives, voting ballots of the books of Leo Politi, and their own Young Author stories. Music, food, and games followed with visitation by parents and friends. It was a memorable event! This community celebration, developed with the children was not even a thought when I began my research, but turned out to be the most powerful literacy event of all. It proved that the accomplishments of the group as a whole was possible only through the combination of the strengths and talents of its members.

The mystery of whole language is still a mystery. I had set a framework for language learning to occur, using literacy events as my connection. The connection had to be made *with* my students, not *for* them. Children came together as researchers, as teachers, but also as children. On the last day of school, while reading *Oh, The Places You'll Go* by Dr. Seuss, I reminded students of the rough situations that each of them had overcome over the year and how proud I was of them.

## DORIS NASH

Conferencing with parents in the fall led me to realize that there was a need for a different method of assessing my students' progress. The mystery of how portfolios would evolve in my classroom puzzled my students as well as me. Although I had read much about portfolios, they were still basically intangible until I witnessed Regie Routman as she modeled her own portfolio at a reading conference in 1993. I realized that, in a portfolio classroom, the teacher must put together his or her own portfolio and share it with the students first. Returning to my classroom, I anxiously shared my bulging but incomplete folder. It included important pictures of family, memorable places, my former students, academic achievements, and landmarks in my own life. My students' excitement and curiosity began to grow as I unfolded bits and pieces of my life before them. Once the torch was passed—from Routman to me and now on to my students—the mystery of portfolios became much less mysterious.

I introduced narrative and expository writing separately so as not to confuse the students, posting the highly developed district expectations for writing as outlined in the rubric as a reference for writing and editing. Before individual writing was initiated, groups were formed to collectively write and practice putting a piece together. Students chose their favorite piece, read it into a tape recorder, and then shared the tapes with the whole group.

To bring some closure to the project, I initiated a student celebration, similar to what I had seen Marianne and Loleta do in their action research. I was not aware of the impact that celebrating would have on my students' self-esteem until I witnessed their excitement about their learning as they stood before their families and friends. Students verbally and visually shared the best of their portfolios with other second graders and parents.

The portfolios revealed the uniqueness of each child—talents, hobbies, interests, and experiences. As I reviewed their written narratives, I recognized that most of their oral sharing and written compositions centered around themselves and what they knew. As I shared my discovery with them, connecting this knowledge with the authors we had read about during the year, they began to understand that authors write about what interests them and often base their stories on their own personal experiences. I learned that whole language and portfolio assessment have been responsible for helping this diverse group explore their talents and take risks.

## LOLETA RUFFIN

During the fall of the year, I was engulfed in whole language literature that informed me about other teachers' research, feeling unsure of how to proceed because I did not think I knew enough. I was filling an empty container that would never be full. I kept waiting until I could wait no longer. I suddenly became aware that I had to begin in order to continue learning.

An effective reading program includes reading to, reading by, and reading with children. I began this year with my intermediate special education students, knowing that I would be instituting a guided reading program in lieu of my traditional reading program. To test reactions, I started reading books to a target group of lower performing students during our reading time, beginning with *Esio Trot* by Roald Dahl and *Carry On Mr. Bowditch*, by Jean Lee Latham. For both selections, we discussed the plot, reacted to the characters, and generated questions for the author. Within this small but intimate group, excitement for reading became a daily occurrence.

After reading these two stories, I began using a variety of guided reading strategies with these special education students. We practiced the following: (a) predicting by looking at the cover of the book or through book talks, (b) relating a story to our own experiences, (c) generating questions to pose to each other about the literature, (d) writing comments and questions to the author, (e) choral reading, (f) skills based on the actual texts rather than through isolated worksheets, and (g) looking for patterns across pieces of literature and within a story.

Each day as we read passages from various novels, the students generated very lively discussions. Sometimes they would amaze me as I listened to them question each other and discuss their answers. I asked myself daily if these were the same students who used to hate reading! This group of children had completely transformed; they now had the ability to delve deeply into a plot and discover some interesting tidbits that even I had not noticed. In addition, they began to take ownership of their learning and make choices. This was an incredible step forward for these children with special needs.

I also involved the children in the evaluation of my action research. They completed pictorial rating scales to evaluate each selection read. There were also pre- and postquestionnaires given, asking students how they were feeling about reading. Finally, for record keeping purposes, I gave the reading test from the basal series at the end of the year. *Everyone* had made significant gains in the areas of comprehension and specific skill development!

This action research was a very positive venture for my students and for me. As we progressed through each piece of literature, I watched my students bring meaning to the printed word and become teachers to each other. Learning to read is achieved through the act of reading to, reading by, and reading with children. We did all of that and more!

## Constructing New "Bridges"

This collaborative teacher research project helped us become meaning makers. We constructed our own stories and shared them with each other in conversation and in writing. Meaning makers produce other meaning makers—and that's exactly what happened in our classrooms during this year of research. This could be the beginning of a tradition.

## REFERENCES

Dahl, R. (1990). *Esio Trot.* New York: Viking.

Edelsky, C., Altwerger, B., & Flores, B. (1991). *Whole language: What's the difference?* Portsmouth, NH: Heinemann.

Goodman, K. (1986). *What's whole in whole language?* Portsmouth, NH: Heinemann.

Latham, J. L. (1955). *Carry on Mr. Bowditch.* Boston: Houghton Mifflin.

Palinscar, A., & Brown, A. (1986). Interactive teaching to promote independent learning from text. *The Reading Teacher, 39,* 771–777.

Politi, L. (1949). *Song of the swallows.* Scribner.

Routman, R. (1993). Keynote Speech. International Reading Association Annual Conference Presentation, March, San Antonio, TX.

Seuss, Dr. (1990). *Oh, The Places You'll Go.* New York: Random House.

Smith, F. (1988). *Joining the literacy club.* Portsmouth, NH: Heinemann.

Wells, G. (1992). *Constructing knowledge together.* Portsmouth, NH: Heinemann.

# TOPICS AND THEMES
# FOR FURTHER DISCUSSION

1. Examine several volumes of a professional journal of interest to you in your subject area or grade level. Determine how many of the articles are written or co-authored by classroom teachers. Describe those you believe are based on classroom research. What were the authors' research questions or topics of interest?

2. Find a journal article written by another teacher–researcher who is interested in the same kind of topics and themes as you are. Write a letter to her/him, responding to the article and what you found interesting, useful, and challenging. Ask for response from the author.

3. Observe a student in a classroom for 3 weeks, keeping anecdotal notes and a journal describing the details of that student's learning, behavior, and interactions with others. What did you learn about that student after such intensive observation? What did you learn about yourself? Compile your notes into a detailed case study and share the study with your colleagues or other teacher researchers for response.

4. Assume that you are interested in an action research project focusing on increasing participation in discussions in your classroom. What kinds of data might you collect? What kinds of "action" might you try? Discuss with colleagues how the students might be involved as co-researchers in this kind of project. What would be their role? How might you analyze the data you collect during this research?

# 4

# LEARNING WITH EACH OTHER: COLLABORATION IN TEACHER RESEARCH

David Hobson
National-Louis University

*A triangular prism hangs from a thin filigree thread in my study windows. I look through it into the yard outside whenever I notice the refracted colors slowly moving around the room as the day progresses. Peering through the prism, I watch just-budding forsythia blur into golden clumps of color, separated now from the distinct arching of branches and framed in a new version of spring. Later, as the sun sets, the forsythia reappear as golden, violet, blue and orange dots across the table where I sit writing. Both points of seeing present shifting versions of the environment surrounding me; these versions depend not only on the slight motion of the hanging crystal itself but also on the angles from which I look through and around the prism.*

—Miller (1990b, p. 86)

Miller uses the image of the prism when she teaches and thinks about curriculum. It seems to me that this metaphor works wonderfully when applied to teacher research, particularly to collaborative efforts made by teacher–researchers. As with a prism, they look from various angles at the phenomenon they are studying and try to think of their own active roles in creating those vantage points. The colors of the prism are refracted, just as a teacher's research is a reflection of a particular situation, itself in continuing motion, yet caught momentarily as a temporary rendering of reality. The moving dots of color in Miller's description remind us that no one construction necessarily signals completion of the inquiry or represents a definitive view. Teacher research is very much a prismatic study, particularly when you add in all of the additional vantage points and ways of seeing that are brought by the members of the teacher research group.

## TEACHING: AN ISOLATING PROFESSION

> We must pay attention to the adults who open the doors, ring the bells, hand out
> the books and the homework assignments. And we need to pay attention not only
> to teachers' relations to the children, but to their relations to one another as well.
> What do they know of one another's work? When and how do they work together—if
> they work together? (Grumet, 1989, p. 21)

Teachers often remark on the fact that they have very rare opportunities to
converse with colleagues. This idea comes as a surprise to many people, particularly to those entering the profession. The image of being isolated doesn't
easily fit with the picture many of us have of teachers. But Huberman (1993)
reminded us that many teachers derive their most important professional satisfactions from interactions with students instead of with peers. It is not from
students that teachers are so isolated; it is from other adults. To many teacher–
researchers, finding ways to overcome the customary isolation from their peers
becomes an integral part of their research.

The isolation in schools begins when the new teacher starts out, and learns
that entry to the teacher's world of work is done "person by person, each
working largely in isolation from others" (Lortie, 1975, p. 74). This situation
becomes the permanent state of affairs for their teaching, "the base of their
occupational culture" (Hargreaves, 1993, p. 72). The teacher can hardly escape
the architecture of schools that organizes classrooms into cellular patterns
separating each one from the others. A teacher's whole day may be spent in
one just one room. An elementary teacher put it this way:

> I live in my own little world in my classroom. Sometimes I think that my children
> and I share a secret life that is off limits to anyone else. We just go about our
> business, like so many peas in a pod. (Lieberman & Miller, 1984, p. 6)

The high school teacher may also be confined to a single classroom all day;
it's the students who move from one place to another around the building.
Meanwhile, teachers can find it extremely difficult to steal a few minutes to
converse with a colleague and may even choose to spend their lunch breaks in
their rooms catching up on paperwork. Teaching can be a lonely profession
even when the isolation is somewhat self-imposed.

Being private is thought by some to be a rule of thumb of the teaching
profession:

> What does it mean to be private? It means not sharing experiences about teaching,
> about classes, about students, about perceptions. (Lieberman & Miller, 1984, p. 8)

Or, in the words of one teacher, "You seal off the room and you deal with the
students. It is safer to be private. There is some safety in the tradition, even
though it keeps you lonely" (p. 9).

The classroom tends to be a territory staked out by the individual teacher and its boundary is not to be violated lightly. Schools are simply not organized to facilitate interaction among teachers. Choosing a degree of isolation is a way to fend off the disruptions and distractions that so often come from being too caught up in an overwhelming system. Flinders (1988) saw this response "as protecting the time and energy required to meet immediate instructional demands," noticing that "it is not uncommon to respond to increased job demands by closing the office door, handling luncheon appointments, and 'hiding out' in what ever ways we can" (p. 25). There is little or no time allocated for teachers to get together and the schedule is often so tight and complicated that even if there was some time, few teachers would have the luxury of having it at the same time or day or place. Teachers are typically divided from each other by grade level and subject area differences. They rarely set foot in each other's schools or visit their colleague's classrooms. Moreover, few teachers have experienced teacher education or staff development programs that acquainted them with how to work with colleagues as well as with children. All of these factors combine to separate teachers from each other. "The very act of teaching is invisible to one's peers" (Lieberman & Miller, 1984, p. 9).

## TEACHERS WANT TO COLLABORATE

Teachers are very interested in sharing practice, even eager to do so, given the necessary time and resources, but some are unaccustomed to this practice and somewhat afraid of exposing themselves to potential criticism from their peers. In schools, there is often little time and less reward for teacher talk. We perceive teacher talk as a means of diagnosis, a time to think out loud, to explore, analyze, and to problem solve. Teacher talk involves time to listen, to share, and to interact. Given a safe place to air their uncertainties, teachers love to talk together, to share practice, and to wonder out loud about what to do with many of the real issues they face in their everyday teaching lives. They can give each other a kind of feedback available from no other source that reduces their anxiety about being effective teachers. Rather than the more usual "listening to experts" approach that seems to characterize so much of formal teacher development, teachers seem most open to the teachings and wonderings of their colleagues. They listen closely to the stories that seem to come from an experience base that all can recognize. Teachers can give each other a hearing and can offer each other empathy, understanding, and practical help.

Teacher research offers classroom practitioners an opportunity for availing themselves of the resources of colleagues on the issues and concerns that have practical importance to them. Teacher research does not consist of a set of tasks imposed from above by school authorities. It need not be characterized by the sort of "contrived collegiality" described by Hargreaves and Dawe (1990), which occurs on those occasions when teachers are "invited." Suzanne Goff describes her own research in which she established a teacher support and collaboration group in her elementary school (see Suzanne Goff's Teacher Research). She writes of the frustration teachers experience year after year without any real affirmation for what they achieve. Establishing teacher research community groups enables teachers to celebrate their successes with each other, create and re-create ways of helping groups of children learn more effectively, and strengthen the connections teachers have with each other. We illustrate the importance of structured and unstructured time in those group contexts and we discuss the possible roles of a group facilitator who shares in the construction of such a climate where problem solving, sharing, and affirmation can take place.

There are many interactive contexts in which teacher research happens. Two teachers may embark on a project together as occurred when a high school English teacher and a kindergarten teacher put their students together in a reading and tutoring program and studied what happened. Or perhaps the group numbers three as was the case with the collaborative research reported by Marianne Newton, Doris Nash, and Loleta Ruffin (see their Teacher Research). A cross disciplinary grade level team of four may embark on a project together. The context of a teacher–researcher study group of six is a powerful one, as evidenced by the work of Miller (1990a, 1992) who chronicled nearly 3 years of meetings of such a small group as they worked on "extending the concept of teacher-as-researcher into reciprocal and interactive forms" (p. ix). I found that a teacher education course of 15 provided an excellent context for conducting a collaborative interview project with retired teachers (Hobson, 1994). The student–teacher seminar comprised of pre-service teachers along with their cooperating teachers and university supervisors provides yet another context for conducting classroom inquiries.

Whatever the context, participants enjoin the process of conducting some classroom-based teacher research. The group is meant to be a place where teachers can get some help with that process.

## GROUP BUILDING: LEARNING TO WORK TOGETHER

Teacher–researchers often form groups in order to gather additional perspectives on their classroom inquiry. Occasionally, teachers may have worked in the same building for 20 years, eaten lunch in the same room, and endured faculty meetings together, but these shared experiences do not necessarily make it easier for these teachers to become a cohesive group. In any case, every group that has a new purpose, or a new configuration of members, is in some fundamental ways a new group.

Probably the two most pressing questions present in such a first gathering are these: Who are these people? and do I feel that I belong here? Learning how to work well together is an important initial task. One way to address these concerns is to spend some time talking with one another and to surface some of the content of the conversations with the whole group. There are many wonderful sources for group-building activities that you may want to consult. Many researchers have investigated the subject and written about it, including the following: Brandes and Ginnis (1986); Cohen (1986); Hanson (1981); Lippitt, Hooyman, Sashkin, and Kaplan (1980); Pfeiffer and Jones (1969); Schmuck and Schmuck (1992); and Watson (1974). Often, working with just one other teacher–researcher for a while is an effective way to begin building community in a research group. Two strategies for building group cohesion that are particularly useful for groups of teachers about to embark on teacher researching are called *paired interviewing* and *pairing and sharing*. Both help to lay the groundwork for collaboration in classroom inquiry.

*Paired Interviewing.* Each teacher chooses a person with whom to pair up, each interviewing the other for a set period of time. A few prompts may help the process get rolling:

- Why are you here?
- How did you decide to join? Was it really an option?
- What are you concerned about in your classroom?
- Are there common things that we want to work on as a group?
- Do two or three of us have a similar research interest?
- What works for you?
- What can you share that was a huge flop?
- What are your expectations for this group?

Responses are recorded by the interviewer using magic markers on a large piece of newsprint, which is posted on the wall for sharing with the entire group. In the debriefing that follows, each participant introduces the teacher interviewed to the others. Polaroid photographs can be taken and attached to the newsprint.

This is an effective first meeting start-up activity because it allows teachers to arrive at different times without being disruptive, it minimizes the directiveness of the facilitator, it provides an orientation to the content and process of what is to come, and it encourages teachers to make a transition from the world of schooling to this community of adult learners. It maximizes interaction, it allows the participants to learn a lot about each other in a short period of time, and it serves to dissolve anxiety associated with any new social situation.

It is important for teachers to become comfortable with each other as rapidly as possible. Both facilitating a high degree of interaction between group members and helping a lot of information to surface quickly contribute to a climate in which teachers can feel an increasing sense of belonging.

Often teachers who are beginning to think about developing some teacher research initiatives have a variety of concerns and worries that may be nagging at them. Many teachers have rather narrow notions of how research is defined, much of this learned in their own university experiences that may have become quite dated during the intervening years. Getting these issues expressed and responded to by members of the group often contributes to developing a more comfortable atmosphere for all present.

**Pairing and Sharing.** Members of the group are asked to write in an effort to identify and briefly describe the issues and concerns uppermost in their minds about joining this teacher research group. Here are some possible prompts:

- Why did you join us for this teacher research discussion?
- Is there an aspect of teacher research that concerns or interests you?
- What obstacles do you need to overcome in order to do research in your classroom?
- What do you have going for you?
- What are your hopes for this group of teacher–researchers?
- What are your fears concerning this venture?

The teachers write in their journals for perhaps 10 or 15 minutes about the beginnings of the teacher research group, perhaps using one of the prompts as a jumping off point. After 15 minutes, the writings are exchanged with another teacher in the group and read. Each teacher offers a response to the writing of one colleague, starting at the point on the page where the author left off, perhaps complimenting or expressing appreciation for points raised, asking a question or two, sharing corollary thoughts or experiences, or maybe expressing additional ideas. The notebooks are exchanged again, read and responded to. There may be several rounds of exchanges, but it is important to finish with the original journal writer bringing the entire dialogue to a close.

Often, after a period of written pairing and sharing, there will be a need in the group for some verbal interaction. Particularly in this circumstance where one purpose of the activity is group-building, time should be taken to bring some of the content of the exchanges into the whole group. Each pair may be asked to briefly describe the substance of their exchange and to prepare to report on their findings to the group. Similar ideas are often developed in several dyads and a lively discussion will ensue. Some of the concerns will pertain to various elements of the research process and so can be used to begin to define and clarify the research initiatives that are already taking shape. Many of the topics, especially at the beginning, will be focused on individual and social concerns involving participation in the group. It often comes as a great relief to hear various members give words to the feelings of stagefright, uncertainty, confusion, and general anxiety that often accompany participation in new social situations that may call for a degree of risk taking. Sharing these concerns is one effective way that a group can begin the process of building its own identity.

## LISTENING AND RESPONDING
## TO OTHER TEACHER–RESEARCHERS

Teachers are quite familiar with this process as it is applied to students. A child is invited to sit for 15 minutes in the author's chair, for example, in the expectation that others will listen and respond. Just as we put children in the author's chair in classrooms, a teacher research group can allow its own members to avail themselves of the resources of the group. It may be difficult for the kindergarten and the fifth-grade teacher to listen to each other because their worlds seem so far apart. (That may also be true for teachers who teach on the very same grade level!) However, just as we encourage students to learn to listen to each other in the author's chair, and see what they can contribute and learn for themselves, so each teacher can take the experience he or she is hearing about, respond as a colleague, and see how this teacher research can be applied to his or her own situation. Everytime you listen to someone else, you gain something.

Ron Lippitt, an early proponent of working with groups to gain knowledge, described a support group in Ann Arbor that he belonged to that encouraged any member to use the time of the group in a particular way—for example, for brainstorming, for responding to draft writing, for role playing, or problem solving. One member of the group acted as secretary, and members scheduled increments of the group's time on a first come-first serve basis. I have found this is a practice that lends itself well to a group of teacher–researchers because it permits exploration of various subjects from many different vantage points.

> When I have been listened to and when I have been heard, I am able to reperceive my world in a new way and to go on . . . It is astonishing how elements which seem insoluble become soluble when someone hears; how confusions which seem irremediable turn into relatively clear flowing streams when one is understood. I have deeply appreciated the times that I have experienced this sensitive, empathic, concentrated listening. (Rogers, 1969, pp. 225–226)

Early in the process of teacher research collaboration, teachers might ask, How do we want to give and receive feedback regarding what we're trying in the classroom? What kinds of feedback and response would be most useful and helpful? Giving helpful feedback is a skill; learning to do it is unlikely to be accomplished from reading guidelines like these, but through practice. In a group of teacher–researchers, where the giving and getting of feedback is such an important element, it is important to provide frequent opportunities for such practice. In one particular collaborating session, for example, one teacher gave several specific suggestions for ways to help students in another researcher's classroom solve word problems. The next time the group met, the first order of business was to see whether the feedback was helpful, whether the strategies suggested were used and if so, with what measure of success. Giving "feedback on the feedback" in this way helped all of these teacher–researchers develop additional insight on how better to elicit helpful responses next time.

## Receiving Feedback

Elbow (1973) offered excellent advice regarding listening to feedback that is perfectly applicable to teacher–researchers receiving response to their work in progress. He suggested that you might need to bite your tongue because if you can't help from talking, you will keep your responders from sharing their reactions with you. Try not to make apologies or give explanations or ask questions until you are sure that the responders have finished telling you how they perceived the experience of your work. It is very tempting to try to shape the kind of response you are getting, but try to resist this temptation. In short, according to Elbow:

> Be quiet and listen. (Elbow, 1973, p. 101)

Tape recording sessions will help teacher–researchers remember the feedback they receive from colleagues. Sometimes it's helpful, at the end of a feedback session, to take a few minutes in which everyone can write exit slips describing the substance of what occurred.

## Brainstorming

Every teacher has experimented with brainstorming as a way of working with kids, of generating a large number of ideas quickly, of encouraging creativity and lateral thinking, and of bringing everyone in a group to the common task. The key is to keep the ideas flowing from the group as fast as possible, just writing everything down on the blackboard (or, even better, on newsprint so you can take it away with you), and not stopping to comment on anyone else's ideas. The scribe writes everything in no particular order and makes no attempt to rank or organize the responses in any way so that the suggestions quickly become anonymous. It's important to write down as much of what the brainstormer says as possible. The scribe must take particular pains not to influence the content by inadvertently using the power of the chalk. It is very important for the facilitator to model the behaviors of not commenting, not shaping, not interpreting, not censoring, not rescuing the group from a momentary silence, but instead respecting each and every one of the contributions that naturally flow.

After the brainstorm is completed, there are several ways to proceed. If the work in question is a group production (for example, if the group is developing options for some action it may want to take), the group may organize the ideas into categories, or put them into order of importance, or arrange them in order of some developmental priority. If the purpose of the brainstorm is to generate ideas in response to the request of a group member, then it may be best to leave the categorization to the individual teacher-researcher. If the purpose is to generate different ways of looking at this collection of ideas, then it might help to make copies of the list of ideas for everyone in the group, scissor them apart, and ask each person to organize the resulting puzzle pieces into some schema. These conceptions might then be handed over to the individual teacher–researcher for further work, or can be reported out in the group and discussed further.

## Being Interviewed

Hunt (1987) offered this very practical technique. First, the teacher describes the research topic in 10 words or less. Next, the teacher prepares a rough interview guide on the topic chosen. This consists of four questions drawn from Kolb's (1984) experiential cycle:

1. What has your experience with this topic been?
2. From your own experience, what do you think are its most important features?
3. In terms of your own experience with this topic, what are your hunches about how it works (i.e., how do you make sense of it)?
4. Based on your understanding of this topic, what is the first step to take in investigating it?

Finally, the teacher–researcher asks another group member to conduct the actual tape recorded interview. In this way, the teacher becomes the first participant in his or her own research. This is a reversal of roles, but a reversal defined such that the teacher-researcher's own ideas can be brought out. Hunt (1987) called this "the Golden Rule in developing research methods" (p. 118). He continued, "becoming a participant in your own research project is a very valuable source of feedback for tuning into whatever methods are used. . . ."

Teacher–researchers are often amazed when they listen to the tape recorded interviews and discover how much they already knew about the subject. Bringing tacit knowledge to explicit awareness in this way comes as a wonderful surprise and can form the basis for many other techniques for accomplishing similar discoveries.

## Periodic Conferencing

The periodic conference is a way to use oral discourse as a means for discovering the progress one is making. I have found that a monthly conference arranged between two teacher–researchers works very well. An oral report on progress to date on the research project is given, concluding with an identification of apparent next steps. The interviewer reflects, asks clarifiying questions, draws out, and tries to develop a clear understanding of what the teacher–researcher is reporting. The interviewee keeps the tape.

One month later, the process is repeated, again with a tape recorder, but starting at the place on the tape where the conferees left off at their last meeting. The main purpose served by this technique is a clarifying one. Speaking is much like writing; one can do it to learn. Recording the conversation on tape opens up the possibility of giving the oral discourse a rehearing. The accumulating record of several conversations over a period of time provides a sense of continuity and developmental process. It is very difficult, when one is fully invested in a conversation, trying to find the right words, stopping and starting, working through the various confusions, to leave the interpersonal interaction with a clear understanding of just what transpired. Having the tape recording for later listening allows one to recapture the conversation and perhaps to extend it further.

## Interactive Journal Writing

Miller (1990a) and the five classroom teachers she collaborated over several years with attempted to develop collaborative reflections on the contexts and assumptions that influenced and framed their practice. They tried to invent forms of inquiry both in their classrooms and in their teacher research group that would "extend the concept of teacher-as-researcher into reciprocal and interactive forms" (p. ix). Miller describes the "formation and constant reformation of their collaborative processes" and their recognition "that 'finding voices' is not a definitive event but rather a continuous process" (p. xi). One of the principle processes they explored was interactive dialogue journal writing:

> I proposed that we keep journals as yet another space for dialogue to take place. The teachers agreed that they would engage in dialogue journal writing with me; that is, we would write back and forth to one another about whatever issues emerged in our individual and collective inquiries. . . . The goal of dialogue journal writing is to carry on a discussion about some important topic over several days, within a classroom context, or over several weeks or months, within a collaborative context such as our research group. (p. 26)

Response feeds the interactive journal writing process. Infrequent response generally causes the process to atrophy and fall into disuse. What kinds of journal responses might one teacher make to another as they both conduct their own teacher research projects? What forms of written feedback from a colleague would be useful? Here are some possible sentence completions which can be used as prompts:

> I'd love to hear more about . . .
> This part confuses me, I'm not sure what happened . . .
> How did you feel about this?

When you described _____, it made me think of . . .
I was wondering about the part where . . .

## Networking With Other Practitioners

The group of teacher–researchers is, of course, itself a small network. In the collaborative research project I conducted (Hobson, 1994) with a group of teacher–researchers involving the interviewing of 34 retired teachers, we found all of our interviewees from among our personal network of colleagues, friends, and acquaintances. The power inherent in activating even a small human network is enormous. It is hard to imagine any practical inquiry into behavior in a classroom that would not in some way parallel activities that other teachers are already conducting somewhere. It may be a relatively easy task to identify these human resources by calling upon those networks already in place.

## Gathering Information Outside the Classroom With Other Teachers' Help

A teacher-research group can also provide support in identifying relevant information for each other. When a group of colleagues is directly connected with the work you are doing, it's incredible how much related information they stumble on in their travels that finds its way quickly to you.

## Collecting Data With the Help of Colleagues

There are many ways that teacher-researcher colleagues can support each other in gathering data. Do you need to try out a paper and pencil instrument to see how it works? A teacher–researcher might do a trial run in her class. Do you need additional pairs of eyes, ears, and hands to make observations in your classroom? How about trading such a task with a teacher–researcher in your group? Maybe you need a set of student writings in response to a particular topic or issue? The teachers in your group could produce student responses that may help you to proceed. Collecting data need not be a solitary task. Get help! *Collaborative Analysis: Finding Meaning Together* by van Manen (1990), described the structure of a collaborative conversation as resembling what Socrates called the situation of "talking together like friends":

> Friends do not try to make the other weak; in contrast, friends aim to bring out strength . . . They do this by trying to formulate the underlying themes or meanings that inhere in the text or that still inhere in the phenomenon, thus allowing the author to see the limits of his or her present vision and to transcend those limits. (pp. 100–101)

Teacher–researchers may select sections of tape-recorded conversations that seem especially salient and play them for a group of teacher–researchers. The group could write responses to the taped selections and then discuss their perspectives. Many new insights develop through this procedure. It is also useful to do with videotaped incidents and events. Bringing the combined perspectives of a group of people to the task of making meaning can open up many new ways of thinking about the data one has in hand.

Although the classroom may often serve to isolate the teacher from other teachers, it is a place where teachers are in almost constant interaction with *students*. It is from a teacher's relationship with his or her students that many of the deepest satisfactions of teaching spring. Therefore, it seems to make sense that we consider the role of students in classroom research. *Every single one of the teacher research strategies we've described in this text can be used by and with students at all levels.*

> Whenever people decide to learn, they undertake research. If teachers wish delib-
> erately to learn about their teaching, they must research. If children wish to learn
> about electricity, they must research. . . . All teachers should be experts in "action
> research" so that they can show all students how to be "action researchers."
> (Boomer, 1987, p. 8)

The teacher research group is one place where the pleasures of teaching and learning are to be found. A student research group is another. One teacher thought she might try to bridge the gap between these two contexts:

> . . . Last year the light dawned! I had been learning about the importance of personal
> and group reflection, a significant life and learning skill. I had discovered that
> learning comes from thinking for yourself and listening to input from others. Sud-
> denly, I became excited. How could I teach my 21 third graders what I had so
> painlessly learned. . . . What had been the process? How could I duplicate this
> experience in my classroom? (Nalle, 1993, p. 45)

## COLLABORATION IN THE CLASSROOM:
## CO-RESEARCHING WITH STUDENTS

In their study, Lieberman and Miller (1984) found that elementary teachers believed that the only significant rewards of the teaching profession lay in the students' "words, behaviors, expressions and suggestions" (p. 2). Although we would like to think there are numerous other rewards inherent in teaching, interaction with students and success with their learning seem to be of major significance to teachers who continue to return to the classroom year after year.

If the students are the reason that many teachers continue to teach, how might their role affect the process of being a teacher–researcher? Paley (1986) discussed the role of young children in that process. She wrote about when she began teaching kindergarten—full of curriculum guide activities, scheduled reading time, nap time, calendar time, play time and, at first, unaware that the "distractions might be the sounds of children thinking" (p. 122). She continued:

> Suddenly, I was truly curious about my role in the classroom, but there were no researchers ready to set up an incriminating study to show me when—and perhaps why—I consistently veered away from the child's agenda. Then I discovered the tape-recorder and knew, after transcribing the first tape, that I could become my own best witness. (p. 123)

She learned then that the act of teaching can become a "daily search for the child's point of view" (p. 124).

Similarly, Sitton (1980) saw the child as the informant of the teacher, which certainly represents something of a shift in roles. Sitton maintained that good teachers, and teachers who survive, have always done this. In order to view students as the ones who have information to share with us in the adult world, we must first find out what *they* know (p. 544). Then teaching becomes informed and can be adjusted—to a child's world and to what the child brings to the classroom. This process is what Jervis (1986) referred to as "a teacher's quest for a child's questions" (pp. 132–133) and it can be the beginning of a teacher's own inquiry.

Such a process of co-researching doesn't just happen with high school students. Nancy Hubbard, a second-grade teacher, explains: "Throughout the project, I found that I was not the one who would always have to plan the lessons. During my research, the children's questions and interests guided the direction of the curriculum. They posed the questions, stated the problems, and we solved them together" (see Nancy Hubbard's Teacher Research).

A special education teacher–researcher was very interested in the role of special needs children in the regular education classroom. As she read more about special education, she noticed that mainstreaming and inclusion were always presented from the viewpoint of adults. Parents, teachers, legislators, lobbyists, and administrators were well represented. "Where is the voice of the children?" she commented. Her research focused on those voices; she asked them what they thought about being included in regular education classrooms. She encouraged them to write about it, talk about it, reflect on it. She was the observer, the inquirer, the learner.

Similarly, a fifth-grade teacher was exploring the ways to make reading more enjoyable for her class. She tried several different methods, tapping into the very latest ideas from the literature, and having some success, though not at all what she had envisioned when she began her research. She realized that she would have to keep searching. Finally, after thinking about it for awhile, she decided to ask her students for their solutions. That was just what she needed. The *children* had a few ideas which moved them forward, one of which was what they called "Reading Teams." Reading Teams became the central element of reading literature in her class for the rest of the year. It was *the children* who had devised the method; the teacher observed, questioned, and learned.

These stories illustrate a legitimate kind of partnership between teacher and student that reflects a mutual respect between parties who are seeking to increase learning in a classroom or school. There are a variety of ways in which students can play an essential role in teacher action research. One way is to teach students research methodologies in order to engage them in the data collection within a school. The Stay in School Partnership Program in the city of New York did that with urban youth who were in danger of dropping out. In order to find out what programming might be useful, they needed to know what the lives of the students were like and how school fit into those lives (Farrell, Peguero, Lindsey, & White, 1988). Students were selected to interview other students, tape conversations with their peers, and then participate in the analysis of the data and contribute to the formulation of research questions based on their research. The students found that the words "interesting" and "boring" came up often when they talked with their peers about school. With that information, researchers together sought to discover exactly what those words meant, with students offering a variety of examples in both categories!

At Aloha High School in Portland, Oregon, students conducted interviews on school climate issues (Johnson & Henstrand, 1993). They believed that this method would yield more honest responses from students as they attempted to find out what the climate for education was like at Aloha. They asked questions such as, "What makes you want to come to Aloha each day?", "How do you get along with people at Aloha?", and "What helps you really learn in classes at Aloha?" This data, analyzed and interpreted by teachers and students together, served as a starting place for an ongoing research project on meaningful education at the high school.

Students who participate in action research as data collectors as well as data analyzers have the opportunity to offer constructive questions that adults may not think of, which may yield useful responses from their peers. They may also offer some interesting interpretations of results that present a youthful perspective on the issues at hand. This method of involving students can take place at the classroom level as well as the school level.

Perhaps historically, we have underestimated the role students can play in making constructive educational decisions. Teachers who have asked the students have consistently been surprised and pleased at the power of the suggestions and ideas the young learners have offered. Such a means of researching what is meaningful calls for a shift in thinking and a shift in control in some respects. It also yields a measure of ownership and investment in the outcomes of teacher research projects to the students. A teacher asked recently, "Do you think I should *tell* my fourth graders that I will be doing research on methods of teaching science with manipulatives this year?" The response from her colleagues: "*Tell* them! How about *asking them to be researchers too!*"

"In a community of learners, adults and children learn simultaneously and in the same place to think critically and analytically and to solve problems that are important to them. In a community of learners, learning is endemic and mutually visible" (Barth, 1990, p. 43). Teacher–researchers we know are very reluctant to view their students as the "subjects" of their research. Students can be catalysts for change; they can offer a fresh perspective with sometimes jarring honesty. Students are not pawns in the research process; they are collaborators and participants in what Barth terms, "the community of learners."

> Through dialogue, the teacher-of-the-students and the students-of-the-teacher cease to exist and a new term emerges; teacher–student with students–teachers. The teacher is no longer merely the one-who-teaches, but one who is himself taught in dialogue with the students, who in turn, while being taught, also teach. (Freire, 1972, p. 67)

Teaching, after all, is a process of engaging learners in trying to make meaning, to make sense of our world. Designing environments and facilitating processes that foster inquiry is the primary task of teachers. Great teachers visibly enact the process of inquiry with their students. They are constantly wondering, looking, gathering information, studying it to reveal meaning, and thinking again. Teachers and students reinforce this process in each other, celebrate each other's developmental reachings, and lead each other along. In these ways, teachers and students together will develop a knowledge lived, not merely displayed in their work.

## REFERENCES

Barth, R. S. (1990). *Improving schools from within*. San Francisco: Jossey-Bass.

Boomer, G. (1987). Addressing the problem of elsewhereness: A case for action research in schools. In D. Goswami & P. Stillman (Eds.), *Reclaiming the classroom: Teacher research as an agency for change* (pp. 4–12). Portsmouth, NH: Boynton/Cook Heinemann.

Brandes, D., & Ginnis, P. (1986). *A Guide to student-centred learning*. Oxford: Basil Blackwell.

Cohen, E., (1986). *Designing groupwork: Strategies for the heterogeneous classroom*. New York: Teachers College Press.

Elbow, P. (1973). *Writing without teachers*. London: Oxford University Press.

Farrell, E., Peguero, G., Lindsey, R., & White, R. (1988). Giving voice to high school students: Pressure and boredom, ya know what I'm sayin'? *American Educational Research Journal, 25*(4), 489–502.

Flinders, K. (1988). Teacher isolation and the new reform. *Journal of Curriculum and Supervision, 4*, 17–29.

Freire, P. (1972). *Pedagogy of the oppressed*. New York: Herder and Herder.

Grumet, M. R. (1989). Dinner at Abigail's: Nurturing collaboration. *National Education Association, January*, 20–25.

Hanson, P. (1981). *Learning through groups: A trainer's guide*. San Diego: University Associates.

Hargreaves, A. (1993). Individualism and individuality: reinterpreting the teacher culture. In J. Little & M. McLaughlin (Eds.), *Teachers' work: Individuals, colleagues, and contexts* (pp. 51–76). New York: Teachers College Press.

Hargreaves, A., & Dawe, R. (1990). Paths of professional development: Contrived collegiality, collaborative culture, and the case of peer coaching. *Teaching and Teacher Education, 6,* 227–241.

Hobson, D. (1994). Across the generations: Conversations with retired teachers. In P. Joseph & G. Burnaford (Eds.), *Images of schoolteachers in twentieth-century America* (pp. 78–85). New York: St. Martin's Press.

Huberman, M. (1993). The model of the independent artisan in teachers' professional relations. In J. Little & M. McLaughlin (Eds.), *Teachers' work: Individuals, colleagues, and contexts* (pp. 11–50). New York: Teachers College Press.

Hunt, D. (1987). *Beginning with ourselves.* Cambridge, MA: Brookline.

Jervis, K. (1986). A teacher's quest for a child's questions. *Harvard Educational Review, 56*(2), 132–150.

Johnson, D. G., & Henstrand, J. (1993). Action research: Using student interviewers to link research and practice. *Teaching and Change, 1*(1), 29–44.

Kolb, D. (1984). *Experiental learning.* Englewood Cliffs, NJ: Prentice-Hall.

Lieberman, A., & Miller, L. (1984). *Teachers, their world and their work: Implications for school improvement.* Arlington, VA: Association for Supervision and Curriculum Development.

Lippitt, R., Hooyman, G., Sashkin, M., & Kaplan, J. (Eds.). (1980). *Resourcebook for planned change.* Ann Arbor: Human Resource Development Associates.

Lortie, D. (1975). *The schoolteacher: A sociological study.* Chicago: University of Chicago Press.

Miller, J. (1990a). *Creating spaces and finding voices: Teachers collaborating for empowerment.* Albany: State University of New York Press.

Miller, J. (1990b). Teachers as curriculum creators. In J. Sears & J. Marshall (Eds.), *Teaching and thinking about curriculum* (pp. 83–96). New York: Teachers College Press.

Miller, J. (1992). Shifting the boundaries: Teachers challenge contemporary curriculum thought. *Theory into Practice.* Vol. 31, No. 3, Summer, 245–251.

Nalle, K. (1993). Democratic processing of children's classroom concerns, *Teaching and Change.* Vol. 1, No. 1. 45–54.

Paley, V. G. (1986). On listening to what the children say. *Harvard Educational Review, 56*(2), 122–131.

Pfeiffer, W., & Jones, J. (1969). *A handbook for structured experiences for human relations training.* Vols. 1–4. San Diego, CA: University Associates.

Rogers, C. (1969). *Freedom to learn.* Columbus, OH: Charles Merrill.

Schubert, W., & Schubert, A. (1984). *Sources of a theory of action research in progressive education.* Paper presented at the annual meeting of the American Educational Research Association, New Orleans, April 23–27, 1984.

Schmuck, R., & Schumuck, P. (1992). *Group processes in the classroom* (2nd ed.). Dubuque, IA: Wm. Brown.

Sitton, T. (1980). The child as informant: The teacher as ethnographer. *Language Arts, 57*(5), 540–545.

van Manen, M. (1990). *Researching lived experience.* Albany: State University of New York Press.

Watson, G. (1974). *Verbal and non-verbal methods for working with groups.* Vol I and II. New York: Harper.

# Taking a Risk: Learning About Physics With Young Children

Nancy Hubbard
Batavia Public Schools

The questions seem to be universal. Will we ever have enough time to teach it all? Will we cover all the material this year that we are expected to cover? Why does our district continue to add new things to teach, but they never remove anything from the curriculum? These are some of the questions I asked every year, but, however inadequately, I managed to get through most of the required subjects. At one time, the teaching of reading and math occupied most of the available teaching time during the school day. If there happened to be any surplus time, I taught either social studies or science. Not only did these concerns frustrate me as a teacher, but they also restricted my growth professionally. My worries about "getting everything in" kept me from trying new ideas. Worst of all, it kept me from taking risks.

In my second-grade classroom, I knew that I was accountable for realizing a particular set of objectives with my students. After all, they would have to be ready for third grade, and if they didn't know it, there are those who would believe it to be my fault. How could I risk venturing out and trying something new?

During the previous year I had taken a class in reading methods in Great Britain. One of the subjects taught there was technology. Technology in the United Kingdom concerns innovations as they extend human capabilities. Some of what I saw and experienced was discovery and some of it was inventing and building.

Much of what I encountered was physics, and I certainly didn't teach much physics in my second-grade classroom! It seems as though our curricula and our school districts emphasize primary reading and math so much that we all too often push aside science. Science is always present, however. Like adults, children are by nature technological creatures. They need to know. They want to find out. Humans have continued through history to use their intelligence, talents, and abilities to raise their standard of living, engaging in technological activities to solve their problems. Our children are born into a society of fast-paced technology. In their homes, at their schools, and even at play, they face machines and gadgets that have made an enormous impact on their lives. These things have made their lives so much easier. Their televisions and video games entertain them, their appliances work for them, their vehicles take them wherever they wish to go at a moment's notice. And these things have now become mundane in their everyday lives. They are as commonplace as sleeping and eating, and even more, they are taken for granted. Because they don't notice them, they have little idea about the ways in which they work or how they evolved.

Lederman (1990) suggested that children, between the ages of 5–7, are at their peak as physicists. Lederman stated:

> Seven year olds scare me. They are always asking questions about how and why things work. And what do we do? We tell them to shut up. From then on they lose interest. We take naturally curious, natural scientists and manage to beat that curiosity right out of them. (Lederman, personal communication, October 25, 1990)

I wanted the children to notice what was around them. I wanted them to begin to wonder. Because I had concerns about the lack of physical science education in my own classroom, I felt that it would be to my advantage to do some teacher research on this topic.

I decided to explore how whole language and physics might be merged in my second-grade classroom. Finding material on this subject would be my next venture. It was important that I seek assistance from those involved in the professional areas of research and physics. I tapped a number of resource persons in the community. Among them were research engineers, middle school physical science teachers, high school physics teachers, and physicists and researchers at Fermi National Accelerator Laboratory. After presenting these people with a list of whole language units, they returned to me a myriad of wonderful, stimulating ideas. I had some real concerns regarding whether or not my second-grade students would be able to grasp physics concepts. Those concepts are difficult enough for adults.

Mr. William Hall, a research engineer for Amoco Research Center and father of five, expressed his thoughts on this idea:

> Most of the principles of physics are easy enough to be intuitive for primary school children. Our worst sin is to muddle their minds with the 'formulas and math' of physics. Our greatest challenge is to understand a given principle so completely and firmly that we can teach it in its beautiful simplicity. It's sort of like watching an Olympic class athlete ... you pick up the essence of what's supposed to be happening without the confusion caused by a novice's flailing arms. (Hall, personal communication, 1990)

However, as wonderful as my collaborative contacts were, the children eventually became my most important resource.

School districts often require the teaching of core chapters in science and social studies. Unfortunately, either because of lack of time or lack of knowledge, teachers refrain from teaching important areas other than core chapters. It simply seemed as though there wasn't enough time to do it all and do it right. I believed, however, in spite of the time constraints, that the hands-on approach was best, and this approach is the most time consuming of all. Most teachers realize that both children and adults learn best what they do themselves. They also learn best when they have incorporated their own ideas into the decisions about what it is they want to learn. They tend to share more, present more, and further pursue their interests when they are able to help make decisions about the curricula.

In the end, my students were working on the research project collaboratively with me. For this reason, integrating science into whole language units was probably the easiest part of the project. My students were more comfortable in the understanding of physics than I was. Once they can begin to understand the basic idea—that something *is*, even though they cannot explain why—they can begin to draw pictures and diagrams of what it is that they see. They can also label those pictures in a way that they are able to understand, or at least talk about them.

This kind of "understanding" was new to me. In the past I had always believed that in science, children must be able to understand thoroughly an idea before advancing on to another. But after a period of 12 weeks, I began to realize that this was not necessarily true. Dr. Leon Lederman, Nobel prize-winner for physics, stated that children learn technology by observing, guessing, and estimating. He feels they need to understand relationships and get a "feel" for the way things work, even if they are not yet able to understand why. He believes that they are able to understand concepts like relativity, motion of particles, and gravity, even if they are not able to talk about them in any depth (Lederman, personal communication, 1990). Although this concept seemed foreign to me, it proved to be true. The children understood physics, they loved it, and they begged for more. They not only read more, but the more they read, the more they wanted to "do."

Throughout the project I found that I was not the one who would always have to plan the lessons. Rather, ideas evolved from things such as toys, literature, or perhaps a trip that someone had taken. One of the most significant lessons during the research developed during a thematic unit on insects. I had brought out a copy of the book *"I can't," said the ant; A second book of nonsense* by Polly Cameron. It was a big book, large enough for all to see. The skills that I had chosen to review that day were use of quotation marks and rhyming words. In the story, a teapot has fallen to the floor and broken. An ant passes by and the teapot implores it to help. "I can't," said the ant. Other inanimate objects speak up, always in rhyme, and encourage the ant to help, often giving specific suggestions. In the end, the ant assembles a crew of his ant buddies, along with two spiders, to mend and return the teapot to its place on the kitchen counter. The spiders spin long strands of silk from the teapot up to and over the handle of the cabinet door, and down again to the floor. As the children looked at the picture on this particular page, one remarked that it looked as if the spiders were using the cabinet handle as a pulley. Another child asked what a pulley was. So we set up pulleys, hanging them from strings suspended from the rafters. We pursued the study of pulleys for quite some time that day, the children freely experimenting with them. As they experimented, they kept notes and visual records of what they discovered in their science journals. Afterward, when we met as a large group, we discussed those journals and the discoveries, challenges, and successes that they contained. At the end of the day, two girls asked if they might borrow the pulleys for the weekend. What a pleasant surprise it was for us all when, on Monday, the girls who had borrowed the pulleys had also researched, with the aid of a parent, the use of pulleys in their homes. They reported to the class that there were pulleys in the window, garage door openers, toys, and tree houses. It was especially interesting that this research had been done by the girls, as it has traditionally been said that girls have not been interested in mechanical things. They put on an excellent, motivating presentation for the class.

The fascination with pulleys continued, and one of the children brought a diagram of an elevator. Some of the other children wanted to know how it worked. Not knowing myself, we pursued the research together and before long, they were building elevators for their teddy bears out of shoe boxes, pulleys, and counterweights. Throughout this whole week, the children had observed, questioned, researched, built models, experimented, and produced a product, and it was all done by their own initiative. All that was necessary for me to do was to provide the opportunities along with a few simple supplies and books.

The outcomes significantly changed my style of teaching. I realized that teaching integrated science was very similar to teaching reading in a whole language program. In the area of language arts, I had been teaching reading, writing, listening, and speaking through the theme approach. Similarly, over those 12 weeks of conducting the research, I found that I had indeed covered a significant amount of material required by the science curriculum. It was simply covered in a different way, through integration with literature. We not only covered science objectives, but the children had also experienced reading, writing, listening, speaking, problem solving, and cooperative grouping processes. It was possible to teach *more* in a shorter amount of time! I knew that in the future, my whole language themes would more often revolve around scientific areas of study in the second grade curricula.

Although I had always given lip-service to child-centered classrooms, the child-centered approach still had room for significant improvements, especially in the area of science. During my research, the children's questions and interests guided the direction of the curriculum. They posed the questions, stated the

problems, and solved them together. At the same time, as I circulated throughout the room, I asked them the questions that provoked them to ask more
questions of each other and think in more depth. Throughout the research
weeks they learned, as I had in my own continuing education, that solving
problems and doing difficult tasks and experiments were easier to do collaboratively. When it was enjoyable, the children often referred to it as "play" rather
than fun. If it was very difficult and they were not so very willing, they could at
least take refuge in the fact that we were doing it together.

I had assigned "technology groups" at the beginning of the research and the
children continued in those groups for the entire 12 weeks. During that time I
realized how it was important that the children work together in a unified group.
It became apparent that I would have to teach strategies for not only problem
solving, but for self-assessment of the group. As the children would experiment
or try a new idea the children began asking questions such as: What did we do
right? Should we use new materials? Should we abandon the idea and come up
with an entirely new idea? Why did this happen? What did we do incorrectly?
As it is for many adults, the idea of questioning themselves was difficult for the
children, and it was clear that they needed a great deal of practice in this area.
As in many cooperative groups, the children had a tendency to blame each
other for failures and often felt that their own personal ideas were the only good
ones. As the research progressed and the children became more comfortable
with each other, they became increasingly better at cooperative strategies and
group dynamics. Each day before we did any group task, it became necessary
to review strategies for successful group work. In the same manner, the class
met as a whole following the completion of the task to process what had just
transpired. Those strategies I continued to use on a daily basis after the research
was over. I found that problem-solving groups were more successful when the
children had specific skills on which to focus. The children, too, must have found
some merit in learning the art of group dynamics. At free exploration time they
would find themselves organizing their own groups to present plays, make craft
projects, play with blocks, or invent. I often overheard them assigning jobs,
encouraging each other, or suggesting other ideas or options.

My role in the learning process became different from any way I had known
in the past. Throughout the projects and activities, I visited work stations and
small conversational groups. Sometimes the children would appear frustrated
and have many difficult questions. I desperately wanted to answer their questions and yet I knew that it would be more beneficial if they could discover the
answers through their own discovery. I found myself answering their questions
by asking more questions of them.

Student growth is directly affected by the role of the more skilled members who
are generally the teachers. In their roles, teachers must be able to proffer tasks
that bring about suitable reorganization of children's thoughts. They must be able
to guide and support student ideas rather than simply transmit the correct ways

to them. In a constructivist setting, the students are involved in a discovery process. They are discovering and inventing while at the same time negotiating solutions, sharing supplies, explanations, and ideas, and continually evaluating. Students use the tasks proposed by the teacher in order to allow their own thinking to become more powerful, more abstract (Clements & Battista, 1990).

From the perspective that learning science is the social construction of knowledge, the children are constructing knowledge while engaging in social talk and activity about problems or tasks that they share. Making meaning becomes a process that involves persons-in-conversation. It is a process in which individuals are introduced and guided by those who are more skilled. The more experienced members can help by structuring tasks in order to enable the less skilled members to perform and internalize the processes. It has been suggested that if the more experienced members, generally teachers, are to lead others toward the conventional science ideas, then their intervention is imperative in order to provide background information and evidence, and make the tools of the scientific world available to the students. The critical feature is the nature of the dialogue between students and teachers. First, the teacher needs to provide some ideas to the students where and when it is necessary, and the students take those ideas from there and make sense of them. Second, the teacher must be an excellent listener. When teachers really listen to children, then they can interpret what the children are understanding, and, in turn, guide them into further dialogue, action, and understanding (Driver, Asoko, Leach, Mortimer, & Scott, 1994).

As the children shared with each other, I in turn shared with the children. It was then that the concept of collegial sharing became an important part of my professional growth. Some of my colleagues had noticed that there were some unusual projects evolving in our classroom, and they would inquire as to what was taking place. As I shared the essence of what was happening, more ideas began to surface. They shared ideas that they had tried in their own classrooms, as well as ideas that they had heard about. Other teachers began sharing with me articles from various professional journals and children's magazines that would be of some interest and benefit to our projects and studies. Occasionally, a teacher would bring her students into our classroom to see a particular project. There were mixed reactions—some were fascinated and others shook their heads in skepticism. Even though opinions varied, there was enough support to urge me to forge ahead.

Not only did support come from my colleagues, the public loved the unconventional ideas. Our local village newspaper reporters with cameras in hand came several times during those few weeks. Pictures and short articles about the unusual methods of teaching physics to children were very appealing to the readers. It was especially appealing to those readers who had never had a chance to do those types of activities in their school experiences. Besides being good public interest stories, they were wonderful public relations stories. The public was not the only stakeholder that was pleased; our principal was glowing.

The principal in our building was more vital in this research than he had ever realized. He was a person who not only endorsed the changes that were taking place, but also ignited new ideas, encouraging them to materialize. When administrators empower teachers, giving them the freedom to take risks in the classroom and try some new and innovative ideas, tremendous events ensue. This "permission" is extremely important to classroom teachers. For too long teachers have been given scripted manuals and pre-made worksheets. They have been instructed by school boards and charged by administrators to teach "the right way," while being given the tools—text books and reproductible worksheets. The message has been clear: this is the way it should be and it is the best way, the only way. Teachers have accepted these tools of the trade because "the experts" have made them. All too often, teachers have not realized that they themselves are the experts. The self-esteem and self-confidence of classroom educators will remain low as long as these messages are in place, for this kind of thinking does not allow educators to think for themselves. In order to refashion this type of thinking among classroom educators, school leaders must have confidence in their staff and allow them to grow, even if it might mean occasional failure. Leaders who keep abreast of current issues and practices, who are willing to take risks of their own, are able to encourage teachers' professional growth and promote change in education.

Becoming confident in my own teaching and research has probably been the principle victory for me as a teacher. I am more likely to take risks today, particularly in the area of making decisions within the curriculum. Even though I know I must reach the outcomes created by my school district, I now realize that I am no longer bound to presenting the curriculum as it is presented in the teaching manuals. My students and I have become co-creators of curriculum. I know that not only are my own ideas valid, but there is also tremendous validity in student-created ideas. My research disclosed that children truly do learn best the things in which they are interested. Additionally, it revealed that children can make meaning through working dialogue together. They worked most intensely on those assignments on which they were allowed to help make decisions and diagnoses, and on those in which they were given sanction to make meaning of what they heard and saw.

My research unveiled the idea that student-created ideas were as valid, if not more valid, as my own plans and ideas. Because I was not consumed with thoughts of executing the lessons exactly as planned, I became a keen observer of children.

I have continued to be an observer and a researcher. I do not always take daily written notes or record my findings in a journal, although I do it much of the time. More often than in the past, I find myself watching and thinking more about children, their learning and my own learning. Through this watching and thinking has come a great deal of questioning. Now I have more questions about what it is that I am teaching, why I am teaching it, and how I am teaching it.

The more questions I ask of myself, the more proficient I become at asking questions of others. As the children are asking in their own research, I am also constantly asking, either silently or aloud to the class, "What went right? What went wrong? What happened here? What could we have done differently? What would we continue to do in the same way?"

Other questions come to consciousness as I think of both the near and distant futures: What other related areas could we explore? How could I teach that skill or idea within the framework of a new thematic unit? Because I have empowered the children to be more in control of their own learning, I now think more in terms of outcomes rather than in terms of teaching objectives. Now I believe more in the process than the product. My students and I deliberate over what was really learned in that lesson or unit. Being a teacher-researcher has become for me an instrument for reflection and change. It has allowed for both renewal and growth in my personal life and my professional life, and what I have learned will continue to nurture my teaching in my future.

## REFERENCES

Cameron. P. (1961). *"I can't," said the ant: A second book of nonsense*. New York: Coward-McCann.
Clements. D., & Battista, M. (1990). Constructivist learning and teaching. *Arithmetic Teacher, 38*(1), 34–37.
Driver. R., Asoko, H., Leach, J., Mortimer, E., & Scott, P. (1994). Constructing scientific knowledge in the classroom. *Educational Researcher, 23*(7), 5–12.

# FINDING MEANING: CHEMISTRY RECONSTRUCTED WITH HIGH SCHOOL STUDENTS

Craig Hill
Lake Forest Academy

## BACKGROUND FOR MY TEACHER ACTION RESEARCH

I have been teaching chemistry for 3 years at a college preparatory high school where the enrollment is selective. The school claims to have "the best and the brightest" student body. Ninety-nine percent of the graduates go on to college.

As a college student, I realized that chemistry had meaning for me. Thinking back, it was when I was in organic chemistry class that I first took responsibility for my own learning. I discovered that chemistry is central to an understanding of the natural world, not just an academic activity.

The "stuff" of chemistry has been changing in recent years. Historically, chemistry has been about things such as atoms, molecules, protons, ionic bonds, and electron clouds. There has been much emphasis on scientific fact and not process. Textbooks are overflowing with scientific terms; students believe that to be good at science, they have to be good at memorization. Many of my students ask, "Why do I need to know this stuff?"; the material seems meaningless to them.

I have been intrigued by a book by Rutherford and Ahlgrem (1990) called *Science For All Americans*. The book is part of the first phase of a project by the Association for The Advancement of Math and Science, which was prompted by a report that students in the U.S. were not among the top achievers in math and science knowledge. Rutherford and Ahlgrem call for a reform in the way science is being taught in our schools, noting that the present way of teaching science is effective only for the privileged few. They stress the importance of having scientifically literate citizens and that the purpose of science education should not be exclusively to produce scientists.

Not long after reading Rutherford and Ahlgrem's book, I began to look for new and different ways of teaching chemistry to produce scientifically literate citizens. I came upon a new term—"constructivism"—and it seemed to make sense. Basically, constructivist theory is based on the idea that: (a) knowledge is constructed from previous experiences, (b) teachers cannot transmit knowledge to their students, and (c) learners are responsible for all that is learned (National Center for Improving Science Education, 1991). Constructivist theory suggests that teachers should teach science by letting the students *use the process of science to learn science*. The way students learn is to take previously known concepts and adjust them to new concepts. It is that active process that changes and builds on students' knowledge. A person has to *experience* the knowledge and let it soak into previous concepts in order for knowledge to either be gained or dismissed. I realized that, if I taught with that process in mind, students could begin to answer the question, "Why do we have to know this stuff?" for themselves.

## MY CLASSROOM RESEARCH—WHAT I SET OUT TO EXPLORE

As a teacher, I was getting very frustrated with many of my students' lack of motivation and understanding of chemistry, as well as with their fear of or inexperience with independent thinking. Even with a variety of in-class activities ranging from labs to videos to debates, the students were not excited about the subject. Statements like the following were common: "Mr. Hill, you are a good teacher. Why do you have to teach such a boring subject?" or "I'm not going to be a doctor—why do I have to learn this?" Is this attitude actually due to the subject of chemistry, I wondered, or is it due to the way in which I've been presenting the subject to them?

It seems as though I have been an actor on a stage performing and the students were the audience. Each day, four shows in all, I would perform chemistry. Sometimes the audience would love it and at other times the performance would be a flop. I began to investigate how to alter the "shows", based on the constructivist principle that each student is different. I began my classroom research with a unit on nuclear energy. My first task was to find out what kind of prior knowledge my students had about the subject. I decided to discover that through a pretest, the results of which would help me to decide on an objectives list which would represent what the students needed to know for the unit. Each student was then required to complete a portfolio that demonstrated an understanding of each of the objectives. Student autonomy, which is a major tenet of constructivism, was stressed; each portfolio was to be designed and created by the individual student, utilizing the experiences and knowledge gained by the student during the unit.

I imagined that with such freedom would also come some pain: pain of not knowing how to demonstrate understanding through means other than a paper-and-pencil-test, pain of having the rules changed in the middle of the schooling game, pain of having no clear sense of what the teacher expected. I was challenging not only their existing knowledge of an academic subject, but also their existing idea of schooling! Is this too much at once? Will the students take ownership? Will they find what they are learning to be meaningful? Will they understand these new roles for teacher and students—or will they feel manipulated? These were my research questions; I was ready to roll.

## WHAT WE DID—STUDENTS AND TEACHER FACE UNCERTAINTY

After the pretest, I designed the list of objectives for the nuclear energy unit as planned. I explained to the students that there were 11 such objectives and that their chemistry portfolios were to be developed around these objectives. It was my goal to have *them* design the assignments and create the tasks that would help them to achieve these objectives. Assignments would then be placed in individual student portfolios. We brainstormed ideas on what the portfolios could include, and we generated formats for assignments such as making a movie, designing maps and flowcharts, and conducting original experiments. However, as the session continued, I could see the students were feeling uncomfortable with so much uncertainty and possibility. One student asked where I fit in with all of this and I told him I was like the coach. "I will help when I see you struggling, but you have to work through your own difficulties." Another student asked if he could just listen to me and get the information that way. I explained to him that *he* was the performer this time and that I was the coach on the sideline. "To learn chemistry, you have to experience chemistry yourself," I counseled him.

Now that I look back on it, it seems that the cognitive demands I placed on the students were enormous. I asked my students, who were my co-researchers in this effort, to comment. One stated it beautifully: "Mainly, no one knew how to get started. To design an assignment, you must first understand the material. But no one understood it at first. How much confusion would we have saved if we'd just read the book and thought about it before thinking of tasks?"

Another student offered his comment in class one day: "I have an idea. How about you teach and we learn?" This remark smacked me on the side of the head! Clearly, he was resistant to this approach for learning. Yet another student helped me understand: "For some of us, it's very easy to make A's when you write stuff down for later processing. Later, you really think about it. Sometimes you actually listen to what is said in class, sometimes you just write it down and maybe think about it later. But when you have to both find the material and also think and learn, and you still want an A, it becomes complex."

The traditional role of the teacher is the researcher of information which is then presented to the class. However, in the constructivist classroom, the *students* assume the role of researchers. This gives the student a double role—that of the learner and that of the teacher. The increased activity of the student may lead to the impression that the "adult teacher" in the room is not doing any work. In the constructivist classroom, the teacher coaches the students instead of playing the game for them.

## THE RESULTS—PORTFOLIOS AND PROGRESS

### From the Students

Evaluation of the portfolios was more for product than for process. The products were those that the students designed in order to demonstrate their understanding of the objectives of the nuclear energy unit. There would be three evaluators: (a) the individual student, (b) the student's peers, and (c) the teacher. The student's self-evaluation would count for 25%, the peers would contribute 15%, and I was responsible for 60% of the grade.

I also asked the students to evaluate the process for learning we used during this unit. They wrote responses to items on a questionnaire given them at the end of the unit and kept notes in journals throughout the 3 weeks. In short, the students liked the independence associated with this method of teaching, but felt the need for more structure as well. This left me in a quandary: If *I* assigned the students the tasks to do, in an effort to give them more structure, their independence to find meaningful tasks to demonstrate their understanding would be lost. They would once again be doing the teacher's "busy work", instead of finding meaning for themselves. The more structure however, the less anxiety over the amount of responsibility. The tradeoff is that with more independence, more meaningful learning can occur.

Students felt that they would have benefitted from more checkpoints in order to keep themselves on task. Some felt that the teacher needed to use more time for "teaching," as they perceived it. Generally though, the students felt that they learned a great deal. One boy wrote, "Now that I understand this, I could do it again. I understand more about nuclear energy than anything else we have done all year. When I am responsible for me, I know what I can and cannot do. It is not easy to be lost in a classroom of oneself. Sure this new teaching method is a real pain in the behind, because it makes you really work, and it does become frustrating. But, it *is* successful."

## Feedback From a Colleague

I felt that one of my fellow teachers would be a valuable source of feedback as I tried this new kind of teaching in my chemistry class. After observing my teaching and looking at some of the materials the students and I were generating, Mr. D. wrote his reactions. His ideas and conversations with me about constructivism helped me to refine my ideas. Here is part of a letter he wrote to me which summarized his response to my action research:

> Here are some thoughts about the approach you used in your chemistry class in your most recent unit. You asked the students to design their own activities to demonstrate their understanding of the topic being studied. They concluded the unit by handing in a portfolio of their work. My reactions are based on observing the class on one day and looking in at other times, as well as participating in frequent discussions with you.
>
> 1. I like the philosophy underlying this approach. I think it encourages independent thinking and time management and gives the students the opportunity to really learn the material and not just memorize it. If you use the method throughout the year, it won't come as such a shock to students who are more comfortable with the lecture-memorize-test format.
>
> 2. You began with a question something like, "What can you do to demonstrate your understanding of this topic?" That is a very tough question. How can you demonstrate real understanding and not just memorization? It is an impossible question to answer if you do not yet have some understanding of the topic. An alternative question might be to ask them to come up with projects which would show how particular concepts work. At any rate, I think in some ways the toughest part of this approach is to enable the students to get started.
>
> 3. For the system to work, the teacher must be prepared to "lower the boom" on those students who turn in shoddy work. Students have to learn that the teacher is serious about this work and that they will be held accountable.
>
> 4. Evaluation of individual projects can be difficult. I think it is a good idea to involve the students in the evaluation process. I wonder too if the teacher should not formally evaluate effort and progress at certain points during the unit rather than appearing to base his or her evaluation solely on the quality of the portfolio.
>
> Thanks for involving me in this process. Our discussions have been helpful in thinking about my own teaching. Mr. D.

## From Me—The Classroom Teacher–Researcher

Throughout this adventure, I kept a classroom journal that I have found to be useful as a researcher. The journal entries I made before the classroom research started reflected some of the concerns I had about my teaching and the class.

The entries also set me up with some very high expectations for the constructivist method. I was written up in the school newspaper not long after my unit began; I was feeling very good about myself and my new adventure! Then, as we proceeded through the uncertainty, my journal revealed my own misgivings. "Is this method really working? Are the students doing anything? Am I helping them? Am I comfortable with this style?"

Now that the unit is over, I have the opportunity to look back and see what happened. I had hoped that the students who were bright but unmotivated in science would begin to learn, seizing this chance to take control of their own learning. What actually happened was that the motivated students continued to do well and quickly adapted to the constructivist way of learning. I have to admit that the students who were unmotivated stayed that way through the nuclear energy unit. I might explain this by saying that the students believed that this way of teaching was just another trick to motivate them. I'd like to hope that if this method was used from the beginning and continued throughout the year, the unmotivated students might not feel so manipulated.

This experience with constructivist teaching has solidified my views on learning. Instead of memorizing random facts, students can be challenged to discover their own learnings. Conceptual conflict does need to occur in order for meaningful learning in science to happen. I felt that it was difficult for my students this year to deal with a new way of learning along with a new concept in science. I will introduce increased autonomy to students next year much more slowly. From the first day, the students will gain experience setting educational goals and achieving them, but they will have more regular checkpoints in place and other aspects of responsibility will be monitored more throughout a unit of study. Ultimately though, the students will experience chemistry labs in which *their* questions are explored and not someone else's. *Their* ideas and prior experiences will lead to their learning of chemistry.

## ACKNOWLEDGMENT

Thanks to Mr. D., my colleague, for his feedback and support.

## REFERENCES

National Center for Improving Science Education. (1991). *The High Stakes of High School Science*. Andover, MA: The Network, Inc.

Rutherford, J. and Ahlgrem, A. (1990). *Science for all Americans*. Oxford, England: Oxford University Press.

# TOPICS AND THEMES
# FOR FURTHER DISCUSSION

1. Discuss or write about how you "hear your own voice" in your curriculum. How is your presence evident in what is taught and how it is taught? Then describe how the students' voices are present in curriculum decision making in your class(es). What other sources of curriculum exist for you and your students?

2. Describe a time when something you and your students were studying seemed to take "a life of its own." What happened and why? What were the results? What did you learn? What are the implications for curriculum when this happens?

3. Conduct a discussion with a small group of students about a specific area of the curriculum or classroom procedure which you are curious about. Then design a plan in which the students you teach could be co-researchers to explore this topic further in the classroom. What contributions do the students make that you, as a teacher, could not make?

4. Find one other faculty colleague who would be willing to work with you on a collaborative research project for a brief period of time (2–3 weeks). If you are a preservice teacher, that colleague may be your cooperating teacher or university advisor; if you are an inservice teacher, perhaps a teammate or department member may participate. Decide on a common interest area and collect data in each of your classrooms. Meet frequently to discuss what you are finding, then prepare to share your work with a larger group of teachers.

What was it like to collaborate in this manner with another teacher? What did you learn from each other that you may not have learned on your own? What were the challenges involved in this procedure?

5. Establish a communication—in writing, by E-mail, by telephone, or in person with an experienced teacher-researcher at another school. You might find such a person through journal publications, through membership in a professional organization, conference attendance, or through a community network of teachers. Keep in touch with this person, sharing ideas, learning from him or her, for several months. Discuss or write about issues of support from colleagues, students and administration with this teacher-researcher. How can the experiences of a teacher-researcher from another school be useful to you in your situation?

6. List your own support system for classroom research; who could you call upon for feedback, response, suggestions, encouragement? What steps do you need to take to increase that network, if that is warranted? Who could provide the positive peer pressure you need to sustain research as a means of professional development?

# 5

# LIVES OF INQUIRY: COMMUNITIES OF LEARNING AND CARING

Linda S. Tafel
Joseph C. Fischer
National-Louis University

*Ours is the responsibility of conserving, transmitting, rectifying and expanding the heritage of values we have received that those who come after us may receive it more solid and secure, more widely accessible and more generously shared than we have received it.*

—John Dewey (1934, p. 87)

## INTRODUCTION

Teachers' visions and hopes for better schools shape the kinds of inquiry interests they explore during their professional lives. Teacher research is enriched through collaboration with colleagues and students. This happens when students and teachers mutually construct a classroom culture for learning, caring, and inquiry. It happens when teachers, in dialogue with colleagues, seek to understand the learnings, relationships, and events that unfold in their classrooms. We view all this as a life of inquiry—vital and essential for teacher growth and professional development.

If schools are to become communities of learning, caring and inquiry, they must find ways to cultivate trusting relationships among teachers and help them feel valued as colleagues and professional educators. Such valuing is evident in the opportunities and recognition teachers receive for doing research, for taking ownership of professional development activities, and for assuming leadership in their schools and professional community.

In this chapter, we examine the interplay between teacher research and professional development, and demonstrate that both are needed for helping schools create a community of learning for students and teachers. We point out how teacher research and professional development have basic goals and methods in common. These include sharing insights gained through experience, reflection, and systematic inquiry. They involve building collegial relationships, dialogue among teachers, and sharing strategies and stories of teaching.

In the first section of this chapter, we discuss how teachers' visions for professional development provide guidelines for creating more effective and meaningful staff development programs. The second section presents a case study of one teacher, Ann Watson Cohn, whom we have worked with during the past 3 years. It illustrates how her professional life of inquiry unfolded, and demonstrates the affinity between teacher research and teacher development. The last section presents a rationale and framework for schools to consider as they build communities of learning, caring, and inquiry.

## TEACHERS' VISIONS FOR PROFESSIONAL DEVELOPMENT

When teachers are asked for suggestions about effective and meaningful professional development activities, their most frequent response is that they want more opportunity to reflect on their work, and to discuss their teaching and learning with colleagues. This is significant to note, for if schools are to benefit from teacher knowledge and learning, a culture for inquiry, reflection, and dialogue must be created. Our discussions with teachers about professional development reveal a continued quest to learn about teaching, and portray the kinds of school climates that foster or hinder such learning. In this section, we examine the kind of visions and frameworks for professional development that teachers hold.

That teaching must be considered an intellectual rather than a routine task (Dewey, 1933), has been a frequent response in our research with teachers concerning the efficacy of professional development programs they have experienced. Similarly, a growing consensus among teachers is that professional development plans should be based on a holistic view of learning, provide opportunity for sharing and dialogue among colleagues, affirm and make use of what teachers have learned through experience and reflection, and be an integral and continuous part of the life and culture of the school. These findings will be elaborated in the teacher stories that follow.

In thinking about her teaching career, Penny Silvers, wrote: "My professional growth and development has been a 'work in progress' filled with many drafts, revisions, conferences with significant others, and attempts at making sense out of my chosen career. It has been a messy and not always predictable learning process. But along the way, there have been opportunities to take learning risks, support from other professionals, and reflective moments that have guided me toward the shaping and developing of my personal vision of what school could be."

Silvers asked a group of colleagues what they found meaningful in any staff development they experienced. In her journal describing their conversation, she wrote: "The main theme that emerged was that the staff development that was planned by the teachers and which gave them an opportunity to talk together, share ideas, and work toward a common goal—that came from within—meant the most to them." This idea of interacting with colleagues is echoed by Astrid Martindale, who noted: "I have found through trial runs at different schools, that teachers don't want to listen to me or anyone as a 'how-giver.' They prefer to be interactive. The staff meeting in which I proposed that next year's format for inservices be changed to reflect examining our school culture, looking at our 'we-ness,' our values etc. was eagerly accepted. I was, am, overjoyed."

A persistent theme of our dialogue with teachers is that episodic inservice events had little impact on their development and learning, and, generally that the school culture itself did little to encourage teacher learning and development. Penny Silvers talked about this: "I did not gain a strong sense of myself as a professional educator from school itself. Operating from a traditional perspective, the schools where I taught, treated teachers as workers, complete with in-service training, summative supervision, and accountability for student performance on standard measures. I had to find support for my own professional growth outside of school, from colleagues with similar interests, professors who were willing to engage in teacher research with me, and my own reading and reflection."

Bruce E. Ahlborn, found that his best staff development experiences were with colleagues who encouraged him to try out new strategies in his teaching. "Up until 3 years ago, I had never experienced a sustained constructivist approach to inservice or staff development. The topics ... did not provide any sort of activating event that would translate into my classroom and have a beneficial effect on my students. But I do recall events staffed by certain local high school teachers who demonstrated things that they were doing with their students and these presentations were useful and different because I tried their techniques with my students. My students liked these new techniques so I kept doing them and modifying them as I went along."

In formulating her vision for professional development, Carol Porter suggested that: "Teachers might invite other teachers into their classrooms to observe the application of new strategies or create a video to share with others. By providing an audience for learners we are providing a reason for them to be reflective practitioners who stand back from the learning and seek to understand it. Through this type of analysis, teachers can begin to construct interpretations that will begin a new cycle of inquiry." In this vein, Ahlborn believes that teacher development should be "people-oriented and as such will consider the culture of the setting as well as the state of the individual in regard to professional and intellectual growth. . . . We need to think of ourselves with the same high regard that Dewey advocated for children."

In thinking about what influenced their learning about teaching and their professional development, many teachers cited a colleague or mentor who both affirmed their learnings and nudged them toward other inquiry and self discovery paths. They paused to reflect on the images they hold of themselves as teachers, what this meant in their development and how they felt about it. Their visions for professional development are grounded in people who are examples of these images. This is the case for Janell Cleland who remembered the impact her English department chairperson had on her life. They frequently went to the library together pursuing research interests. In her journal to us, Cleland wrote:

> For the first time I wasn't looking for activities that would work in class the next day. I wanted to know why some things worked in class and why others did not. Was there a pattern to successes? I explored the writing process with students, telling them we were in this together. We read sections of *Beat Not the Poor Desk* in senior English class and decided together how we could adapt and apply it to ourselves. We created a learning community and took risks. We collaborated and learned together. We revised and improved; it was an exciting two years for me.

Teachers want schools to become intellectual environments in which to teach and learn with their students. This has been a persistent theme in our ongoing conversations with them. Bruce Ahlborn found a personal affinity with Robert Schaefer's book *The School as the Center of Inquiry* (1967), and in thinking about his students, offered: "When students respond enthusiastically to a particular approach or when a class is alive with the wonder of a new insight or buoyant in the mastery of a new skill, the teacher attains a high pitch of contained excitement and pleasure." He hopes that schools can be places for excitement, wonderment, inquiry and discovery for teachers as well. In reflecting upon a summer course he led for teachers, Ahlborn found an interconnection between caring relationships and teacher learning:

> It is important to note that these places exist in the world of teachers, and that those of us who design experiences for other teachers and then engage them in these experiences must be sensitive to the needs of our colleagues as they react to the experiences we have constructed for them. Do we care enough about the individuals involved with us to find out what they do and how they think about themselves and how they picture themselves professionally? The answer to these questions is an emphatic yes, if you plan to "work with" as opposed to "work on" the people in your program. If you want to develop a culture of trust that helps people move through change . . . you have to begin with the individual.

A major theme in these reflections is that when schools recognize and affirm their learnings and experiences, teachers continue to inquire about their work, share their learnings with their colleagues, and grow professionally. This becomes possible when schools are committed to building a culture of caring and respect for teachers and for students. Several other themes stand out in the teacher stories and visions for professional development presented here.

Teachers told us that their most meaningful professional development entails observing their students, trying out hunches, testing out various practices, reflecting on their work, and being intellectually curious about teaching, learning, and the world of schools. For them, to grow professionally means to live with ambiguity and uncertainty, to take risks, and to learn that mistakes are a natural part of trying out something new. They believe that professional development must be a continuous journey of inquiry, of evaluating and valuing their learning, and of constructing meanings through reflecting on teaching. In their visions for themselves as teachers, they view teaching and learning as inseparable, and believe it is a life's work.

Teachers believe that relating and caring relationships must be central to teaching. In our dialogues with them, they say that to grow professionally involves enhanced communication and empathic understanding between teachers and students, and among teachers. This implies that teachers learn and grow professionally within a school community that honors learning—among students, colleagues, and mentors who share common goals and values, and who trust and respect each other. They have come to realize that caring relationships are required to facilitate learning and inquiry concerns of teachers and students.

Embedded in their views of meaningful professional development is their belief that to teach means to **practice** the teaching profession. This act of practicing is as true for education as it is for law, medicine, science, art, or any other profession that engages one's intellectual curiosity and involves finding value and meaning in one's chosen work.

Practicing in the teaching profession includes facing the new, exploring ideas with students, finding new ways to connect with students and helping them relate to each other, experimenting with new strategies, and finding new awareness of self and profession. This life time of practice is greatly enhanced by sharing with colleagues our questions, wonderments, perplexities, and insights about our teaching and our learning. With kindred spirits and dedicated companions, dialogue about practice can be affirming, joyful, and often ennobling.

## A PROFESSIONAL LIFE OF INQUIRY

> ... it is important to move back in inner time and attempt to recapture the ways in which the meanings of teaching (and schooling) were sedimented over the years. To look back, to remember is to bind the incidents of past experience, to create patterns in the stream of consciousness. We identify ourselves by means of memory; and, at once, we compose the stories of our lives. (Greene, 1991, p. 11)

As we examine teacher reflections of professional development, it is evident that in continuing to learn about their work, teachers practice research. This is not a surprising finding when we consider that research is fundamentally a reflection and learning process. In our work with teachers, we have found, as Schon (1983) did in his research, that teacher research involves "a continuing process of self-education," and that as teachers become researchers-in-practice, "the practice itself is a source of renewal" (p. 299).

In studying the role of reflection in teacher development and learning, Richert believes that "Good teaching does not rest on a set of static, prescribed rules and technical strategies. Rather, shifting circumstances suggest teachers be reflective in their approach to classroom practice. Reflective teachers approach teaching as problem solving; they see teaching circumstances and conditions as problematic rather than given, and they approach each situation with an openness to both the known and the unknown" (cited in Lieberman & Miller, 1991, p. 114).

To illustrate the interplay between teacher research and teacher development we turn to our work over the past three years with Ann Watson Cohn who reflected on her professional development through a series of dialogue journals and discussions with us. Ann taught at the Baker Demonstration School of National-Louis University. As with other teachers cited in this chapter, she found that reflecting on her teaching is essential to her professional growth and satisfaction, and that there is a close affinity between intellectual curiosity and development as a teacher. In an early journal to us, Ann described her professional growth as a journey of unfolding questions.

One of the most important influences on my teaching during that first year or two was my belief that my colleagues knew a great deal more about teaching reading, or math, or science or social studies, than I did. Lunchtime conversations often centered on instructional problems my peers had. Words, terms, and phrases unknown to me popped up with tantalizing and embarrassingly frequent regularity. Sometimes an instructional activity would be described that was unlike anything I had heard of. I remember to this day someone excitedly describing a successful reading/writing activity involving predictable books. I had never heard of using repetitive stories to generate children's own stories! What a good idea. How did one do this? When could I try it? I immediately started experimenting with this notion in my classroom while looking for additional information about it. And so it went. I heard colleagues talk about things unfamiliar to me, scavenged for information on it, and experimented with everything in my classroom. There was no formal plan to learning, but I certainly had plenty of new questions to answer each week. I didn't like not knowing.

As I reflect on my first years at Baker they were clearly a time of knowledge building. My questions were guided by what I heard around me. Further, . . . I was free to explore within my own classroom. Lots of mistakes were made by me in those days, but I watched, reflected and improved with each successive try. Freedom to experiment with new ideas, latitude within a curriculum to do so and an environment that encouraged and supported creativity in teaching certainly helped my growth as a teacher during those first critical years here.

Ann came to see her personal reality as a teacher as one of exploring ideas and meaning making. She talked about how her world of teaching began to expand "beyond the walls of her classroom." She looked more deeply at what her questions revealed about her teaching and learning. Her questions were becoming more focused and often found their source in her observations of her students.

Like most classroom teachers I first viewed the walls of the classroom and the space between them as the only legitimate area of concern for me. Gradually I extended this view to include school-wide issues. I also began to alter the kinds of questions I asked about teaching. Prior to teaching the reading methods course at the end of my second year at Baker, I asked questions about subjects I felt I ought to know about. They were motivated by fear of being found inadequate (by my administrator, my peers, and by myself). In hindsight I realize this fear had slowly been diminishing each time I worked with a college student in my classroom or spoke to visiting teachers about the kinds of things we did in the room.

Three important outcomes resulted from these experiences. First, my teaching in reading shifted from a skills-based approach to a process-oriented one as a result of the reading and research I did for that course. This in turn influenced instruction in all areas of the curriculum because I now was much more comfortable with the notion of being guided by the children's needs. I planned and altered instruction much more often based on observations of my students. Secondly, I began to believe that classroom teachers could contribute to the field of education in places outside those four classroom walls.

The third outcome was a change in the type of questions I asked. Instead of a scattered and random approach to gathering information about teaching dependent upon what I heard or didn't hear, I became more deliberate in my choice of questions. I began by updating my knowledge of math. My need was to find out how to make my practice in this subject area more developmentally appropriate, effective, interesting and challenging for my students. Two well taught courses provided me with an excellent background which in turn led to a further change in the type of questions I asked.

Up until this point I was curious to find out the pieces of information I felt I lacked, but this gradually began to alter. As I attended to the cues the students gave me each day and taught accordingly, questions began to emerge based on these observations. This latest batch of questions tended to be about the ways in which children come to learn, rather than about a broad subject area. I wanted to know things such as: How do children come to understand addition? How do they make the connection between problem-solving strategies and the symbols that represent the operations? How do I help children use all the cuing systems in order to read fluently? or even, What are some ways we can integrate reading, literature, mathematics? The shift in questions was from a reactive to a proactive stance, and more importantly the source of my questions moved from other adults to the children themselves.

Other questions in the Baker/National environment also affected my teaching in subtle ways. The opportunity to do presentations at state, regional and national conventions gave me a chance to share some of my classroom "experiments." The positive feedback I received on each of these occasions reassured me that I was asking worthy questions and making practical discoveries. It also convinced me further of the need for teachers to share their work with other teachers in public ways.

The final factor to affect my teaching was the role of the teachers at Baker in the school decision-making process. The opportunities to raise, address, and resolve issues affecting us gave me an important sense of not only ownership, but also responsibility. This carried over into a sense of responsibility for my own professional learning. If I didn't know how to teach math well, then it was my job, not someone else's, to improve that knowledge. Faculty decision-making, opportunities to discuss ideas, public ways in which to share them even before they're completely polished and refined (I know that's a radical idea!), freedom to experiment in one's own classroom and most importantly the chance to do this on your own schedule, guided by your own interests all have the potential to transform teaching practice for teachers.

From her tentative time of anxiety entering a new school, Ann Watson Cohn gradually found a sense of confidence in herself as a teacher, recognition from colleagues, and ownership of her teaching. Her questions unfolded from ones concerned with how to be a competent teacher of content, to ones of how students learn, and what is behind their learning. It did not take long before her observations of students and reflections on her personal interests became the foundations of her inquiry. Eventually, Ann worked with colleagues on school-wide concerns to build a community of caring, learning, and inquiry at Baker school. She portrays the kind of commitment to other teachers that Maxine Greene believes can lead to "richer ways of being human" (see the following quotation).

## BUILDING COMMUNITIES OF LEARNING, CARING, AND INQUIRY

> I am suggesting that a concern for personal reality cannot be divorced from a concern for cooperative action within some sort of community. . . . Coming together to determine what is possible, teachers may discover a determination to transcend. (Greene, 1991, p. 13)

Currently, visions about how we might best live together in schools are often clouded and sometimes contradictory. Lieberman and Miller (1991) and others have painted pictures of what a "professional" school culture might look like. Whereas Yee and McLaughlin (cited in Lieberman, 1988) described school as a place to have a career, other models for professional or staff development continue to perpetuate the "working on" framework. Tafel and Bertani (1992) argued for an alternative view of "working with" teachers as key to meaningful professional development agendas. The old inservice model, with its many deficit or deficient assumptions about teachers dies hard.

Schaefer (1967) provided one of the first visions of the school as the center of teacher inquiry. "What could be more engaging than inquiring into the myriad mysteries of the child's world or learning more about ways of fostering the individual student's search for meaning?" But Schaefer lamented that "teachers have not been freed to study their craft.... Instead, they have had to bear a heavy burden of guilt for being unable to resolve difficulties ..." (p. 59). In outlining what it would take to move from a "blame the teachers" stance toward a school that inquires, Schaefer called for those innovations, which to this day, have remained unimplemented in most schools—true colleagueship among teaching peers, reduction of bureaucratic control of the teaching profession, and a culture of collaboration.

In working toward visions of what might be, we and our teacher colleagues remain hopeful (as Schaefer was) of remaking a profession. Through our work together, we have come to recognize the chicken–egg relationship between all that takes place with a school culture. Teachers cannot inquire without becoming researchers. Inquiry and research agendas can and have provided the context for professional growth. They help build a framework for "having a career" and for discovering meanings through reflection and inquiry on one's teaching.

As we have worked together, we have been intrigued by and embraced Roland Barth's (1990) vision of the ideal school:

> A place where teachers and principals talk with one another about practice, observe one another engaged in their work, share their craft knowledge with each other, and actively help each other become better. In a collegial school, adults and students are constantly learning because everyone is a staff developer for everyone else. (p. 163)

What do school communities that value learning and inquiry look like? First, we believe they begin with a value base that establishes a commitment to build and sustain a community for inquiry among teachers, among students and between and among teachers and students. Elementary teacher Nelda Hobbs loves to tell the story that there's a big difference between "doing school" and "being a community." So many of our teacher colleagues lamented the lack of excitement, the focus on meeting state-mandated objectives, the humdrum of the school experience for both students and teachers. In a community that values learning and inquiry, ideas, activity, questions, unsolved mysteries are all exciting, perplexing, and challenging. There is energy, enthusiasm and wonder.

There is, fundamentally, a culture of care. In describing such a culture, Nel Noddings (1984) stated, "We must recognize our longing for relatedness and accept it, and we must commit ourselves to the openness that permits us to receive the other" (p. 104). She describes the relatedness between teacher and student: "The special gift of the teacher, then, is to receive the student . . . Her commitment is to him, the cared-for, and he is—through that commitment—set free . . ." (p. 177). We believe teachers can and must create such a culture of care for and with each other. One must meet the other in caring. The teacher's special gift, then, is to receive not only the student, but also her teacher colleagues, to be committed to them as both teachers and learners, and to extend together their individual and collective inquiry.

Throughout this chapter, we have sown the seeds of a view of teacher inquiry and development that moves us away from the old inservice model. Within a culture of care, we begin with tales of classroom life—stories of children, of lessons, of activity, of good days and bad, of laughter, engagement, and joy of learning. Then we share those stories openly and with commitment to each other and to thinking about how to continue to grow—teachers growing in their understanding of their professional role, their craft, their art, and helping children grow as learners. Through the sharing of stories about school and classroom life emerge questions that can guide our shared inquiry about how to do what we do better. Through our inquiry comes insight, the ability to deepen our understanding, to recognize both our strengths and our need for growth and continued inquiry.

With our teacher colleagues, we will continue to construct our theory about how best to build and sustain the relationship between teacher inquiry and professional development. Our tentative conclusions reflect recurring themes in our research and ongoing dialogue with teachers. They can be summarized as follows:

1. Caring relationships and dialogue with colleagues are essential for supporting teachers' questions and pursuing their research. A professional life of inquiry is possible when schools value collegiality and encourage sharing ideas and learnings among teachers and students. This means telling others about the insights, struggles, and reflections we experience in our teaching. It requires building a school culture in which teachers feel safe in trying out new ideas and exploring ways to improve their teaching. It requires a community of learning, caring, and inquiry.

2. Teacher ownership must be an essential feature of both teacher research and professional development initiatives. Teachers need to feel that they have ownership of their teaching, that their decisions are elicited and valued, and that they are responsible for building curriculum and creating communities of learning and inquiry. In studying the field of teacher action research, Susan Jungck, points out that teachers have a central and unique role to play: ". . . the researcher's personal involvement is so integral to the process and outcomes,

that an axiom in interpretive research asserts the researcher *as* key instrument." Happily, this is a growing realization and position among the education research community. Teachers, finally, are being recognized as uniquely able to provide the greatest insights and understanding about teaching practice and student learning. As schoolpeople more fully embrace this recognition, teacher research initiatives will be encouraged, supported, and appreciated.

3. Constructing knowledge through reflections on practice is a main goal of teacher research and professional development. This entails both a personal responsibility for pursuing one's inquiry, and being encouraged to ask questions, to reflect on teaching practice, and to share learnings with colleagues. It means there are internal and external dimensions involved in teacher research and teacher development. Again, we find Jungck's discussion of interpretive/constructivist research especially insightful and helpful. In a summary statement, she wrote: "Therefore, inner reflection and meaning construction, outer observation and activity, and changes perceived through a time frame, thematically characterize the experience of teacher researchers." We have pointed out in this chapter how teacher development is an inner journey of inquiry and reflection within a context of observing students and dialogue with colleagues.

4. The kinds of inquiry questions that teachers pursue are founded on personal values and beliefs that guide and inspire their teaching and learning. In fostering positive school change, we need to understand the nature of, and factors that influence, the ethical decisions teachers make in their teaching and the kinds of questions that intrigue them. Reflecting on practice helps teachers become more aware of the values operating at the basis of their instructional choices, and helps clarify why certain kinds of questions about teaching intrigue them. Ultimately, knowing and caring about students and learning is the common ground of teacher research and teacher development.

As teachers work with their colleagues, they can invite each other to the possibility of creating a caring culture in which wonderment, discovery, relating, and inquiry become the central work of schools. Hopefully, they will continue to cherish this as their vision for schools and as their legacy to the teachers who follow them. In our dialogues with teachers, we are inspired by the many who have begun their journey toward building communities of caring, learning, and inquiry. They have made this their life's work. Influenced by the philosophy of Jean-Paul Sartre, Maxine Greene sees this quest of relating to and caring for others as our life's *project*. Because her teaching and writings have deeply influenced our dialogues with teachers, we would like to end this chapter with her words to us:

> As we grow older along with others and experienced diverse teachers and teaching situations, we build up a structure of meanings. Many of these meanings derived from the ways in which our choices and purposes were supported or frustrated

by other people's choices and purposes in the shifting social worlds of the class-rooms we came to know. . . . We may be moved to choose our project because of certain lacks in a social situation in which we are involved: We may want to repair those lacks and make that situation what it might be, rather than what it is. Or our choice of project may be connected with our notion of what we want to make of ourselves, of the kinds of identity we want to create. (cited in Lieberman and Miller, 1991, p. 506)

## REFERENCES

Barth, R. S. (1990). *Improving schools from within: Teachers, parents, and principals can make the difference*. San Francisco: Jossey-Bass.

Buber, M. (1947). *Between man and man*. Boston: Beacon Press.

Dewey, J. (1933). *How we think: A restatement of the relation of reflective thinking to the educative process*. Chicago: Henry Regnery.

Greene, M. (1991). Teaching, the question of personal reality. In A. Lieberman & L. Miller (Eds.), *Staff development for education in the '90s: New demands, new realities, new perspectives* (pp. 3–14). New York: Teachers College Press.

Lieberman, A. (Ed.). (1988). *Building a professional culture in schools*. New York: Teachers College Press.

Lieberman, A., & Miller, L. (Eds.). (1991). *Staff development for education in the '90s: New demands, new realities, new perspectives*. New York: Teachers College Press.

Noddings, N. (1984). *Caring: A feminine approach to ethics and moral education*. Berkeley: University of California Press.

Schaefer, R. J. (1967). *The school as a center of inquiry*. New York: Harper & Row.

Schon, D. A. (1983). *The reflective practitioner*. New York: Basic Books.

Tafel, L. S., & Bertani, A. A. (1992). Reconceptualizing staff development for systemic change. *Journal of Staff Development, 13*(4), 42–45.

# 6

# SUPPORTING TEACHER RESEARCH: PROFESSIONAL DEVELOPMENT AND THE REALITY OF SCHOOLS

Gail Burnaford
National-Louis University

*Action research incorporates many of the qualities of an 'ideal' staff development program. It is individualized and can be used by a teacher at any developmental level. It assumes teachers are knowledgeable and gives them power to make decisions. It can be carried out collaboratively. It is an on-going process and for that reason can be more effective than a typical one day in-service presentation. One of the more significant qualities of action research is that it puts the teacher in the position of accepting more responsibility for her (his) own professional growth.*

—Wood (1988, pp. 16–17)

## TEACHER RESEARCH AS PROFESSIONAL DEVELOPMENT: MEANINGFUL INSERVICE EDUCATION?

This chapter seeks to address issues surrounding teacher research when it becomes the central ingredient in one's own professional development and growth. When a teacher, or group of teachers, elects to pursue teacher research as an element of yearly goal setting and of the yearly plan for learning and renewal within a school building, then that research has been legitimized as professional development. There are a variety of terms for this endeavor; schools often use the phrase "institute days", "staff development", "release days", or "inservice time" to refer to time in which, ideally, teachers can learn and grow within the profession. All of these terms, however, seem to semantically associate such endeavors with the organization of schooling rather than with the personal and professional needs and interests of teachers. For this reason, I have chosen to use the term "professional development" to refer to the planning and realization of programs to enhance the lives and work of teachers. This chapter explores the ways in which teacher action research can play a role in such professional development in schools.

How can we envision the teacher as one who actively pursues his or her own knowledge, organizes the means by which that knowledge can be utilized in the classroom, and then evaluates how successful it has been? The traditional inservice model in which teachers are herded into a cafeteria or gymnasium, instructed in a "better way to do it" for half a day, then encouraged to go back to the classroom and "do it" is all too familiar and too ineffective. What are the alternatives to the inservice paradigm of preach then teach, and how might teacher action research play a role in teachers' own professional development?

Barth (1990) described a school in Bennington, Vermont, where the teachers are not inserviced. "Instead," he writes, "they engage in continuous inquiry about teaching. They are researchers, students of learning, who observe others teach, have others observe them, talk about teaching, and help other teachers. In short, they are professionals" (p. 46).

What if teachers were in charge of their own professional development? What kinds of activities might they plan? What kind of meaningful work might they do together and independently to improve their teaching, learn more about their subject areas, or learn how to share resources with other teachers? What kinds of support would be useful to teachers as they pursue their own growth and knowledge? Although action research can be pursued at any level of schooling, it is not typically a part of the culture of schools as we know them. Schools are not usually places of inquiry. Action research is not merely a planning process distinct from change; it *is* change, and as such, is difficult to implement in school systems. The most general complaint about traditional inservice programs in schools is the lack of sustaining influence they have (Siedow, Memory, & Bristow, 1985). A few months after a typical inservice program, teachers scarcely remember the topic and freely admit that they did not actually *apply* a great deal of what they heard during the inservice in their classrooms. Such programs are "conducted reluctantly, attended unwillingly, and (are) soon forgotten" (Siedow et al., p. 28). The status quo is comfortable; it provides a sense of security and therefore sustains itself. Teacher action research, on the other hand, is itself change and changing.

There is also a strong perception that traditional inservice programs must yield immediate, practical, easy to adapt "tricks". The rule is to include something they can "use on Tuesday", preferably with handouts attached, or the program will probably be considered an absolute waste of time. Such skill-based models for staff development may work when the strategies to be communicated are "technical", but they are not at all effective when *skills* are not at the heart of the process and when persons must learn in the context of their own routine, figuring out appropriate and meaningful application of larger principles of learning and teaching (Little, 1993). Viewing the process of teacher action research as the primary means of professional development challenges teachers to acknowledge that there are no such quick solutions to problems they face in the classroom. "Tricks" or gimmicks that can be demonstrated in one inservice session are usually not profoundly influential over a long period of time. A process of teacher action research, in which the teacher elects a theme or line of inquiry and chooses how and when to implement change in the classroom, is more inclined to be more deeply held and more noticeable in practice over time.

Little (1993) suggests six principles for professional development in schools that may be useful for us to consider here. She maintains that professional development:

1. Offers meaningful intellectual, social, and emotional engagement with ideas, materials, and colleagues.
2. Takes explicit account of the contexts of teaching and the experience of teachers.
3. Offers support for informed dissent.
4. Places classroom practice in the larger contexts of school practice.
5. Prepares teachers (as well as students and parents) to employ the techniques and perspectives of inquiry.
6. Should involve governance that ensures a balance between the interests of individuals and the interests of the institution. (Little, 1993, pp. 138–139)

Teacher action research seems to most readily address number 5, although on closer examination, we can see that research done by teachers and students in classrooms can incorporate all of the other considerations for effective professional development that Little suggests as well.

Does action research actually have the capacity to change the culture of schooling in this manner? It is possible that "the act of institutionalization could unwittingly and unavoidably alter the process" (King & Lonnquist, 1993, p. 13). It is important for us to distinguish between forms of action research that have been driven by universities and project coordinators in central offices, and *teacher* action research. King and Lonnquist pointed out that, "to the extent that action research works only to reinforce existing practice or to implement programs mandated by people outside of classrooms, it will not be the vehicle of meaningful empowerment and change that is implicit in its promise" (p. 14). Much so-called action research operates in schools as a means to reach goals set by administration; such projects cannot rightly be called *teacher* research and cannot be viewed as emancipatory professional development (Lather, 1986).

Perhaps in ensuring that action research remains within the control of classroom teachers and their students, rather than being driven by external circumstances or management, we might remind ourselves that in such meaningful research, people reflect on, and improve, their *own* work and their *own* situations (Griffiths, cited in Lomax, 1990). The researchers—who are classroom teachers—formulate the research questions; the researchers gather and analyze the data; the researchers share what they are learning with a larger community.

## SUPPORT FROM COLLEAGUES FOR TEACHER RESEARCH: A NECESSITY FOR PROFESSIONAL DEVELOPMENT

In some sense, changing the means for professional development in schools to a model of teacher action research suggests some significant changes in the *relationships* among people in the school building. Colleagues become a part of the inquiry process, as do administrators.

Although collaboration in and across school communities is an important source of support for teacher research as professional development, it is equally crucial to discuss the ways in which those communities can affirm the needs of individual teachers who are at different points in their careers and have different expectations for their own professional development. Research suggests that meaningful education for adults is experiential, life-centered, and self-directing (Knowles, 1980). Given these three characteristics of what might be termed "effective professional development," we would do well to explore the characteristics of people in a school building that may have an impact on the success of teacher research ventures there.

One factor that influences the effectiveness of professional development initiatives are the teachers' years of experience in education. Teacher research assumes no hierarchy with regard to experience. Still, the level of experience affects the nature of research undertaken. Kelli Visconti describes herself as a "twenty-something" teacher who did a research study about herself in the teaching profession (see Kelly Visconti's Teacher Research). She had been teaching just 4 years and was curious about how teachers do what they do for 30 or 40 years! She designed her research to find out more about herself and about the profession she chose just out of college. Clearly, her study was very different than if it had been conducted by a 30-year teaching veteran. But, nonetheless, it was valuable for Kelli as a teacher and as a researcher.

Kelli is not in the majority in the teaching field however; statistics reveal that the teaching force is quite a bit older than "twenty-something" and that many have been teaching for a long time. In 1989, the average age of the teaching force was approaching 50, with 75% in the teaching profession for at least 10 years and 50% in the profession for 15 years or more (Evans, 1989). Can teacher action research be a viable source of professional development for these experienced teachers too?

Reform in professional development typically has not adequately addressed the age and experience characteristics of the teaching profession. One study

affirms that, not surprisingly, "teachers at different developmental stages reacted differently to collaborative action research; behaved differently in action
research teams; thought differently about authority and leadership; conceived
of change differently; and understood the goals and outcome of research differently" (Oja and Pine, 1987, p. 101). Teachers who have been in a school for 15
years or more do not often want or need the typical inservice courses. Their
needs are more personal and individualized, related to their own teaching areas
or a more specialized interest area such as changing technology. Experienced
teachers value choice and options in their professional development.

Other factors affecting the nature of teacher research projects in the school
setting include the scope of teachers' interests and experiences to date, the degree
of risk involved, in taking initiative and the nature of feedback or responses
needed for a continuing commitment. In addition, the "status" of a teacher, with
regard to tenure, stability of teaching assignment, length of time in the district,
and leadership in the building are all factors in how the research will be viewed
by colleagues in the building. Finally, a teacher's relationships with the principal,
department chair, or team leader are also elements that affect the nature and
impact of the research.

How can change and improvement move beyond an individual teacher–researcher's classroom, if that is desirable? How can collaboration truly be a factor
in continuous improvement of schools? According to Fullan (1990), schools that
are characterized by norms of "collegiality and experimentation" are much more
likely to implement innovations successfully (p. 12). Similarly, successful teacher
research can have a "spin-off" effect on increasing collegiality among teachers.
Fullan reminds us that professional (staff) development will never have its
"intended impact as long as it is grafted onto schools in the form of discrete,
unconnected projects" (p. 21). How then can seemingly disconnected teacher
research projects be more than one-shot attempts at growth and become part
of a more consistent, collaborative means for professional and school development?

In order to effect wider changes, beyond the individual classroom, teachers
will have to share what they learn on a consistent basis with others in the school.
This sharing can be done during staff meetings or district inservice sessions. It can
also be done through the circulation of written summaries, teacher research
newsletters, and more widely distributed publications. "People do not *grow* by
having their realities only confirmed. They grow by having them challenged, as
well, and being supported, listened to, rather than defended against that challenge" (Kegan and Lahey, 1984, p. 226). Although teachers may be reticent at first
to share what they have done in their classrooms—"No one's interested", "I don't
want to show off," or "They might find something wrong with it,"—schools that
create a climate for such interaction over time can move toward more significant
change beyond the classroom level.

Although chapter 4 in this text discusses teacher collaboration in greater
detail, it is important for us here to address the organizational and institutional

structures that encourage collaborative teacher research that serves as professional development in schools. Teaming is one such structure that can work to enable teachers to experiment in their classrooms while sharing their experiences with other teachers who meet with them regularly. Wood (1992) wrote of three teachers who stay with the same groups of children for grades 1 and 2, meeting daily with each other to share stories, trade ideas, and write about what they are learning. He also described the initiatives of a team of five Milwaukee teachers who rewrote the entire school curriculum around a series of six themes. Their efforts moved on to encompass a whole-school philosophy and organizational structure, engaging the parents as well.

In Winnetka, IL, the teachers have organized themselves into the Winnetka Teachers Institute. The institute gathers ideas from the teachers on professional development topics they are interested in. Study groups form based on those interests and teachers work together to further their own learning. At Waukegan High School, in Waukegan, IL, Paul Spies (1994) and several of his colleagues reorganized part of the ninth grade into interdisciplinary learning teams in order to more fully meet the needs of their urban students.

All of these endeavors involved the collaboration of "teams" of teachers who planned and implemented their own means of professional development. All were forms of teacher action research, which were both personal and collective in nature. Change, in each of these instances, began small—perhaps with one piece of the curriculum as the focus for research. It then expanded, as the teachers saw the obvious connection between the processes they were engaged in and the rest of school life. What do the products of this type of work look like? They might be articles for publication, scrapbooks, student drawings, or self-evaluative journals. They might also be curriculum designs or models, narratives, or sketches. They could include videos, exhibitions, or lesson plans. Ultimately, these teams of teachers made choices and decisions for themselves as to the focus of their inquiry and subsequent action. They found new ways of showing what they know and what they are doing.

In Carol Pelletier's (1993) school, the teachers organized Teacher Book Clubs, in which interested teachers met for 5 half-day release times to collaboratively analyze selected educational texts. The books clubs were successful due to the integration of the content with the teachers' own routines. Pelletier noted that the book clubs provide a means for learning to be reflective as well as knowledgeable about professional literature. The reading of this literature then encouraged participants to pursue various kinds of "action" within their classrooms.

Teacher study groups are another means of professional development that are closely related to teacher research models. In 1987, the Massachusetts Field Center for Teaching and Learning initiated such a program by awarding $700 grants to teachers in teams. These teams then collaborated to investigate issues, coordinate workshops, conduct research and surveys, and design programs (Hartley, 1993). These teams found the collegial support they needed to pursue their own growth through these self-directed groups. In addition, the teachers found recognition within the professional community for the work they did and the learning that they shared with other teachers. Small grant projects such as this often provide the necessary impetus to engage in collaborative processes for professional development. Some professional organizations, such as the National Council of Teachers of English (NCTE) offer similar grants, specifically targeted for teacher–researchers. State and local affiliate organizations also often have money available for teachers.

The Coalition for Essential Schools program also supports the concept of teacher research in the classroom in its structure based on teacher-driven decision making in schools (Sizer, 1992). The coalition encourages exploration of reform and restructuring of schools, based on the nine principles. The specifics of implementation and evaluation are left to the faculty of Essential Schools who determine the direction they will go and the initiatives they will pursue in a given school year.

Schoolteaching has often been termed an isolated profession—one in which teachers must learn to teach in what Lortie (1975) called "the Robinson Crusoe syndrome." Even after teachers are experienced, those who choose to be innovative and dynamically concerned with their own professional development may continue to feel like Robinson Crusoe, totally dependent on themselves for survival. One could say that this isolation does afford teachers a degree of limited freedom to try out new things, use innovative materials, and alter the curriculum as they deem necessary and worthwhile.

There are informal, implicit communities of teachers in schools, however, who respond negatively to any teacher who seeks growth and innovation. Negative "peer pressure" from colleagues can be difficult for teacher–researchers to resist (Renegar, 1993). Two urban teachers were exploring innovative reading and writing strategies in their elementary classrooms. They remarked that they felt what they were learning and doing in terms of literacy with the children in their urban school was alienating them from their peers (Vida Schaffel discusses this phenomenon in her Teacher Research as well). They wondered whether it might be to their benefit to find a school in which such efforts were applauded and encouraged rather than viewed with suspicion. Pre-service teachers who engage in action research may especially feel this reserve when they enter the classroom prepared to explore alternatives. Negative peer pressure can defuse the energy needed to work toward change.

In many school settings, it is presumed that "good" teachers are entirely self-sufficient, have no questions about their practice, and have no inclination to try something new (Cochran-Smith & Lytle, 1993). But what if schools were places where the very best teachers were those who *had* questions and continually asked them? What if it was the expectation that teachers, each and every year, would pursue a line of inquiry—as the means of professional development—that would then be shared routinely in faculty gatherings or district meetings?

The culture of schooling would most assuredly change, improvement would be a way of life, and colleagues would begin to listen to—and learn from—each other. Groups of teacher–researchers can work together, supporting each other's efforts, advocating for each other in the larger faculty, and providing the necessary *positive* peer pressure to make that happen.

## PRE-SERVICE PROFESSIONAL DEVELOPMENT: CAN TEACHER RESEARCH WORK FOR APPRENTICE TEACHERS?

In the past 30 years, there has been a considered effort to help preservice teachers become more reflective as they are learning about teaching (Zeichner, 1986). Many pre-service courses and student-teaching programs require journal keeping as a component that encourages pre-service teachers to internalize what they are learning, analyze it, and make meaning from it. It seems though that when pre-service teachers actually enter the school building to engage in observations, internships, and student teaching, they become more and more concerned with learning "what works" in the immediate situation; reflection seems to focus more on that than on any form of critical analysis or personal assessment. Consequently, by the time many preservice candidates finish their internships, they have become "passive technicians who merely learn to execute pre-packaged instructional programs" (Goodman, 1986, p. 112). Many such pre-service teachers have learned, by that time, to adopt the attitudes and methods of their cooperating teachers.

Where then does action research fit into a program that promotes promising professional development and growth in preservice teachers? Schon's (1987) description of "reflection in action" might hold part of the answer. In order for practicing teachers to learn to reflect, weigh alternatives, and test their own assumptions about learning and teaching, they need experience in posing a problem or question, adapting that line of inquiry to a particular context or situation (i.e., the classroom, in which some field experience is occurring), and experiment with some designed plan to discover its implications and consequences. Such practice situations can encourage preservice teachers to learn to "engage in self-monitoring of practice" (Ross, 1987, p. 134), which is a highly desirable trait of effective teachers. As apprentice teachers engage in action research, they develop an increased awareness of the decisions they will be making as teachers.

Although this kind of activity sounds highly beneficial for pre-service teachers, we must acknowledge the various interests at stake when practicing teachers enter the school system and engage in classroom research. Not only must we consider the interests of the pre-service teacher, who is learning to be reflective while being encouraged to take informed risks with a measure of support from the university and the cooperating teacher, but we must also be aware of the interests of the school system, the cooperating teacher, and the students in the classroom. Research has not typically been part of the initial teacher preparation any more than it has been part of the professional development/inservice planning in school districts. Sensitivity, communication, and collaboration are all essential elements in these endeavors.

We in the field of education also need to hear about teaching from apprentice teachers who are just entering the profession. "The perspectives and voices of student teachers themselves are critical to, but almost always missing from, the literature on learning to teach" (Cochran-Smith, Garfield, & Greenberger, 1992, p. 289). Rarely have pre-service teachers had the chance to construct knowledge about their work. Further, student teachers who have the rich opportunity to interact with experienced teachers who are also doing classroom research will realize that all are continually learning about teaching in this profession. Such an experience "tells prospective teachers that novices and experienced professionals alike are continually learning to teach, and it emphasizes that one of the best ways to link theory and practice is through a process of self-critical and systematic inquiry about teaching, learning, and schooling" (Cochran-Smith et al., p. 290). Seeing the student teacher as a researcher "assumes that research—or thinking critically about the process in which you are engaged—is not something you do *after* you have learned how to teach. It is something you do *in order* to learn to teach" (Bowen, 1992, p. 294).

Typically, pre-service teachers who are engaging in action research do so within the parameters of an action research course as part of their program. Within that model, the students are carefully supervised and communication is continuous between the school and the university. Or, an action research course serves as the preparation for conducting the research, providing a time for learning about methods of research, determining topics of inquiry, and practicing self-reflection. The actual research can then be completed during a student-teaching experience. Sometimes, the demands of the preservice teacher education program are such that an action research component can only be introduced and implemented during the student teaching or internship experience. The latter is not ideal, given the other constraints and time investment which is necessary during student teaching (Ross, 1987). In any case, communication and consent of the classroom teacher is essential during such endeavors. (For more information on the specifics of implementing action research in a pre-service program, see Ross, 1987).

Teacher-centered action research suggests "personalized professional development, or, as one staff developer noted, the 'cheapest form of meaningful inservice work available'" (King & Lonnquist, 1993, p. 18). Teachers' main reasons and opportunities for meaningful professional development begin "with a teacher's experience of what it is to teach and to be a teacher—in general and particular circumstances" (Little, 1993, p. 147). In classroom research, teachers (and students) consider those circumstances and then make judgments about what is worthwhile before they take action. It is "classroom-based study, planned and carried out by the person most likely to be interested in and affected by the findings—the teacher" (Brown, 1990).

## SUPPORT FROM SCHOOL LEADERS: A MATTER OF PRIORITIES

Although we claim that action research is most meaningful when it is embraced by individual teachers who see the need and the results in their own classrooms, we cannot ignore the role of school leaders if we are prepared to affirm the value of teacher research as a primary means of professional development in schools. What attitudes and interpersonal skills are needed on the part of building administrators while teachers are shaping their own professional learning through classroom research? What kinds of impact should a principal have on the conceptualization, implementation, and evaluation of such research? How could building leaders participate in such research, while preserving the autonomy and safety in risk taking which is necessary for the process to take place?

In part, action research potentially alters the concept of 'failure', as King and Lonnquist (1993) pointed out. Teachers who try something in their own classrooms, reflect on outcomes, and retry based on the data gathered cannot be perceived as having failed at anything. They are continuing to grow from their experiences and newfound knowledge. Moreover, they are continuing to reach beyond their own experiences to consider what others have discovered in their classrooms. Principals must acknowledge that there is no room for a judgment of success or failure, no place for rating the research by teachers as an A, B, or C. In fact, external evaluation, in and of itself, often fails to promote teacher improvement or growth. Classrooms in which there is ongoing research into the processes of learning become climates for formative assessment of instruction and curriculum. Establishing and maintaining that climate of safety and freedom to take risks in the school building is a central role for school leaders.

It may be that another means for administrative support of research lies in leaders' own understanding of Schon's (1987) conception of "reflection-in-action," which is an integral part of teacher research. Traditional school organization seems to work *against* such reflection; in order for teachers to be reflective, however, it's necessary for *schools* to be so (Skrtic and Ware, 1992). Some suggest that the preparation of administrators could contain a reflective element, in which they too participate in action research with continuing reflection and analysis. Daresh (1992) claimed, "more emphasis on developing reflective skills will significantly improve the field of administrator preparation" (p. 220).

Administrators also have the responsibility to help make it possible for teachers to work together on research endeavors. Promoting collegial exchanges, affirming the sharing of research results, providing avenues for publishing and presenting research in faculty circles, will contribute to a climate of inquiry and collaboration in a school building. "The educational administrators of the future must be much more comfortable about working in a world marked by collegial relationships with teachers and other educators" (Daresh, p. 233). Again, there are implications for how we prepare people to become administrators; leadership becomes facilitative in a school building in which teachers are making decisions about their own professional development. Creating communities *within* schools is a feature of being a facilitator of learning among faculty members.

Administrators can also play a valuable role in mobilizing resources and making them available to teachers who need them for classroom inquiry. Often, curriculum coordinators are aware of minigrants that teachers can apply for; making those available to teachers can offer incentives. Each year in the Chicago Public Schools, teachers can apply for $500 minigrants from the Rochelle Lee Foundation to purchase trade books for their classrooms. These grants have served as the impetus for several teacher researchers to do classroom studies on the use of trade books in the reading curriculum. Administrators can encourage and assist teachers with grantwriting seminars; they can even have staff members who are expert in writing grant proposals available to other teachers who are interested but not yet experienced in that process. Targeting district funds that are allocated for staff development and directing them toward teacher research efforts is the most helpful means principals have of demonstrating their own belief in the value of classroom inquiry as professional development. Funding those initiatives speaks volumes to teachers who may be willing, but feel they are not yet able.

Perhaps the most significant contribution administrators can make, however, is *time*. Teacher–researchers repeatedly confirm that they need time to plan for, conduct, and evaluate research efforts in their classrooms. If administrators value this kind of work, and believe that it actually does contribute to more effective teaching and learning in their buildings, they will safeguard time for it. Time can be allocated as part of faculty meetings, paid release days, summer workshops, or after school meetings. Incentives can be established to use part of team or department planning times to set goals for individual or team action research that would benefit all members. Inservice days could be devoted to collaborative and/or individual reflection and discussion of ongoing research projects. "When teachers are given time for reflection and experimentation and have some choice in the direction this reflection and experimentation will take, they engage in studying and enhancing the practice of teaching" (Tracy & Schuttenberg, 1990, p. 54). Reserving sufficiently large chunks of time is important when ideas are being generated and response to perspectives are being shared. When such blocks of time are available, teaching becomes viewed as the complex act that it is. Administrators can help teachers see their research efforts as being long-term and responsive to the input from students, parents and community by building in time *permanently* for research-related activity.

Finally, building administrators can be important resources to teacher researchers if they learn to *listen* to teachers talk about what they are doing and why. A demonstration of interest in a project often sparks renewed reflection and commitment within a teacher–researcher. Just having a building administrator who knows and cares about what the teachers in the building are concerned with and interested in can be a powerful support system for classroom researchers.

I have identified six ways in which building administrators can facilitate teacher research as professional development in schools by: (a) providing a climate of safety and freedom to take risks, (b) being reflective leaders, (c) making it possible for teachers to collaborate and share their research with each other, (d) mobilizing resources to support classroom research, (e) providing time consistently for research, and (f) listening and being informed about the research teachers are doing in the building. School leaders who believe that change comes through individual teachers in individual classrooms become advocates for teacher research and demonstrate that advocacy in these ways.

In Little's (1993) analysis of professional development, she said that she places teachers at the center. Other realities, such as the politics of the school board, the pressures of state mandates, the demands of parents and community, and the directives from the front office are secondary to the needs and concerns of the teacher and his or her students. It stands to reason then that we examine the potential role of teachers as leaders in their own professional development.

Many school districts have already discovered that professional development days are far more effective if they are organized, implemented, and evaluated by teachers. How can teachers assume more of the leadership for using classroom research as professional development? First, teachers can value other teachers' learnings; they can encourage, praise, and demonstrate curiosity and interest in what their colleagues are doing in their classrooms. Second, they can be willing to communicate their own classroom research within and perhaps beyond the school community, making it available to building administrators and seeking feedback from a variety of constituencies. Third, they can assist the building principal in finding ways to organize professional development time to include teacher action research. Principal preparation can be designed in such a way so that principals are charged "with the mission of developing a community of leaders within their schools" (Troen and Boles, 1993, p. 27). Principals can participate in teaching teachers how to be leaders in their buildings and teachers themselves can learn how to be accepting of leadership emerging from their own ranks.

Teacher action research is about pre-service and inservice teachers taking responsibility for their own professional development and growth. It is a means by which we in the profession can participate in school change that matters to us and to our students. Schwartz (1992) reminded us that "meaning is slippery", but, as teachers we know that learning itself is pretty slippery too (p. 111). Classroom research offers us practical possibilities to continue our own growth and learning.

It encourages teachers to listen to children and to each other, plan and enact change, and reflect on what we bring to our classrooms and the profession of teaching. What better means of professional growth are there than that?

## REFERENCES

Barth, R. S. (1990). *Improving schools from within.* San Francisco: Jossey-Bass.

Bowen, B. (1992). Response. In N. A. Branscombe, D. Goswami, & J. Schwartz (Eds.), *Students teaching, teachers learning* (pp. 293–295). Portsmouth, NH: Boynton Cook/Heinemann.

Brown, D. S. (1990). Middle level teachers' perceptions of action research. *Middle School Journal, 22*(2), 30–33.

Cochran-Smith, M., & Lytle, S. L. (1993). *Inside outside: Teacher research and knowledge.* New York: Teachers College Press.

Cochran-Smith, M., Garfield, E., & Greenberger, R. (1992). Student teachers and their teacher: Talking our way into new understandings. In N. A. Branscombe, D. Goswami, & J. Schwartz (Eds.), *Students teaching, teachers learning* (pp. 274–292). Portsmouth, NH: Boynton Cook/ Heinemann.

Daresh, J. C. (1992). Reflections on practice: Implications for administrator preparation. In E. W. Ross, J. W. Cornett, & G. McCutcheon (Eds.), *Teacher personal theorizing: Connecting curriculum practice, theory, and research* (pp. 219–235). Albany: State University of New York Press.

Evans, R. (1989). The faculty in midcareer: Implications for school improvement. *Educational Leadership, 46*(8), 10–15.

Fullan, M.G. (1990). Staff development, innovation, and institutional development. In B. Joyce (Ed.), *Changing school culture through staff development* (pp. 3–25). Alexandria, VA: Association for Supervision and Curriculum Development.

Goodman, J. (1986). Making early field experience meaningful: A critical approach. *Journal of Education for Teaching, 12*(2), 109–125.

Griffiths, M. (1990). Action research: Grassroots practice or management tool? In P. Lomax (Ed.), *Managing staff development in schools: An action research approach* (pp. 37–51). Clevedon, England: Multilingual Matters LTD.

Hartley, S. (1993, April). *Teacher study groups: Making sense together.* Paper presentation at the Annual Meeting of the American Educational Research Association, Atlanta, GA.

Kegan, R., & Lahey, L. L. (1984). Adult leadership and adult development: A constructivist view. In B. Kellerman (Ed.), *Leadership: Multidisciplinary perspectives* (pp. 199–230). Englewood Cliffs, NJ: Prentice-Hall.

King, J. A., & Lonnquist, M. P. (1993, April). *Lessons learned from the history of collaborative action research in schools.* Paper presentation at the Annual Meeting of the American Educational Research Association, Atlanta, GA.

Knowles, M. S. (1980). *The modern practice of adult education.* Chicago: Follett.

Lather, P. (1986). Research as praxis. *Harvard Educational Review, 56*(3), 257–277.

Little, J. W. (1993). Teachers' professional development in a climate of educational reform. *Educational Evaluation and Policy Analysis, 15*(2), 129–152.

Lortie, D. (1975). *Schoolteacher.* Chicago: University of Chicago Press.

Oja, S. N., & Pine, G. J. (1988). Collaborative action research: Teachers' stages of development and school contexts. *Peabody Journal of Education, 64*(2), 96–115.

Pelletier, C. M. (1993, April). *Professional development through a teacher book club.* Paper presentation at the Annual Meeting of the American Educational Research Association, Atlanta, GA.

Renegar, S. L. (1993). Peer pressure among teachers: Enemy of educational excellence? *Kappa Delta Pi Record*, Spring, 68–82.

Ross, D. D. (1987). Action research for preservice teachers: A description of why and how. *Peabody Journal of Education, 64*(3), 131–150.

Schon, D. A. (1987). *Educating the reflective practitioner*. San Francisco: Jossey-Bass.

Schwartz, J. (1992). On the move in Pittsburgh: When students and teacher share research. In N. A. Branscombe, D. Goswami, & J. Schwartz (Eds.), *Students teaching, teachers learning* (pp. 107–119). Portsmouth, NH: Boynton Cook/Heinemann.

Siedow, M. D., Memory, D. M., & Bristow, P. S. (1985). *Inservice education for content area teachers*. Newark, DE: International Reading Association.

Sizer, T. R. (1992). *Horace's school*. Boston: Houghton Mifflin.

Skrtic, T. M., & Ware, L. P. (1992). Reflective teaching and the problem of school organization. In E. W. Ross, J. W. Cornett, & G. McCutcheon (Eds.), *Teacher personal theorizing: Connecting curriculum practice, theory, and research* (pp. 207–218). Albany: State University of New York Press.

Spies, P. (1994). Learning teams: The necessary design of secondary schools for the 21st century. *Teaching and Change, 1*(3), 219–237.

Tracy, S. J., & Schuttenberg, E. M. (1990). Promoting teacher growth and school improvement through self-directed learning. *Journal of Staff Development, 11*(2), 52–57.

Troen, V., & Boles, K. (1993). Teacher leadership: How to make it more than a catch phrase. *Education Week*, November 3, pp. 27, 29.

Wood, G. H. (1992). *Schools that work*. New York: Penguin Books.

Wood, P. (1988, April). *Action research: A field perspective*. Paper presentation at the Annual Meeting of the American Educational Research Association, New Orleans, LA.

Zeichner, K. (1986). Individual and institutional influences on the development of teacher perspectives. In J. Raths & L. Katz (Eds.), *Advances in teacher education: Vol. 2* (pp. 135–163). Norwood, NJ: Ablex.

# STAY IN OR GET OUT?
# A "TWENTY-SOMETHING" TEACHER
# LOOKS AT THE PROFESSION

Kelli Visconti
Skokie Public Schools

## LEARNING TO BE A TEACHER–RESEARCHER

I had been teaching for just 4 years and was in my 20s. Now that those first few years had passed, I felt that I knew more about what teaching was all about and I could take a breath and look around a bit. I became curious as to why teachers become teachers and why some leave the profession and some stay. How could some of my colleagues teach for 20 years? And, perhaps more important, why didn't I feel like I could do this for 20 years?

I began to realize that I seemed to need a new challenge every so often. Was that why I couldn't seem to stay satisfied with this career? Did I have to constantly move on after I "conquered" a certain task? I was very interested in the fact that I was so dissatisfied with teaching after I had spent a large portion of my life gearing up for this career. I was so curious about this topic that I became somewhat obsessed with finding the answers to my questions. So began my research.

It turned out that my research was a collaborative process in that I spent a lot of time interviewing teachers formally and informally about the profession. I tested out my theories and questions on many of my teaching colleagues so that I could further analyze my own presence in the teaching profession. By talking about my feelings toward teaching, I realized that I was not alone. I began reading other people's thoughts on teachers. By reading articles and books, and by discussing teaching with many people, I was able to understand my discouragement more fully—and do something about it.

I read through professional journals and books about the teaching profession and started making notes to myself. I also continued to write in my journal about my own feelings and my daily experiences with my fifth-grade students. My questions continued to guide me: Was this the profession for me? Was it possible to feel burned out while still being "twenty-something"?

Dan Lortie was one of the first authors I read. His book, *Schoolteacher* (1975) described why many teachers enter the profession: to work with children, to service others, to return to the school setting, to have the security of a steady salary and adequate benefits, and to have summers and holidays off. I found that these were the reasons I became a teacher too.

Shively (1991) stated that the teaching profession has many critics. "While teachers must be certified and meet high educational standards, we are under the jurisdiction of an elected school board. Every parent, every citizen feels in a position to evaluate teachers because they were once students" (p. 86). Shively helped me to realize that I was not alone in my occasional feelings of disappointment, stress, and discouragement. She suggested that there may be legitimate reasons for teachers to feel this way; I was beginning to sense that I was "on to something." I was definitely experiencing a feeling of powerlessness that other teachers often share.

Then I read some of Meek's (1988) material. He declared: "I think America is ambivalent about teachers. There is some evidence that the public is willing to support teachers in terms of greater compensation, and there are efforts to improve conditions for teaching. But, at the same time, teachers continue to be treated as second-class citizens—in education, the greatest status accrues to those who work least closely with children ..." (p. 12).

I also explored some of the literature regarding teacher burnout. I learned that burnout is a result of stress, tension, and anxiety, and it seemed to me that teachers who are experiencing feelings of burnout can have a detrimental effect on their students, colleagues and on the reputation of their schools.

## WHAT I LEARNED

After doing all of this reading and talking with other teachers, my research, in the end, circled back to me. I remember feeling very frustrated with this situation because the answers to all of my research questions could only be found within me; my colleagues, my principal, my family could not tell me. Only I could decide if teaching was the right profession for me.

I had been keeping a personal research journal over a period of several months. To come to some decisions, I began reading through all of my journal entries and highlighting sentences and paragraphs that had to do with my attitudes toward the teaching profession. I put all of these quotes onto index cards and then tried to categorize them according to topics: "good day at work," "bad day at work," "conversations with other teachers," "nonteacher comments about the profession."

I also taperecorded interviews with three teachers from my school and my principal. After transcribing these interviews, I tried to match their conversations with the topics that emerged from my journal writing.

There were several themes that were generated from these data sources, which are reflected in my journal entries:

### Being a Twenty-Something Teacher: I'm Not Alone

I've been sharing some of my findings on teacher burnout with some of my young colleagues who are feeling burned out. They were so relieved to hear that they are not the only ones feeling this way. They want me to keep them informed! A second-year teacher told me about her first year of teaching and how terrible it was. She was pressured by other teachers to be at school by 7:15 a.m. every day and to stay until 6:00 p.m. She commented that everyone did it; if you went home at 3:30, you were viewed as someone who wasn't dedicated to her job. As a first-year teacher, she just couldn't keep up with these expectations. She says that she "never feels good enough as a teacher"; there's always something she should be doing to improve her work.

As a teacher in her 20s, I have a very different lifestyle than most of my colleagues. A typical evening for me after school would include relaxing in front of the TV for a few hours at my apartment while I eat dinner. Then I might get changed and drive to the health club for a two-hour workout. By the time I get home, it's probably 11:30 or midnight. That's not what I picture many of the teachers at my school doing.

### Teachers *Are* Experts and Deserve Respect

I am an example of a hard-working teacher who feels emotionally drained by my career. What rewards do I have to show for my work at the end of a day, a week, a year?

Teachers need time away from children in order to regroup. Summer vacations, weekends, and holidays are all important opportunities for teachers and students to refresh themselves.

### Renewal Comes From Experimenting: Teaching As Learning

Change in a classroom is a way of addressing the frustrations which can lead to burnout. Because I became more excited about my job during this research, I am beginning to do more creative projects with my students. I am also beginning to communicate more with each student on a level that I never had before. I began journaling with my students, and responding to things they had written. Because I was a learner again, I was able to relate to the children as learners. It wasn't the content of the curriculum that changed, but the methods that I used.

### Renewal Comes From Dialogue With Other Teachers: Teaching As Collaboration

Throughout my research, I have been finding that many teachers feel the same way I do. Knowing that other teachers share my views gives me confidence to deal with issues *outside* the classroom, while still concentrating on being a good teacher and making learning memorable for children *inside* the classroom.

The four themes—(a) I'm not alone, (b) teachers are experts and deserve respect, (c) renewal comes from experimenting, and (d) renewal comes from dialogue with other teachers—that emerged from my research revealed action plans for my own professional development. The focus for such growth seemed to be in collaboration and the willingness to take risks. After realizing what it could mean to work with colleagues and support colleagues in their work, I began arranging my own "inservice" opportunities in my building and in the professional community. Even though I am a young teacher, I learned that I too am responsible for continuing my own learning in my profession. I think I became much more involved in the whole environment of my school while I was doing my research. I began to be very interested in the teachers, the students, and the principal because I felt more a part of the school climate. I felt as if I was much more invested in my school during my research than I had been in previous years. I discovered that I needed and wanted feedback from my colleagues. I came to believe that we need to hear from each other that we are doing a good job. Maybe that's why we talk so much about our jobs during lunch and after school. Because of this new realization, I began to seek the feedback that helped me grow. If I was unsure about the way to handle a situation with a student in class, I asked a colleague for advice. If I found something that worked well for me, I was ready and willing to share it with a team member. I wrote: "This year, things feel different. I feel as though I am more comfortable with the staff than I was last year." It seemed to me that burnout could be avoided if teachers work together, creating a community and a climate in a school where each teacher can be an individual, and yet, have colleagues for support and encouragement.

*To be a better teacher, I need more of my own self in my job. I need to be more committed to it; to stop thinking of it as a job, but as a learning experience; to think of it as an experiment each year; a research project perhaps.*

This last entry from my journal is probably the most important learning from my research. Being a twenty-something teacher has its disadvantages and its advantages; as a very young teacher, I was able to use the opportunity of being a teacher researcher to step back from my career choice and survey it. I learned much about my colleagues, my school, and the profession in general. But most of all, I learned about myself.

## REFERENCES

Lortie, D. C. (1975). *Schoolteacher: A Sociological Study.* Chicago: The University of Chicago Press.
Meek, A. (1988). On teaching as a profession: A conversation with Linda Darling-Hammond. *Educational Leadership, 46*(3), 11–17.
Shively, J. (1991). Why I entered teaching, why I stay. *Educational Leadership, 49*(3), 84–86.

# Experienced Teachers and Action Research: A Model for Professional Development

## Suzanne Goff
### Wilmette Public Schools

Me, a researcher—why? When I began my teaching career I was just like any other wet-behind-the-ears beginner. I was interested in getting my feet wet, being with children and earning my first paychecks. I wanted to be a good teacher, and, in my thinking, that didn't include research. Thinking about my past experiences with any undergraduate research I had completed certainly was not a part of my thinking in those beginning years.

As I think back on my undergraduate years (more than 20 years ago), most of my research involved short-term assignments of the traditional kind that might have looked something like this:

Focus on a topic.
Gather good references.
Find some great quotes.
Develop a good introduction.
Fill in the middle with experts' thoughts.
Then write a convincing, sometimes personalized conclusion.

I got A's for that approach. But it didn't draw me in, consume me. It didn't make me want to know more. The assignment was completed; it was time to move on.

There was one type of undergraduate research that became in itself motivating and kept me completely involved. When I was expected to set up my own structure for collecting real-life information, establish my own criteria for change, then look for results, my motivation never wavered. Being involved with situations that I knew were real became tremendously invigorating. When a project asked me to observe a child, keep notes, and gather data about the child's history as well as the learning situation she was in, I was completely devoted to working hard at the project. Knowing that a child's behavior or her attitude could be influenced by my planned interaction with her had meaning. At the same time, I was discovering causes and effects on the child's learning as well as my own. That type of investigating had a personal impact. In my inexperience, this was not research; this was getting ready to be *the teacher.*

After 18 years of learning in the classroom, I was ready to pursue a master's degree. I enrolled in a program that kept the same teachers and group leader together for 2 years. Our study and learning was directly related to our class-room. In fact, no one was in the program unless they had a teaching position. I wanted to make connections with other teachers, stay in the classroom, and apply what I would learn in the program to my students' learning. The structure definitely fit my schedule, my philosophy, and my style.

Many of us were not in the "research" state of mind. We might have been very involved with curriculum, writing it, reshaping it, molding it to fit each year's group of children, but most of us had not had any commitment to this kind of study since our undergraduate years. More importantly, we were not at all prepared for the personal ownership that came with our projects.

Most of our past experiences asked very little of us in the way of creating the research. Professors initiated and established most of the parameters. Not so in this program. When we asked, "How?" the answer was, "You decide." When we wanted topics to choose from, we were met with questions like, "What's really creating a need to know for you?" or "What have you always wanted to understand about yourself and your teaching?" We asked, "How long should it be?" or "On whom do we focus?" or "What should we look for?" The answers were very unsettling for many of us, and for some, sheer frustration—"It must come to you" was what we heard. Our research group leader was relentless with her goal to make us independent researchers:

> You need to look at the 'what-ifs' in your life as a teacher. What if a change could take place that would make your teaching more than it is now? Think about the possibilities. . . . Choose one that keeps coming back to you.

She reminded us of a list of "what-ifs" the group had generated earlier during a class session. We briefly looked at them. Then, on an index card, we were to write one that continued to intrigue us. I wrote, *"What if experienced teachers could observe each other and help each other with their teaching skills? What if there was a way for experienced teachers to mentor each other?"*

From my inexperienced vantage point of research, this was a rarely-dealt-with concept. I had heard of many mentoring programs for novice teachers and how valuable they could be. I had not heard, through my 18 years of teaching, of any program that was specifically built to help the *experienced* teacher. The idea was invigorating to me and one that I wanted to explore. It sat in my head and wouldn't leave. My research had its beginning. I began to delve into my memories of early teaching and wondered, "What could have happened in my early years as a teacher that might have sparked such an idea of teacher collegiality? Why *this* concept?"

In my teacher-researcher group, we were asked to write a proposal statement ... just one sentence or phrase that would capture the idea of my "what-if" professional dream. I worked with a partner. We tried a variety of titles. None really seemed to fit until I began to use the word "support." I clearly wanted the concept to be teacher-based and not controlled by a whole system or any administrative decisions. Philosophically, grassroots had always had more impact for me. I was very excited and at the same time very tentative. Support, where and how? Then it exploded onto the paper.

## TEACHER-INITIATED PEER SUPPORT: HELPING EACH OTHER TEACH

There it was! It sounded right and it expressed what my hope was for my project: teachers helping one another, teachers starting the journey to self-improvement through support—lending a thought, holding a hand, sharing a feeling.

My partner had excellent questions about how I would start, and these helped me sort out where I would begin:

Who do you want to work with?
Would the support look like mentoring?
What kind of time will you need?
Will you have a problem starting this in your school?
What if you get no one to volunteer?

I soon discovered that in the past decade, teacher interaction and the concept of collegiality was at the forefront of staff development research. After I got over the initial feeling that I had not come up with a brilliant new idea for research, I became very excited about the prospect of looking for a model to work with for teacher support. I decided to begin with goals that focused on the experienced teacher's need for peer support. I wrote: *"The most fruitful professional experiences in teaching often involve the support and cooperation with a fellow teacher. If this resource could be effectively utilized on a consistent basis, the opportunities for personal and professional growth might be the answer to the growing concern for improved staff development."*

My early research asked questions that helped me begin my search for answers. I was looking for one remedy to my concern about the lack of teacher interaction. It wasn't until I was well into my research that I discovered that the search for *one* answer was interfering with the possibilities. But I believed the questions I had been asking myself were real to teachers:

> What if a teacher could use another teacher for his or her own professional development?
> What if peers who are experienced and who wish to improve could provide quality help to one another?
> Could teachers observing each other and mutually giving constructive feedback become the optimum tool for teacher inservice?
> Does collegiality have real potential for teacher growth?

I had no idea what a tremendous task I was asking of myself, nor was I really aware of all the factors involved in the success of such a dream. I wrote in my initial plan, "I believe that many teachers would be willing to be a part of such an experience. . . . I hope to present a model for a peer support system that is useful and realistic." My literature search uncovered a vast amount of information. I found myself delving into historical and philosophical backgrounds that are an integral part of collegiality, many of which had *never* entered my mind at the beginning of my search. As I look back, I can say that this stage of naivete—of confusion, of surprise—is all part of research. Valuable lesson learned.

At the time, I was looking for a prescription that could work for my colleagues and myself; instead, I was finding walls to climb and barriers that talked about limited teacher interaction, schedules and structure. No wonder the word "collegial" had not become part of our professional heritage.

Viewing the topic from the point of view of the veteran was in my initial proposal, but not specifically so. I did discover that the thoughts about teacher interaction from a new teacher's point of view and those from a teacher with 15 or 20 years experience were distinctly different and for very sound reasons. New teachers are expected to perform as adequately as a veteran teacher the first day on the job. They are given the same responsibilities as veterans. If one were to consider any occupation and the expectations of the beginner, none can come to mind where the novice must accomplish the same work performance as a veteran—except in the role of teacher. The teacher who has made it through those first difficult years and still finds tremendous value in the profession is looking for something more than learning to become a "good" teacher. I realized the issue for teachers like me was not the need to survive but the need to excel. *The difference between mediocrity and fulfillment was the driving force.*

The study done by the Holmes Group (1986) confronted the "careerless" aspect of the teaching profession and how it affects the experienced teacher. "Good teachers must be knowledgeable, but they have few opportunities to use that knowledge to improve their profession or to help their colleagues improve" (Holmes, p. 6). Listening to fellow veterans' concerns gives a perspective to the quality of effectiveness with children. Self-assessment and self-affirmation are professional tools for teachers that can be destructive or they can empower. Collegial interaction can enhance growth. Schools need to be professional communities where the veteran and new teacher alike can "offer their artistry to one another" (Eisner, p. 12). Wow! That sounded good!

The issue of privacy has been a major stumbling block to teacher interaction to the bewilderment of educators and administrators who long to see teachers working together to enhance their own learning as well as the growth of the profession itself. Is the chance for collegiality controlled only by the structure of the system? Or is it the choice of the teacher?

Taking risks among peers, opening oneself up to scrutiny, being considered the "guiding light" or "expert," and fearing self-examination are all part of the realm of privacy in the profession. What a dilemma for many teachers—wanting to use the rich resources and gaining affirmation opposed with the feelings wary of misunderstandings, being judged, and taking a chance to change. The culture of privacy in teaching has created much of the caution and hesitation to work with one's colleagues.

All these issues: school structure, professionalism, the needs of the veteran teacher, staff development, and teacher privacy emerged as not sought after from my research. They all helped me create a mindset that was to balance my perspective—a perspective that helped prepare me for the experiences I had with my fellow colleagues when I began my search for *the model* for peer support. My respect for research and what personal impact it can have skyrocketed. It created a permanent change in my thinking.

New questions arose about my goals. As I continued to discover more through my research, I wondered about how my colleagues would respond. Were there others like me who had had meaningful teacher-to-teacher experiences? How many teachers were dealing with the issues of privacy and the frustrations of the school structure? I began to realize the impact that my school administrator and the structure of the school culture would have on the success of my model. I had learned a great deal which tempered the optimism with which I began my research.

When I first met with my group, my goal for a particular collegial model was still in the forefront of my research hopes. We met periodically during the school year and found ourselves to be, more than anything else, a resource for reflection. A critical discovery for me during our interaction was that *a definite form for working together was not necessary.* Five teachers and I became a source of professional rejuvenation and affirmation.

I asked for volunteers from my school staff of 30, hoping to get one or two willing teachers to work with me in my research. Interestingly, five *veteran* teachers joined me. I initially struggled with how to lead the group to some action. I was not aware that our sharing and reflecting were the beginning of our growth of a support group.

My journal entries were revealing. A change in my research goals was evolving, and learning what "support" meant to my colleagues and to myself was becoming a reality:

> I am not sure how to lead this group or even if I should lead in any particular direction. It is a bewildering role for me to play.
>
> I am just beginning to understand that my role in this group is NOT a leader but a fellow member . . . they are eager to talk and express their needs . . . I need to keep my direction open.
>
> The last thirty minutes of our time together was excellent, because they talked about the future of our group . . . what I had first envisioned is much different from what the group is like now.
>
> Our times together have become very valuable. We have given ourselves time to develop an identity. The future lies ahead.

I was very grateful for the uniqueness of each colleague who joined me in this research. I thought about the personal strengths of the individuals affecting the success of the group. Do these teachers have a common characteristic that helped them become "good at" being collegial? Does the fact that all of us are experienced teachers play a part in our desire to interact? These questions were just a symptom of how this research and *the process of research* influences perspectives. My *ideal model* for collegial support really never came to be. For the time being, I have concluded that veteran teachers may have a need for a different type of support than I originally had thought about when my research began. As I pulled together my research data, I made this entry in my journal:

> Perhaps veteran teachers need a different kind of collegiality. It would provide more peer support and acknowledgement of where we have come. It would include problem-solving together when those yearly struggles keep coming back. A collegiality that is reflective and interactive is perhaps what is needed for the teacher in midcareer. Not separate, or unique from beginning teachers, but in concert with their unique growth needs. To grow and to improve in an atmosphere of trust, I have come to believe, is a very real goal. The quality of life for any professional is affected by the potential for self-renewal. (Goff, p. 135)

During an early summer lunch meeting this year, my new principal and I became acquainted. She immediately recognized through my comments how much teacher-to-teacher support meant to me. I asked her to consider reading bits and pieces from my research. She was enthusiastic and willing. I was not prepared for the commitment on her part to become involved in my goals. They had been hers before we ever met. Her own personal commitment and encouragement have been a source of motivation and hope.

She read my action research cover-to-cover all in a weekend. When I spoke with her the following week, her face clearly showed she was ready to get her feet wet and become an accomplice in my ambitions. A meeting was organized with my group to get input. During her first year as our administrator she has helped maintain a teacher support group—Teacher Study Group—for the whole year! Her sanction of my goals (which are truly hers also) makes them more of a reality for many more teachers who are searching for this type of support.

Here is an excerpt from my research project's conclusion that expresses my thoughts about this growth:

> Cohesiveness and beneficial interaction are absolutely necessary for the health of the whole profession.... As a veteran teacher I have learned to deal with the restraints of the structure. I've learned to refocus and reorganize each year.... What becomes frustrating for a veteran teacher is there is no affirmation that she has learned how to create and recreate every year.... We are looking for a change, and are ready to do something for someone else (besides students). Understanding this has helped me see the image of who I am and who I will be more clearly. (Goff, pp. 134–135)

Three years later, my research is still close, very close to my heart and my everyday thinking. Finding the latest article about collegiality or hearing of a success story about a teacher-to-teacher support idea still holds meaning for me. Feeling confident critiquing new information on the subject is new for me. The sense of being professionally knowledgeable is extremely rewarding. My awareness of child-to-child collaboration has blossomed. This can directly be attributed to my conscious efforts to learn about teacher support for each other.

There are other benefits. I am more boldly asking my colleagues to give me advice, ideas, and reactions. My appreciation for my strengths as well as my weaknesses is real and unashamed. Valuing differences in colleagues has been added to my growth as a teacher. All of this is a direct result of my journey through research.

Reflecting back, I can say that a teacher needs to be in a readiness stage for research to create growth and change. This readiness is no different than what all learners experience. This stage of preparedness is a concept so critical to a teacher. Not recognizing its potential can make the difference between a learner progressing or wandering.

The stage for learning can be set and the appetite can be whetted, but if the learner is somewhere else with her growth, the full impact may not be there. Adult learners are no different. I was a "ready researcher," and I firmly believe that fact has made a world of difference to my growth as a teacher.

As I was nearing the end of my literature search I found a book co-edited by teacher staff developers, Holly and McLoughlin (1989), called *Perspectives on Teacher Professional Development*. In their epilogue they reflected on the growth and change that has occurred in the past decade with their own research. When I read it, I was amazed at how close it came to my belief in my own growth and in the growth of the teaching profession:

- We've begun, but we're not near the end.
- We started as isolated practitioners and we've moved to persons in collaboration and colleagueship.
- We've moved from research *on* teachers to research *with* teachers and lately to research *by* teachers. (Holly & McLoughlin, p. 309)

We have begun, and that's reason enough for me to look forward to my next experience with teacher research.

## REFERENCES

Eisner, E. (1983). The art and craft of teaching. *Educational Leadership, 40*(4), 5–13.

Goff, S. (1991). *Teacher-initiated peer support: Teachers helping teachers.* Unpublished master's thesis, National-Louis University, Evanston, IL.

Holly, M. L., & McLoughlin, C. (Eds.). (1989). *Perspectives on teacher professional development.* New York: Falmer Press.

Holmes Group (1986). *Tomorrow's teachers: A report of the Holmes Group.* East Lansing, MI: The Holmes Group, Inc.

## RELATED READINGS

Barth, R. (1990). A personal vision of a good school. *Phi Delta Kappan, 71*(7), 512–516.

Evans, R. (1988). The faculty in midcareer: Implications for school improvement. *Educational Leadership, 46*(8), 10–13.

Fullan, M. (1990). Staff development, innovation, and institutional development. In B. Joyce (Ed.), *Changing school culture through staff development* (pp. 3–25). Alexandria: Association for Supervision and Curriculum Development.

Glatthorn, A. (1987). Cooperative professional development: Peer centered options for teacher growth. *Educational Leadership, 45*(3), 31–35.

Goodlad, J. (1984). *A place called school.* New York: McGraw-Hill.

Grumet, M. (1989). Dinner at Abigail's: Nurturing collaboration. *NEA Journal,* 20–25.

Joyce, B., & Murphy, C. (1990). Epilogue: The curious complexities of cultural change. In B. Joyce (Ed.), *Changing school culture through staff development* (pp. 243–250). Alexandria: Association for Supervision and Curriculum Development.

Little, J. W. (1989). Teachers as colleagues. In V. Richardson-Koehler (Ed.), *Educators' handbook a research perspective* (pp. 491–518). New York: Longman.

Lortie, D. (1975). *Schoolteacher.* Chicago: University of Chicago Press.

Raywid, M. (1993). Finding time for collaboration. *Educational Leadership, 51*(2), 30–34.

Rosenholtz, S. (1989). *Teacher's workplace: The social organization of schools.* New York: Longman.

Sagor, R. (1991). What project LEARN reveals about collaborative action research. *Educational Leadership, 48*(6), 6–10.

Sarason, S. (1971). *The culture of school and the problem of change.* Boston: Allyn and Bacon.

Shanker, A. (1990). Staff development and the restructured school. In B. Joyce (Ed.), *Changing school culture through staff development* (pp. 91–103). Alexandria: Association for Supervision and Curriculum Development.

Wildman, J., & Niles, J. (1987). Essentials of professional growth. *Educational Leadership, 45*(3), 14–19.

Zahorik, J. (1987). Teachers' collegial interaction: An exploratory study. *Elementary School Journal, 87*(4), 368–393.

# TOPICS AND THEMES FOR FURTHER DISCUSSION

1. Describe the procedures currently in place for professional development in a school system you are familiar with. Then design a model for a process which includes teacher action research. How would such a model be different than the current system?

2. Construct and distribute a survey of faculty in your building to assess professional development needs and interests. How could the data from this survey be utilized to plan professional development for the next 3 years? What did you, as a teacher researcher, learn from this survey process?

3. Observe a school for a week in order to assess the degree to which a culture of learning and caring exists, as Tafel and Fischer describe. What would be the indicators of such a community?

4. Form a Teacher Book Club or Teacher Study Group such as Goff describes at your school. Collaboratively decide what the group's purpose will be. Plan a format for meetings, design a schedule and write a 1–2 page proposal. Discuss the proposal with your building administrator to determine the feasibility of funding and release time. How could such a group contribute to your professional development?

5. Research available grants for teacher research in your state, city or county, and professional associations. Compile a list and distribute in your building. Write a grant proposal and submit an application for funding.

# 7

# TEACHER INQUIRY IN THE TRADITIONS OF SOCIAL SCIENCE RESEARCH: "IS IT REAL?"

Susan Jungck
National-Louis University

## INTRODUCTION

What terms and images come to mind when you hear "research" and specifically, "research in education"? For 10 years now, as I have taught graduate research courses, I have routinely asked teachers to think about and write down their responses to this question. Later, in a group, we share these responses and brainstorm more collective images together. Over the years and through to the present, consistent terms and images dominate their responses:

- large, national-type studies which involve statistics; usually (always?) these studies attempt to *prove* something
- a lot of data
- comparison groups
- boring
- quantitative is all I know—factual type
- control groups
- objectivity
- facts, figures
- lots of jargon
- experimenting
- validating hypotheses
- theories
- cut and dry conclusions

- statistics
- boring in reading
- dusty-shelf material
- library research
- testing ideas
- very involved, a rather awesome task
- fact finding
- no practical application to classroom
- sometimes makes me feel stupid because I can't comprehend [and] knowing and understanding certain ed. research makes me feel smart, superior with it
- it is done by professional scholars (researchers) scientists, etc.—in other words—experts
- not relevant to me
- something I would never do!
- evaluation of teachers (Jungck, 1987)

Overwhelmingly, these teachers' responses correspond to what Agar (1986) and Guba and Lincoln (1994) referred to as the "received view" of the natural and social sciences which has dominated our language for nearly 400 years. Indeed, it is *the* conception of science and research that most of us "received" in elementary school when we memorized what was called "the scientific method." This "received view" is representative of a philosophical paradigm; a worldview consisting of basic beliefs that guide action. A paradigm, according to Guba and Lincoln (1994) "defines, for its holder, the nature of the 'world', the individual's place in it, and the range of possible relationships to that world and its parts. . . . The beliefs are basic in the sense that they must be accepted on faith . . . there is no way to establish their ultimate truthfulness" (p. 107). They go on to say that the paradigmatic beliefs are responses to three fundamental questions: (a) What is the form and nature of reality? (b) What is the nature of the relationship between the knower or would-be-knower and what can be known? and (c) How can the inquirer (would-be-knower) go about finding out whatever he or she believes can be known (p. 108)? Thus, paradigms are not *just* philosophical abstractions; in very direct ways they ground our perceptions of the world, dominate our language, and holistically influence, according to Eisner (1991, p. 8), the very basis of "what we are likely to experience."[1]

---

[1]The "received view" of research reflected in the teachers' comments just mentioned reflect a positivist philosophy, a belief system Guba and Lincoln (1994, pp. 109, 110), describe as:

(Realism) An apprehendable reality is assumed to exist, driven by immutable natural laws and mechanisms. Knowledge of the "way things are" is conventionally summarized in the form of time-and context-free generalizations, some of which take the form of cause-effect laws. Research can, in principle, converge on the 'true' state of affairs. The basic posture of the paradigm is argued to be both reductionistic and deterministic (Hesse, 1980).

Although there probably exists no precise and agreed on definition of positivism, even among positivists, Francis Schrag (1992) claimed that the following prototypical example represents what most would consider positivistic research in education:

> Individuals are selected and allocated to treatment and control groups; the two or more groups are provided alternative 'treatments' and their progress (or decline) on one or more 'dependent variables' is recorded; finally, a statistical evaluation of the results is conducted aimed at assessing whether a difference between the results in the two groups may be caused by chance. (see Wulff, chap. 10)

I see many of these positivistic assumptions reflected in the language of the teachers' responses. Research is done by "experts" and is "something I would never do." Knowledge is investigated by those "professional scholars (researchers)," who as objective investigators are capable of not influencing the objects of their study. Reality is reduced to relationships between precise variables, those "cut and dry conclusions" that, as context-free generalizations, are seen as "not relevant to me." The neat and tidy worlds and results of this approach to research seem apparently unrelated, "boring," and "dusty-shelf material" to many teachers.!2·

---

(Objectivist) The investigator and the investigated "object" are assumed to be independent entities, and the investigator to be capable of studying the object without influencing it or being influenced by it. When influence in either direction . . . is recognized, or even suspected, various strategies are followed to reduce or eliminate it. Inquiry takes place as through a one-way mirror. Values and biases are prevented from influencing outcomes.

(Experimental and manipulative) Questions and/or hypotheses are stated in propositional form and subjected to empirical test to verify them; possible confounding conditions must be carefully controlled (manipulated) to prevent outcomes from being improperly influenced.

[2]Karl Popper's (1968) influential elaboration of a contemporary post-positivistic conception of the "received view" qualifies the assumption of verifiable certainty, the "cut and dryness" of positivism, and describes more what science and scientists can and actually do. Reality or knowledge can never be proved or verified; we can only get closer to understanding it through approximating it by a process he described as falsifying versus verifying hypotheses. In this view, researchers individually are not assumed to be completely objective either; that is an ideal and responsibility shared by the larger collective community of researchers and critics. I have overly simplified the nature of these positivisms, and these teachers' conceptions of it, in my attempt to merely reference a set of beliefs that have dominated the language and practice of education research through most of this century. The significance of this dominant language should not be underestimated. Patti Lather (1991) emphasized the power and significance of the language we use to shape "our experience of 'the real.'" She refers to the contemporary postmodernists' critique of positivism that emphasizes this "in its proposal that the way we speak and write reflect the structures of power in our society . . . language is a productive, constitutive force as opposed to a transparent reflection of some reality" (p. 25). Today critical and postmodernist theorists overwhelmingly emphasize that the language we have available and use greatly influences *what we can consider as real.*

I believe that there have been negative consequences of this dominant positivistic tradition, not in terms of what it has and continues to contribute, but in terms of what and whose knowledge and research has consequently been marginalized. An almost exclusive focus on positivistic research has: (a) emphasized knowedge that is largely reduced to variables, and observable, predictable behaviors, (b) restricted the role of researchers to those outside the classroom, and (c) limited awareness of alternative philosophical frameworks, methods and languages. In particular, the tenets and language of positivism preclude from purview the complex nature of teachers' realities, the influential and subjective relationships they have with those in their environments, and the interpretive and narrative nature of how they come to know and describe their world. It's little surprise, then, that the teachers' responses just mentioned reflect a felt detachment from the dominant "received view" and practice of research that they associate with our field.[3]

Within the historical context, the development and practice of scientifically based knowledge can be seen as Bredo and Feinberg (1982) and Reason (1994) did, a democratizing impulse. Expanding the basis from which knowledge could be developed and legitimated resulted in the expansion of popular participation in the process as well. Meanings are not stable, however; they are relative to historical and situational contexts. A belief system, that in one historical context expanded the nature of what could be considered legitimate knowledge, has in today's context of education functioned to restrain knowledge production. The domination by various forms of positivistic research has come to limit, not expand, the community of researchers and, thus, the forms of knowledge that we generate in our field. As an approach to knowledge it glosses the complexity

---

[3]Historically, the view that knowledge could be *discovered* through observation-based science and reasoning represented an advance over prior traditions that rested knowledge in faith and theological, mythological, and metaphysical systems of thought. Beginning in the mid-17th century, a philosophical shift referenced as the Age of Reason and the Enlightenment, ushered in a new faith based in the potential of science, reason, rationality, and logic as the basis of knowledge and truth claims. Prior to claims that knowledge was based upon science and rationality, knowledge construction and legitimation was limited to those who through divine right and religious ordination had the authority. With the advent of this scientific revolution, these parochial sources of knowledge were challenged and a confidence developed that truth claims could be empirically based and thus verifiable. Knowledge so constructed became more tentative, thereby open to modification and development through rationality and logic. Knowledge production became the legitimate purview of a more broad based community of researchers, less vulnerable to the edicts and self-interests of religious and secular elites (Bredo & Feinberg, 1982, pp. 13–14). This confidence in science and reason persists today, enhanced by the more precise post-positivistic methods and sophisticated quantitative languages. We see this in our field's emphasis on measures of IQs, academic achievement, standardized tests, learning styles and risk factors, all of which are assumed to be scientifically researched and developed descriptions of something real. As such, they are used to make and defend decisions about the ability, readiness, appropriate labelling, grading, promoting and tracking/grouping of students. Thus, we use the modes and methods of scientific rationality to justify our practices, thereby avoiding, sometimes even denying, the role of subjectivity and values in these often controversial and contested decisions.

of teachers' worlds, and misses the cultural realm of meanings and influences that are not directly controllable, measurable, or observable.

The dominant perception and language of what is "real" research has functioned effectively to separate teachers from researchers and teaching from research. Also, by analogy, it supports the myth that theory and practice are separate endeavors. The current teacher-researcher movement addresses much of this. It emerges from an alternative philosophy, communicates through a different language, and proceeds with different methodologies; all of these factors focus on the relationship between knowing and acting, teaching and researching.

## THE PARADOX OF TEACHER RESEARCH: "IS IT REAL?"

There is a contemporary paradox that bothers me and stimulates the remaining focus of this chapter. During the last 10 years, more and more teachers have been encouraged and supported for conducting and publishing research. As Burnaford, Fischer, and Hobson (in this volume) describe, advocates for action research in education and cases of teachers doing research go back more than 50 years; recent years have occasioned a more widely recognized surge of activity. In part, this is attributable to what Cochran-Smith and Lytle (1993, p. 11) referred to as the emergence of more "supportive structures" that value and support teacher research. Professional organizations like the National Council of Teachers of English (NCTE), graduate programs in education, professional development activities, research centers, some government funds, and even more publications devoted to the topic have all contributed to legitimating this research.

The kind of action research that teachers have been doing however, as illustrated so well in this text, is not traditional positivistic research, but what Cochran-Smith and Lytle (1993, p. 13) referred to as "new paradigms and alternative kinds of discourse and analysis." Based on my experience in working with teacher-researchers who are enrolled in my university's master of education degree program, and the first person accounts of teacher research appearing in this text and numerous other recent publications (Bissex & Bullock, 1987; Cochran-Smith & Lytle, 1993; Goswami & Stillman, 1987; Newman, 1990; *Teaching and Change* journal published by NEA & Corwin Press), I am struck by the insight and skills that current teacher-researchers have to understand, affect, and narrate the actions that guide their own practices and those of their students. I believe, that these and most good teachers teach themselves through researching themselves very well. They have, however, less familiarity with the "new paradigms and alternative kinds of discourse and analysis" that philosophically stimulates and grounds their research than they do with the more dominant positivistic paradigm. Consequently, they often appear less than confident that what they are doing is *real research*.

Pat, a former graduate student of mine, illustrated this paradox, a philosophical insecurity that lingers along side experiential expertise, accomplishment, and confidence. Pat was narrating to a group of teacher colleagues a very detailed and reflective account of how her understanding of language development had been deepened through the process of developing a writing workshop in her second-grade classroom that year. She talked about how her own ideas and practices had changed and developed, shaped by her experiences. She talked about "the" current theories of language and writing development and how her understandings both resonated with and challenged them. She had the apt attention of her colleagues, I was inspired, and we were all in the process of celebrating the completion of her written account of this research, when she abruptly stopped. She looked at her newly published book and said, "My husband was disappointed when he read this. He said it didn't sound like research because it was so personal, so subjective. He said, 'researchers don't use 'I'." She asked us, "Is this real research?" Although seemingly confident in her experience and knowledge, she appeared less confident in the legitimacy of her way of knowing. Her colleagues, equally experienced and newly published researchers themselves, weren't so sure either.

In Margery Williams' book *The Velveteen Rabbit* (1983), the rabbit seeks to know the "magic called real." The other toys in the nursery act superior and pretend to be "real"; they were after all, models of things, mechanical in nature, full of "modern ideas" and users of "technical terms" (p. 10). Comparatively, the rabbit feels "insignificant and commonplace," far from what others considered "real" (p. 12). He learns instead that "Real isn't how you are made" or an inherent quality, "it's a thing that happens to you" explains the Skin Horse. "As when a child loves you for a long, long time, not just to play with, but really loves you, then you become real" (p. 12). Through use and through being valued, "reality" is construed and constructed; it cannot be presumed.

The children's book, *The Real Story of the Three Little Pigs by A. Wolf*, Scieszka (1989), provided another relevant response. The wolf tells his version of the story of how the pigs and their houses were destroyed. According to his version, his reality, he is an innocent "victim" framed by the tabloids. According to the remaining pig and the original story teller, he is a "big, bad wolf." According to Scieszka's version, it's a little ambiguous:

> You may think you know the Three Little Pigs and the Big Bad Wolf, but only one person knows the *real* story. That person is A. Wolf. . . . What *really* happened when A. Wolf was at the door? Was it an historic pig out or a Mother Goose frame-up? You read it. You decide. (taken from the book jacket)

Reality is always contingent, constructed, and described from a point of view. Is Pat's research real research?

As "insignificant and commonplace" as the velveteen rabbit, wolf, and these books may seem, they reflect a philosophical belief system which emerged in the late 19th-century as a critique of positivism. I will refer to this paradigm variously as phenomenology, constructivism, or interpretivism. For about 25 years, reseach-ers in education have increasingly conducted research within this paradigm and their work has contributed to a broadening of our perceptions, methods, and language for what is considered "real" research in our field. At the 1994 American Educational Research Association (AERA) Conference, Eugene E. Garcia, the current director of the US Department of Bilingual Education and Minority Language Affairs, references this philosophical and methodological shift:

> The biggest shift in social sciences methodology over the past twenty five years has been the increased emphasis on qualitative, ethnographic, participant-observer approaches. This shift has been supported at the philosophy of science level by the discrediting of the logical positivist's goal of "decontextualized" general law, substituting a recognition of the context-dependence of all scientific statements, and the essential role that quality research must invest in the high costs of providing contextual knowledge. (Newsletter, AERA, Division G, Summer 1994, p. 8)

A constructivist philosophy is fundamental to the shift and methods of which Garcia speaks, and the research of teachers like Craig Hill or Emmerich Koller (in this volume). It basically differs from positivism by assuming that reality and knowledge is created and constructed, not fixed and discovered.[4]

Erickson (1986) characterized the methods and theories of interpretive re-search, with an illustrative prototype that stands in marked contrast to positivistic research:

> Interpretive research is concerned with the specifics of meaning and action in social life that takes place in concrete scenes of face-to-face interaction and that takes place in the wider society surrounding the scene of action. The conduct of interpretive research on teaching involves intense and ideally long-term participant observation in an educational setting followed by deliberate and long-term reflec-tion on what was seen there. That reflection entails the observer's deliberate scru-

---

[4]Guba and Lincoln (1994, pp. 110–111) described these assumptions as:

(Relativist) multiple, apprehendable, and sometimes conflicting social realities that are the products of human intellects, but that may change as their constructors become more informed and sophisticated.

(Transactional and subjectivist) The investigator and the object of investigation are assumed to be interactively linked so that the 'findings' are literally created as the investigation proceeds.

The variable and personal ... nature of social constructions suggests that individual constructions can be elicited and refined only through interaction between and among investigator and respondents.

The inquirer's voice is that of the "passionate participant" actively engaged in facilitating the "multivoice" reconstruction of his or her own construction as well as those of all other participants.

tiny of his or her own interpretive point of view, and of its sources in formal theory, culturally learned ways of seeing, and personal value commitments. As the participant observer learns more about the world out there he or she learns more about himself or herself. (p. 156)

From this description, it's relatively easy to envision teachers doing this kind of research, yet, when Erickson wrote this, it was written from a perspective that presumed the "outside" researcher and elaborated an interpretive framework for doing research on teaching. Since interpretive research only became significant in education research during the 1970s, this article largely functioned to introduce, explain, and validate it as a powerful paradigm. Yet, even within this context, Erickson recognized its logical appropriateness for teacher–researchers as well:

It is a few steps beyond this for the classroom teacher to become the researcher in his or her own right. As Hymes noted (1982), interpretive research methods are intrinsically democratic: one does not need special training to be able to understand the results of such research, nor does one need arcane skills in order to conduct it. Fieldwork research requires skills of observation, comparison, contrast, and reflection that all humans possess. In order to get through life we must all do interpretive fieldwork. What professional interpretive researchers do is to make use of the ordinary skills of observation and reflection in especially systematic and deliberate ways. Classroom teachers can do this as well, by reflecting on their own practice. Their role is not that of the participant observer who comes from the outside world to visit, but that of an unusually observant participant who deliberates inside the scene of action. (p. 157)

Given that neither the focus of this publication nor Erickson's writing was on teacher–researchers, what I find particularly foreshadowing, is the way Erickson chose to end, with a section entitled: "Conclusion: Toward Teachers as Researchers" (p. 156). He made a claim that teachers have a particular vantage point that uniquely positions them as insiders to conduct participant observer research. And beyond that, producing knowledge of their profession is a political and professional imperative:

If classroom teaching in elementary and secondary schools is to come of age as a profession—if the role of teacher is not to continue to be institutionally infantilized—then teachers need to take the adult responsibility of investigating their own practice systematically and critically by methods that are appropriate to their practice. Teachers currently are being held increasingly accountable by others for their actions in the classroom. They need as well to hold themselves accountable for what they do, and to hold themselves accountable for the depth of their insight into their actions as teachers. Time needs to be made available in the school day for teachers to do this. Anything less than that basic kind of institutional change is to perpetuate the passivity that has characterized the teaching profession in its relations with administrative supervisors and the public at large. (p. 157)

I have quoted Erickson's work at length because early on it associated two movements, each of which had momentum individually, in a major and influential publication. Early action and teacher research in education were not always interpretive in nature, and interpretive research in education was not associated at the beginning with teachers. I see the 1980s as a time when these two movements rapidly developed in tandem, and increasingly in conjunction, but this is *not* to say that the growth and validation of interpretive forms of research in education *caused* teachers to suddenly *become* researchers. The occurrence of more and more interpretive research in education more likely provided a new lens through which people could recognize and appreciate alternative versions of *real* research. Having new lenses we were better positioned to "see" the kinds of research that good teachers had always been doing, even encourage it.

I believe that good teachers *have always* conducted this kind of research, though less as a systematic and explicit practice, and more as a natural and necessary one. Thirty years ago, in *Teacher* (1986), Sylvia Ashton-Warner wrote about her teaching experiences in New Zealand, which began in 1932. It is a personal, narrative, and interpretive account of problems (as she saw them) and solutions (as she developed them). She used the first person "I" throughout. Her style was reflective, analytical, passionate, action-oriented, and very subjective. Her methods were not sophisticated, complex, or unbiased. She observed and listened to her students, interpreted her situation, kept a reflective diary, and theoretically related her work to that of Plato, Pythagoras, T. S. Eliot, Fromm, Jung, and others. She planned, implemented, observed, modified, and published her teaching approaches. We are told on the book jacket of the latest publication that her work is relevant to others: "Today her findings are strikingly relevant to the teaching of socially disadvantaged and non-English-speaking students." Is this not research?

## TEACHER RESEARCH METHODS:
## ACTION RESEARCH, PERSONAL EXPERIENCE
## AND NARRATIVE RESEARCH

The cultural anthropologist Clifford Geertz (1973) suggested a perspective that I assume in the remaining section in this chapter:

> If you want to understand what a science is you should look in the first instance not at its theories or findings and certainly not at what its apologists say about it; you should look at what the practioners of it do. (p. 5)

Here Geertz is reflecting a common phenomenological value and research strategy, one "which tries to stay close to the phenomena by avoiding as much as possible all abstraction and imposition of constructs, and by relating always the object of study to the experiences of the subject who does the studying" (Eger, 1993). Teacher–researchers, when they describe and understand their students, classes, colleagues, and curriculum through personal anecdotes and stories are staying "close to the phenomena." I too prefer staying close to the phenomena when discussing some of the methods teachers use in conducting their research. I do this to emphasize that it is the researcher who develops and uses methods, and, interprets and acts on data or information, rather than methods *per se* that is most fundamental to the research. There is nothing inherent in any method, that will automatically lead to worthwhile and meaningful knowledge. Similarly, the worth of any information derived through analyzing observations, interviews, and site documents depends on how a teacher interprets, values, and acts. One of the distinguishing features of interpretive–constructivist research in general, and the teacher–researcher movement in particular, is that they emphasize a researcher's influence as key to the quality and outcome of research and they de-emphasize the idea that methods or data alone are either determinative or suggestive. Methods and data are not seen as independent of researchers; through selecting and implementing methods, and interpreting and valuing data, the researcher's personal involvement is so integral to the process and outcomes, that an axiom in interpretive research asserts the researcher *as* key instrument.

If we observe teachers as they do research, as well as read accounts of their research such as those in this text, we tend to notice among the diversity of methods and approaches, some common themes inherent in the nature of their work. Before discussing the various methods that teachers draw on, I first want to discuss some themes common to their work. In doing research, teachers tend to be, as Clandinin and Connelly (1994) described the process, "simultaneously focused in four directions: inward and outward, backward and forward" (p. 417). I see these directions as perspectives or dimensions through which their research occurs. The authors just mentioned describe what it means to view experience from these various directions:

> By inward we mean the internal conditions of feelings, hopes, aesthetic reactions, moral dispositions. . . . By outward we mean existential conditions, that is, the environment or what E. M. Bruner (1986) calls reality. By backward and forward we are referring to temporality, past, present and future. To experience an experience is to experience it simultaneously in these four ways and to ask questions pointing in each way. (p. 417)

We see examples of teachers simultaneously focusing in all four of these directions in their accounts in this text. Even in the brief descriptive glimpse we get into Jan De Stefano research in chapter 2, she reflects and questions all of these dimensions. Her work spans a 20 year perspective; she situates her current research within the context of her 18 years of experience teaching in, but evolving away from, a "direct teacher-centered method." In her account she narrates her change toward more student centeredness in both her "inward" development and commitment to that philosophy, and her "outward" expression through active curriculum research and development. We see in her account the constant tacking back and forth between an inward focus on her feelings and beliefs and an outward focus on her students and curriculum. For this researcher, a new way of teaching geometry and a new way of thinking about how to teach geometry developed in tandem. Therefore, inner reflection and meaning construction, outer observation and activity, and changes perceived through a time frame, thematically characterize the experience of teacher–researchers.

Differences, however, exist in the degree to which teacher–researchers focus in any of these directions, or assume these perspectives, either in the course of conducting their research or in the outcomes they envision. For example, in Joseph Fischer's typology of research questions, described in chapter 2 of this text, we see different emphases placed on settings and contexts, teaching strategies and content, and visions and hopes for teaching. Teachers' research then, could focus *more* outwardly than inwardly, *more* on understanding a situation than in changing it, *more* intently on the present and future than on the past, or *more* based in narrative reflection than on outward change. Although teachers might not equally or explicitly address or elaborate in their research all the dimensions to their experience, what seems important is the recognition of the dimensional nature of their experiences and the traditions of multidimensional approaches to research. Consequently, research methods that capture, enhance, and illuminate these multidimensional ways of looking and knowing, thereby enabling teachers to "stay close to the phenomena," have emerged as particularly relevant research strategies.

## THREE METHODS FOR RESEARCH: INFLUENCES ON TEACHER ACTION RESEARCH

In particular, three methodological approaches to research, all consistent with the interpretive–constructivist philosophy, have collectively informed much of the recent teacher research: *action research, personal experience or personal accounts, and narrative genres.* Collectively, these methods utilize the power of subjective experiences of the participant to inform all stages of the research endeavor, emphasize the process of constructing knowledge within a context, and focus on conditions and processes of change. Collectively, these methods address, through the data, questions and languages they highlight, multiple dimensions of knowing. Individually each method has particular strengths and teachers tend to draw on them selectively accordingly to their needs, interests, and personalities.

For example, *action research* in the United States is a fifty-year-old tradition associated with social change efforts. Historical accounts, definitions, and interpretations of action research are varied (Noffke, 1994), but Elliott (1991) captured what is central in most, "the study of a social situation with a view to improving the quality of action within it" (p. 69). Central to action research is the aim of improving practice. In the 1940s Kurt Lewin developed a research model that, though modified a bit, persists today as a structure that many teacher–researchers utilize. The model is oriented "outwardly" by focusing research on observation and change in the environment. His model consists of identifying a general idea, information gathering, general planning, developing related actions, implementing and evaluating those actions, and revising the general plan. Researchers are to spiral through conceptualizing, implementing, observing, and revising as they "research by doing." Throughout the cycle there are phases focused on more outwardly observing the effects of one's actions. Data and data gathering techniques tend to focus on collecting evidence about the effectiveness of new strategies and might include things like: interviewing, checklists, questionnaires, inventories, teacher observations and analytic field notes, photos, video- and taperecordings, and document analysis. Both the action research cycle and the kinds of data that are highlighted in it assume researcher reflection and interpretation. Reflection and interpretation tend to be more rational and instrumental to the primary ends of action research, however, which are to develop and evaluate changes in the social environment. Action research tends to be a valued research strategy of teacher–researchers; it honors their keen observational skills, their inclination (indeed obligation) to influence their own environment with an aim toward improving it, and their skill at developing, modifying, and observing simultaneously, on-the-spot! The model systematizes what good teachers tend to do naturally.

We see throughout this volume not only references to the importance of action research as a dynamic model of change, but a tendency to equate action research with teacher research. So too, teacher–researchers routinely describe their research with reference to the temporal component and dynamic of conceptualizing, developing, implementing, and assessing the changes they are making in their classrooms. We see in their practice the realization of the action research model, the production of new or improved practices within their own context. In recent years, action research has become so associated with teacher research, that we are increasingly seeing it recognized in formal degree work, certification programs, professional development, and education reform efforts (Noffke, 1994). Action and teacher research are becoming so linked that, as in this text, we are seeing the phenomena referred to as "teacher action research."

If we consider action research as one methodological strand of teacher research, like the warp in a weaving, then the "personal accounts" (Lancy & Kinkead, 1993) or "personal experience" (Clandinin & Connelly, 1994) strand in interpretive research, like the weft in a weaving, is its complement. *Personal accounts or personal experience methods*, which emphasize the inner dimensions of understanding, experiencing, and interpreting events, are either the oldest or the newest forms of research in education. In a recent book devoted to describing qualitative (interpretive) research traditions in education, Lancy and Kinkead (1993), devoted only a brief section in their chapter on personal accounts research to what they coin as "self-generated case-study" research by teachers. They introduce the methods as so new as to not yet be a tradition, to be in a state of "flux." To them, "self-generated case-study" research by teachers represents only a sub-genre of the new personal accounts methods (p. 169). Although I agree that this is probably the most recent genre of education research to gain adherents, visibility, and legitimacy in the field, I believe that what it represents philosophically and substantively is based on one of the oldest notions of how humans come to know and understand their world.

What is central to this method, and what weaves it so well into the action research cycle, is its directional focus "inward" on processes of knowing and constructing meaning through *narrative*. Bruner (1986, p. 11) described narrative as one of the two fundamental modes (the other being the logico-scientific mode) through which humans order their experiences and construct reality. Similarly, Polkinghorne (1988) asserted how fundamental narrative is:

> Human beings exist in three realms—the material realm, the organic realm, and the realm of meaning. The realm of meaning is structured according to linguistic forms, and one of the most important forms for creating meaning in human existence is the narrative. (p. 183)

Narrative modes of knowing and the methods of personal experience research are focused on interpreting what events mean to the participants involved. As a complement to methods that emphasize behaviors and events, narrative or personal experience research focuses on methods to interpret what events mean. Personal experience methods necessarily and simultaneously focus in directions that Clandinin and Connelly (1994) identify. The personal construction of narrative or story, is the process through which individuals integrate a multidimensional way of knowing. The dynamic nature of narrative is particularly important in research; if we interpret our experiences through narrative, then we can and often do reinterpret those experiences as well. As so many personal accounts of research in this text illustrate, stories of experience and understanding reflect stories of change as well. This represents not only the power of narrative as a way to know, but the potential of this form of research as well to promote growth and change:

> Therefore, difficult as it may be to tell a story, the more difficult but important task in narrative is the retelling of stories that allow for growth and change. (Clandinin & Connelly, 1994, p. 418)

Therefore, the methods of personal accounts research (like autobiography, reflective journals, and field notes of experience) with their essential reliance on the first person "I," are intended to reflect the legitimate and necessary presence of a researcher. Narrative accounts of experience and research reflect the processes through which current understandings are derived as well as their temporality; they are not definitive or static findings.

Thus, we tend to see that teacher research is characterized by a blending of methods that have complementary strengths. Not only do the methods of action, personal experience, and narrative research complement each other, they collectively enable the teacher as researcher to validate and weave together dimensions of their experience. It will be teachers who continue to develop these methods to best enable them who will accomplish this integration and valuation.

## CONCLUDING REAL QUESTIONS

Is teacher research real research? Where? With whom?

When teachers as researchers are affirmed; when teacher knowledge is respected; when teacher language is legitimate; when theory, practice and reflection are united; when teacher–researchers are experts, change agents, producers, and consumers of meaningful knowledge; when teachers pioneer new methods of knowing; who *really* benefits?

## REFERENCES

Agar, M. H. (1986). *Speaking of ethnography.* Newbury Park, CA: Sage.

American Educational Research Association. (1994, Summer). *Newsletter of Division G: The Social Context of Education.* Washington, DC: AERA.

Ashton-Warner, S. (1986). *Teacher.* New York: Simon & Schuster. Original work published in 1963.

Bissex, G. L., & Bullock, R. H. (Eds.). (1987). *Seeing for ourselves: Case study research by teachers of writing.* Portsmouth, NH: Heinemann.

Bredo, E., & Feinberg, W. (Eds.). (1982). *Knowledge & values in social & educational research.* Philadelphia: Temple University Press.

Bruner, J. (1986). *Actual minds, possible worlds.* Cambridge, MA: Harvard University Press.

Clandinin, D. J., & Connelly, F. M. (1994). Personal experience methods. In N. K. Denzin & Y. S. Lincoln (Eds.), *Handbook of qualitative research* (pp. 413–427). Thousand Oaks, CA: Sage.

Cochran-Smith, M., & Lytle, S. L. (1993). *Inside outside: Teacher research and knowledge.* New York: Teachers College Press.

Eger, M. (1993). Hermeneutics as an approach to science: Part II. *Science & Education, 2,* 303–328.

Eisner, E. (1991). *The enlightened eye: Qualitative inquiry and the enhancement of educational practices.* New York: Macmillan.

Elliott, J. (1991). *Action research for educational change.* Philadelphia: Open University Press.

Erickson, F. (1986). Qualitative methods in research on teaching. In M. Wittrock (Ed.), *Handbook of research on teaching* (3rd ed., pp.119–161). New York: Macmillan.

Geertz, C. (1973). *The interpretation of cultures: Selected essays.* New York: Basic Books.

Goswami, D., & Stillman, P. R. (Eds.). (1987). *Reclaiming the classroom: Teacher research as an agency for change.* Portsmouth, NH: Boynton/Cook (Heinemann).

Guba, E. G., & Lincoln, Y. S. (1994). Competing paradigms in qualitative research. In N. K. Denzin & Y. S. Lincoln (Eds.), *Handbook of qualitative research* (pp. 105–117). Thousand Oaks, CA: Sage.

Jungck, S. (1987, November). *Alternatives for curriculum inquiry in teacher education.* Paper presented at the meeting of the American Educational Studies Association, Chicago, IL.

Lancy, D. F., & Kinkead, J. (1993). Personal accounts. In D. F. Lancy (Ed.), *Qualitative research in education: An introduction to the major traditions* (pp. 168–207). New York: Longman.

Lather, P. (1991). *Getting smart: Feminist research and pedagogy with/in the postmodern.* New York: Routledge.

Newman, J. M. (1990). *Finding our own way.* Portsmouth, NH: Heinemann.

Noffke, S. (1994). Action research: towards the next generation. *Educational Action Research, 2*(1), 9–21.

Polkinghorne, D. E. (1988). *Narrative knowing and the human sciences.* Albany, NY: State University of New York Press.

Popper, K. (1968). *Conjectures and refutations.* New York: Harper & Row.

Reason, P. (1994). Three approaches to participative inquiry. In N. K. Denzin & Y. S. Lincoln (Eds.), *Handbook of qualitative research* (pp. 324–339). Thousand Oaks, CA: Sage.

Schrag, F. (1992). In defense of positivist research paradigms. *Educational Researcher, 21*(5), 5–7.

Scieszka, J. (1989). *The true story of the 3 little pigs by A. Wolf.* New York: Penguin Books.

Williams, M. (1983). *The velveteen rabbit.* New York: Alfred A. Knopf. Original work published in 1922.

# Overcoming Paradigm Paralysis: A High School Teacher Revisits Foreign Language Education

Emmerich Koller
Glenbrook North High School

*Whatever you can do or dream, you can begin.*
*Boldness has genius, power and magic in it.*
*Begin it now.*

—Goethe, 1904

## A NEW BEGINNING

At age 50, after 27 years of teaching, I have found something that has made teaching very exciting again. I am quite aware of the fact that by expressing such enthusiasm, especially among some of my more tired colleagues, I run the risk of being trivialized as an idealist, or someone who by some miracle escaped the disappointments that often come with many years in the trenches and therefore not qualified to address true veterans in the field. The fact is that I have not escaped most of the tribulations of public school teaching and I am well acquainted with that burned-out feeling. That, more than anything else, gives me legitimacy and a right to tell my story.

It is my hope to embolden my colleagues out there who might also be willing to dream as I did, regardless of age or specialty, and to encourage them as Goethe does: to begin it now. What follows is an account of how I managed to move from *paradigm paralysis* to a fundamentally new approach to my teaching.

There were several arguments against embarking on such an adventure. Two years ago, I would have argued against expending too much effort for an uncertain outcome. The daily demands of teaching and the extra, often unnecessary burdens placed on teachers by their administrators are often so demanding that any serious consideration of making a radical shift is usually dismissed outright. The other deterring element was the perception that something that works well enough shouldn't be fixed. I am a German teacher at a suburban high school north of Chicago and I have received national recognition for my work. My students have accumulated a record number of awards for their outstanding achievements in German. Obviously things were going well enough. Why change anything?

My reasons for change were, first, that I had been experiencing some dissatisfaction with the way my slower students fared in my classes. Second, I was determined not to allow myself to fade yet; I still wanted to learn and grow. Third, I've managed to maintain the basic belief that most students' potential is much greater than what we educators manage to elicit.

It has always been my professional goal to help my students realize their full potential and never to be content to settle for the average. I think most of my students have sensed my sincerity and faith in them and that, more than anything else, explains their success in the past. But there were others who did not succeed, whom I could not reach. In this I found the frustration and the dissonance in my professional life—the problem that I wanted to tackle and hopefully solve. And so I made it the task of my research project to find a way that would transform both the atmosphere and the learning process in my classroom, to such an extent that it would make learning truly joyful and, consequently, more effective. I decided to seek my solution where I had not looked before, in the exciting new findings of brain research. Isn't it curious that as professionals dealing with the mind, we teachers in general show little interest in the functioning of the brain? Even a cursory glance at brain research and its implications for education made me realize that the task I was about to undertake was not going to be a mere intellectual exercise. For so many years I have successfully used traditional concrete-sequential teaching methods that called for a lot of memorization on the part of my students. I felt safe and secure with that approach. It brought me respect within my profession and my students occasionally feared me as a *macho* teacher, dubbing me "Killer Koller." As I became aware of the unusual methods that brain-based teaching called for and the fundamental changes I would have to undergo, I came to know the real meaning of *paradigm paralysis*. It stands for a real monster that makes any significant change difficult, if not impossible.

## A MONSTER WITHIN US

Confronting my paralysis often reminded me of a story by Dick Gackenbach (1977) called *Harry and the Terrible Whatzit* that I used to read to my little daughter. There was this little boy, Harry, who was deathly afraid of the terrible "Whatzit" down in his basement. One day Harry simply could not avoid going down there because his mom had gone there earlier to get a jar of pickles and had not returned yet. He had to go and help her. Unbeknownst to him, she had gone to the garden by way of another door. Once in the basement, Harry had to confront this double-headed, three-clawed, six-toed, long-horned "Whatzit" who predictably jumped out from behind the furnace, his hiding place. Having no choice in the matter, little Harry confronted the terrible "Whatzit," displaying his courage with a broom stick. To the emboldened boy's great surprise the "Whatzit" turned out to be a cowardly monster who grew smaller and smaller with each threat and swat. Before vanishing completely, Harry magnanimously sent the whimpering, now miniscule monster to Sheldon Parker, who lived next door. Making a significant change, a *paradigm shift*, means confronting a monster within us and it takes some courage and perseverance.

I began with a thorough examination of my perceptions and paradigms. I asked myself, if perhaps I was so blinded by the old methods of foreign language instruction, and even by my past success, that I did not see the new opportunities that could perhaps revolutionize my teaching in such a way that all my students could profit equally well.

## THE OLD APPROACH

There have always been some students who sat there in front of me, whose faces and body language exhibited utter boredom and disinterest. There were some who tried sincerely to learn the language, but after 3 or 4 years have barely mastered the fundamental skills. And there were those who came into my class unable to pay attention due to the emotional pain and stress they were carrying with them. How could I reach such students? Clearly the old approach didn't reach them.

When I first began teaching as a young man, fresh out of college, I was not hampered by any foreign language methods. No one had told me how to conduct a language class before I actually stood in front of my first group of students. For that reason my teaching was unique, unorthodox perhaps, yet effective. Then I had to become certified and I had to take methods courses. To fit into a new school I had to teach German the way languages were traditionally taught in that particular school. To be tenured I had to go along with the latest fad, which was followed by several more "perfect solutions" to language teaching. Paradigm was forced upon paradigm. All along I was able to maintain a reasonable amount of individuality, and when it produced remarkable results, I also regained autonomy in my classroom and some freedom to explore and search for an approach that would add a new dimension to my work. My hope was to blend old and new, to retain those aspects of my teaching that had brought me success and give them new meaning and relevance within the framework of a new approach.

## "ACCELERATED LEARNING": THE NEW APPROACH

As I explored foreign language brain-based approaches, I encountered terms such as suggestopedia, whole-brain learning, optimalearning, the natural approach, total physical response, and superlearning, all of which rest on basically the same assumptions that I discuss shortly. Here in America these approaches all gather under one umbrella, The Society for Accelerated Learning and Teaching (SALT). Accelerated learning stands for brain-based learning, that is, natural learning and therefore accelerated (Rose, 1985; Schuster & Gritton, 1986). Accelerated learning takes into account what we have learned from psychology and the recent findings of brain research. The various methods are still evolving and changing with the increasing understanding of how our brain works. Those who implement these methods are motivated by the fact that even though we are just beginning to understand how our brain functions, we already know enough to see the error of our old ways, and with some courage and imagination we could make drastic changes in our teaching that would bring about dramatic changes in learning as well.

## A PARADIGM PIONEER

Dr. Georgi Lozanov, a renowned psychiatrist, physician, and educational researcher in Bulgaria, was the first to combine the results of psychology, yoga and brain research with education. In 1979, Lozanov coined the term "suggestopedia" to refer to the application of suggestion to the improvement of education and learning (Lozanov, 1979). He has applied his findings to language teaching to prove his theory and he achieved incredible results (Lozanov & Gateva, 1988). His methods have been adopted and used by many schools first in Eastern Europe and Russia, and in the last two decades, throughout the world.

Suggestopedia is a brain-based learning method that is designed to tap our brain's vast, unused capacity. It is estimated that we use only about 5% of our brain's capacity. From psychology, Lozanov incorporates the use of suggestive factors in teaching. We all know, for example, that a teacher's tone of voice, dress, attitude, even facial expression can trigger interest or rejection in students. From yoga, Lozanov took the ideas of mind and body rhythms, as well as techniques for relaxation and concentration. From neurology and biology comes the knowledge of hemisphericity and its importance in education. The left brain hemisphere takes care of verbal–intellectual-sequential functions, whereas the right brain hemisphere takes care of intuitive–spacial-associative ones. Unfortunately, in traditional teaching the left hemisphere is addressed much more and the right hemisphere is often ignored. Lozanov does not advocate that learning become right-hemisphere-dominant, but that both hemispheres be engaged equally, because that makes learning most effective.

In summary, Lozanov's suggestopedia rests on the following tenets:

1. We have a great innate potential that needs to be tapped.
2. Suggestion is the means by which we tap our reserve capacities.
3. We always operate with conscious and subconscious levels simultaneously. These must be carefully orchestrated for best effect.
4. The negative norms in us must be desuggested.
5. Every stimulus is associated, coded, symbolized, and generalized.
6. The teacher's authority and trustworthiness is essential for learning.
7. A child-like and playful state is an effective way to tap reserve capacities.
8. Pseudopassivity is a highly receptive state that is necessary for absorbing information. Appropriate music helps us to attain this state.
9. In communication several levels are operating simultaneously. Those below the level of consciousness such as tone of voice, facial expression, and posture, can be very significant.
10. Peripheral stimuli can be orchestrated to suggest a desired outcome. One must never underestimate the significance of peripheral perceptions.
11. Suggestopedic teaching and learning is always joyful and pleasant. Without this the reserves will not be reached.
12. Music and role-playing are important features of suggestopedia.

I had no difficulty accepting most of the basic principles of brain-based learning as formulated by Lozanov and other pioneers. They made sense to me and often I felt like saying: "Why didn't I think of that?" But it was quite another matter putting these principles into practice. One doesn't need courage to read about and even accept brain-based teaching theories, but one does need a fair amount of courage to set aside old teaching habits, prepare an accelerated learning lesson, and then walk into a classroom and teach it with conviction!

Initially, I could not envision myself implementing these approaches in my classroom. Classical music to read dialogues to? "Surfing" with the music? Warm-up and breathing exercises? Visualizations and mind calming? Dimmed lights? Mind maps? Changing seats all the time? Self-corrected quizzes? No threat, no pressure? I considered all these practices as truly "far-out" and initially I couldn't see myself implementing them in my classes.

## PUTTING THEORY INTO PRACTICE

One of the German classes that I faced each day during my earliest stage of transition was my Academy 3 class, a group of talented students in their third year of German that was just finishing chapter one of Franz Kafka's (1971) *Verwandlung (Metamorphosis)*. I came up with a number of different activities that the students could choose from. These activities included preparing mind maps, acting out parts of the story, and writing poems, songs, and lists of various grammar structures.

Such assignments were quite new to this group and so I was anxious to see what would develop. To my surprise, their reaction was very positive and the activities truly enjoyable. Brian, for example, decided to simultaneously act out and describe the predicament of Gregor Samsa, the hero of the story, who after a night of restless dreams wakes up to discover that he has turned into an ugly bug. Lying there on his back on top of my desk, his limbs flailing helplessly in imitation of the bug's many legs, and recounting Gregor's inner confusion in the language of the author was a scene not soon to be forgotten by his classmates. Jonathan and Emily wrote and presented creative poems. Andy wrote and composed a song about Gregor. For his performance we had to go to a room with a piano because he accompanied himself as he sang his song. All of this was, of course, done in German.

One would not consider these activities as too different or unique to the accelerated learning approach. No doubt, one could find such activities in other foreign language classes. But they were different for this class, and for me it was the easiest possible entry into accelerated learning. Many of the students chose to do a mind map. Such an exercise helps one to organize the main ideas of a theme in a manner that corresponds much more to the way our brain functions. This type of outline is not linear and systematic in the traditional sense. A mind map is an expanding and creative development of a central theme, with major elements branching off from the center in all directions and seeking out, as it were, related and interconnected aspects as they move further from the center (see Fig. 7.1).

I began my first-year German class with some relaxation exercises. A typical accelerated learning session usually begins with a short physical warm-up to get the blood flowing, some breathing exercises to get oxygen into the brain, and a short mind-calming session to make both mind and body relaxed, and thus more receptive to learning. Threat and stress are two of the most serious obstacles to learning. My classes are no exception. Because this was a totally new procedure for my students and a difficult step for me, I first explained the underlying theory behind all these activities. The students' reaction was mixed. None of them reacted negatively, but they did wonder what was happening to me. With a grin on their faces, they asked me if I was all right. The boys seemed to be a little embarrassed, perhaps for me. I did not use music at first. I was sure they would reject it outright. In the end the use of classical music was the most popular feature of this new approach.

Other changes that I made for this class at this early stage were: the introduction of frequent self-corrected quizzes; grouping the chapter's vocabulary according to some meaningful pattern; seating students in a semi-circle; doing mind maps with text and drawings on the board; and assigning mind maps as homework. I encouraged the students to be as artistic as they could be. Once the students were

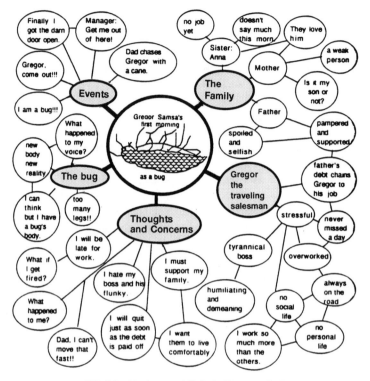

FIG. 7.1. Mind map of Kafka's *Metamorphosis*.

fully aware of what I was looking for, these mind maps became works of art. All of them ended up on the classroom's bulletin board. For most of these students it was the first time they had their work displayed in my classroom. The reason behind this assigment is obvious. Students will remember drawings much better than plain words in a vocabulary list, especially if they themselves did the drawing and writing. It is a right-brain activity. If they also get a positive emotional feedback, such information becomes firmly anchored in their long-term memory. As my confidence grew, I tried other strategies that I thought would be practical and useful and I implemented them in all of my classes.

It soon became clear that my students really liked this new approach. Eric and Danielle, for example, flourished particularly well. The transformation that took place in these two students corresponded perfectly to the predictions of accelerated learning experts. Both of these students had great difficulties in my classes and I often wondered why they even bothered to go on. Suddenly they were receiving As and turning in unexpectedly creative projects. Eric used to hide in class; now he spoke up and wanted to read the text to the accompaniment of the music. I was pleasantly surprised by his good delivery. He and his partner, Dan, were involved in radio and television broadcasting and they made use of their expertise to do projects for their German class. They presented their projects with much humor and enthusiasm to everyone's enjoyment in class.

Danielle, who had received only low grades since her first year, was now in her third year suddenly getting As. She kept saying that what we were doing now was "simply awesome." I have never seen her as excited and happy in my class. On one occasion she did a video with Lisa and she included her entire family who all played parts. After one of the classes, she asked me to see her last four grades in my grade book. They were all As. The moment was as gratifying to me as it was to her. She wished that all her classes could be taught this way. For Danielle, an artistic, creative, and imaginative person, this was the perfect approach because it gave her the opportunity to receive and process information that suited her learning style. Her homework revealed all her talents. I assured her that she was never less smart than her classmates; she just had not been taught in the way she learned best.

In my concluding notations in my journal I noted that accelerated learning works indeed, and that the students liked it and asked for more. A return to the old approach would have caused a rebellion. They were cooperative, enthusiastic, and also creative. Often they suggested original ways to cover the material. They especially enjoyed the Baroque music. They spoke German more freely, their grades were higher than normal and they had smiles on their faces. On the negative side, I found the physical environment not conducive to this approach. The lack of windows, patched linoleum floors, bright fluorescent lights that could not be dimmed, uncomfortable chairs, a less-than-adequate sound system, insufficient bulletin board space, and yellow walls produced a classroom that lacked warmth and friendliness.

## SCHNUPF DIE SCHNECKE

Toward the end of the first semester I introduced a truly mind-blowing teaching aid, a puppet. The purpose was to ease the fear of students who are sometimes timid when they are required to speak in class. It is so much easier to have a conversation with a cute puppet than one's teacher. The puppet is a snail named **Schnupf die Schnecke** (Sniffles the Snail). I introduced Schnupf as a refugee snail from Strasbourg. Bilingual since birth, he now speaks only German. He escaped from France after his entire family was wiped out by escargot-eaters. Schnupf is now a resident of the Black Forest and currently at my school on a cultural exchange. After an initial expression of disbelief by some of my students, Schnupf was soon accepted in class. Once he was actually kidnapped and held hostage an entire weekend by one of the students and threatened to be taken to a French restaurant unless I promised not to give an upcoming test. Another student borrowed him for a weekend and now insists on personally carrying him back to my office after each appearance in class. Furthermore, if Schnupf is not brought to class on a regular basis students begin to clamor for him. Clearly, Schnupf has added a dimension to my class that far exceeds my expectation. I believe Schnupf has allowed some students to escape to a secure world where there is no fear of making mistakes.

## CONCLUSION

After 10 weeks I administered a survey for two reasons. I needed my students' honest reaction to accelerated learning and I also needed their feedback that might support me in my request for more financial assistance down the road. A quick glance at this survey shows that all my students found the accelerated learning approach to be more fun than the traditional approach. Most said that it is less difficult and more interesting. Most of them also felt that they were learning more vocabulary and useful expressions and that they were more comfortable, relaxed, and motivated. Only one student would have preferred the traditional approach. The majority wanted more music, more mind calming, and self-corrected quizzes. They especially liked acting out roles and thought the amount of homework for the course was appropriate.

Because my initial experimentation with accelerated learning proved to be quite successful, I subsequently adopted this approach for all of my classes to the point of writing my own text and producing sound and videotapes to accompany the text.

It has been a most interesting journey that started with a puzzlement caused by seemingly unmotivated and low-achieving students in my classes. Even though a practical solution to the problem was hoped for, it was not anticipated. The journey itself with its discoveries along the way would have been sufficient reward. However, because I have actually found a solution, I consider myself fortunate indeed.

The puzzlement that led me on my journey came from observing some of my students attending but not learning much in my classroom in spite of my best efforts. Juxtaposed to such observations was a basic belief of mine that anyone who learned his native language can also learn a second language if the right conditions for learning can be found.

My own experience with language learning and our poor rate of success in foreign languages convinced me that the methods used in most schools are fundamentally flawed. When I arrived in this country at the age of 19 with no prior knowledge of English, I was not put into a class where I was made to memorize vocabulary words and grammar rules, and I never filled out a worksheet. My progress in such a class would have been slow at best. Instead, I was placed into freshman college classes along with all my new American classmates. The input was massive and it came from all directions. The information was not systematic and no one established an artificial plan of studies for me. No expert educator made me learn the conjugation of verbs first and perhaps the relative clauses last. I was exposed to the simplest and most complicated structures of the language all at once. This type of input was truly abstract–random and my own brain found the language patterns all by itself because our brain is the best pattern-finding machine there is.

We in education have traditionally ignored the capacities of our brain. For centuries we have organized all information, packaged it as we saw fit, then doled it out piecemeal. Because such a process is unnatural, it induces stress in the learner, causing the learner to downshift. The poor performance that follows causes further stress and ultimately failure. With our well-intentioned but ill-guided actions, we educators can actually choke off the brain's natural and almost limitless potential to absorb and synthesize information.

My acquisition of English was not accomplished in the classroom alone; indeed, most of it took place outside the classroom, where learning was truly natural and joyful because it was supported by a universe of stimuli that enabled my whole brain to be engaged. I will never forget my first truly American breakfast. My first contact with a box of American cereal was not just a word on a list, but it was encountered with all my senses. The cornflakes had a taste and smell unlike anything else I had eaten before; it came in a neat, colorful box within which there was a bag, the significance of which escaped me at the time. The crunching sound of the flakes was also unique and in the process of eating them, I also learned the words for milk and sugar, spoon and bowl, sweet and good, and probably many others. And because I actually managed to convey to my breakfast companions that corn is eaten only by farm animals where I came from, I also learned the words for horse, pig, and duck, and some basic cultural differences. I walked away from that first American breakfast table with scores of new words and concepts that I was never going to forget again. Hundreds of such experiences through each day and many thousands in the following weeks and months went into my language acquisition experience.

How can we expect our students to learn a language with little mini-dialogs at the beginning of each chapter, a list of vocabulary at the end, and some grammar drills in-between? I know my experience cannot be duplicated in a high school classroom, but much can be done to make learning more brain compatible.

We know now that a relaxed mind is more receptive to information, that music helps to establish that relaxed state, that the mind absorbs knowledge also subconsciously, that the brain has a vast potential that we are not tapping, that it can deal with much more knowledge than we allow it to receive and that it assimilates knowledge in many more ways than just the linear, logical sequence so common in our schools. All these aspects can be orchestrated in a classroom in such a way that the learner is actually unaware of the intent of these techniques or of the near automatic learning that is taking place. The learner is immersed in an experience that is joyful because learning that is natural is always joyful. Once this condition is established in a learning environment, learning becomes limitless.

Putting into action that which my mind found to be right was very challeng-ing—it meant overcoming paradigm paralysis. As I struggled to put theory into practice I found the challenges formidable but not insurmountable. My transfor-mation was a gradual, sometimes painful, sometimes exhilarating process that continues today and may never be completed. Therein lies not only the chal-lenge but also the reward for daring to do something new, because success lies in the journey, not in the destination.

## REFERENCES

Gackenbach, D. (1977). *Harry and the terrible whatzit.* New York: Houghton Mifflin.
Goethe, J. W. (1904). *Goethe on Shakespeare: Selections from Carlyle's translation of Wilhelm Meis-ters.* London: De La More Press.
Kafka, F. (1971). *The complete stories of Franz Kafka.* New York: Schocken Books.
Lozanov, G. (1979). *Suggestology and Suggestopedy.* The Lozanov Report to the UNESCO.
Lozanov, G., & Gateva, G. (1988). *The foreign language teacher's suggestopedic manual.* New York: Gordon and Breach Science Publishers.
Rose, C. (1985). *Accelerated learning.* England: Clays Ltd.
Schuster, D. H., & Gritton, C. E. (1986). *Suggestive accelerative learning techniques.* New York: Gordon and Breach.

## RELATED READINGS

Caine, R. N., & Caine, G. (1991). *Making connections: Teaching and the human brain.* Alexandria, VA: Banta Company.
Christensen, R., Neal, B. W., & Christensen, J. (filmmakers). (1989). *Paradigms* (a video film). Infinity Limited and Charthouse Learning Corporation.
Connolly, C. (1992, April). *SALT Basics.* Workshop given at the International Society for Accel-erated Learning and Teaching Conference, Minneapolis, MN.
Covey, S. R. (1989). *The habits of highly effective people.* New York: Simon and Schuster.
Dewey, J. (1938). *Experience and education.* New York: Macmillan Publishing Co.
Dhority, L. (1984). *Acquisition through creative teaching.* Sharon, MA: Center for Continuing De-velopment.
Eggers, P. (1984, Dec. 4) Suggestopedia: An innovation in language learning. *Media & Methods,* 17–19.
Ellison, L. (1992, April). *Educator's guide to the brain.* Paper presented at the International SALT Conference, Minneapolis, MN.
Ellison, L. (1990, Fall). What does the brain have to do with learning. *Holistic Education Review.* 41–46.
Ellison, L. (1990). Whole brain strategies do accelerate learning. *Consortium for Whole Brain Learning, 9*(3), 1–2.
Gold, L. (1992, April). *A day unlike all other days.* Workshop given at the International SALT Conference, Minneapolis, MN.
Hart, L. (1983). *Human brain, human learning.* New York: Longman.
Krashen, S. D., & Terrell, T. D. (1983). *The natural approach.* Hayward, CA: The Alemany Press.
Krashen, S. D. (1982). *Principles and practice in second language acquisition.* Exeter, England: A. Wheaton & Co. Ltd.

Rand, P., & Gompartz, R. (1992, April). *Optima learning.* Paper presented at the International SALT Conference, Minneapolis.

Schaefer, D. A. (1980). My experience with the Lozanov Methods. *Foreign Language Annals, 15*(5), 273–283.

Schmidt, C. (1992). *The Lozanov method.* Letter distributed at the International SALT Conference 1992, Minneapolis, MN.

Sternberg, R. J. (1992, April). *The Nature of Intelligence.* Paper presented at the International Society for Accelerated Learning and Teaching Conference, Minneapolis, MN.

# TOPICS AND THEMES
# FOR FURTHER DISCUSSION

1. Prepare an explanation of why teacher action research is "real" research. Include the historical context for such research and contrast this paradigm with other perspectives on research.

2. Read Sylvia Ashton Warner's book *Teacher* and discuss how her work can be and cannot be characterized as teacher research.

3. Jungck describes three methodological approaches to research that have contributed to what we know as *teacher research*: (a) action research, (b) personal experience/accounts, and (c) narrative genres. Summarize each approach; then discuss how much influence each has had or is having on your work as a teacher researcher. Analyze the teacher research in this text to determine the influence of each of these methodological approaches.

4. Write about how your research would be different if it were conducted by an outside ethnographic researcher. How would your role be affected? How would the methods for collecting and interpreting data be different?

5. Emmerich Koller describes what happened in his foreign language teaching as a "paradigm shift." Discuss what this means and then write about the "paradigm" that seems to be influential in your teaching.

# AFTERWORD

Every day, teachers engage in authentic research methods in their own lived experiences. They develop curriculum for their classes, they search for alternative hypotheses when dealing with an especially challenging student, and they base their own methods for instruction on the "data" they collect each year with a new group of children in the classroom. They gather results, draw conclusions, and base future actions on those conclusions. Nonetheless, classroom teachers do not exist *primarily* to produce research. Their job is to do "good work", as Kincheloe (1991) described it, meaning that they are there to promote knowledge, build and utilize critical reflection, feel uncertainty, act according to their instincts and prior experiences and, in doing all these things, pursue inquiry. For them, *purpose* governs standards for research.

How will teachers know when it is research? We see Eisner's (1994) criterion of referential adequacy as one that can be applied to teacher research. Eisner (1994) suggested that we address the question of "whether it's research" to the critical community to which a researcher belongs; in other words, ask *teachers* whether their needs are being met by their own classroom inquiry. Ask *teachers* whether they can and do learn from listening and responding to a community of teacher–researchers as they explore ways to learn and teach in their classrooms.

We believe that the agenda for educational research can and must come largely from this constituency—the teachers themselves. Teacher research as a movement acknowledges that there is much knowledge that can only be generated by those who are in classrooms regularly with children and who try to continually improve the teaching that occurs there. Atkin (1989) asserted: "the progress of meaningful school reform will be stalled until teachers emerge from their marginal positions in the research community and become full partners in the conception and the conduct of educational inquiry" (p. 205).

For this reason, we believe that teacher research must play a significant role in all aspects of teacher education programming. Pre-service or apprentice teachers can benefit from learning the tools of being researcher teachers as they examine themselves and how it will be for them as teachers in the classroom. They can experience a redefined role of "teacher" as one who questions, who asks students to question, and who listens as much as talks. Inservice or graduate programs in teacher education can build on the knowledge base that experienced teachers already possess, and move on to encourage more critical reflection that suggests change in both structure and content of schooling.

When teachers experience the role of being researchers, when they become engaged in a collaborative community that supports them as they take risks and experiment in their classrooms, and when they begin to see their students as co-researchers, things change in classrooms. Cochran-Smith and Lytle (1993) claimed that "what goes on in the classrooms of teacher researchers is qualitatively different from what typically happens in classrooms" (p. 101). Teacher education programs have the obligation to introduce, encourage, and sustain teacher research, which can make such a difference in what children experience in school.

Finally, researchers who are also teachers learn about themselves and who they bring to the tasks of teaching. Their own autobiographies are critical to the challenges of teaching and research that promote narrative inquiry and invite them to connect the personal and the professional. "Research ability provides the vehicle by which teachers reach the emancipatory goal of learning to teach oneself," Kincheloe maintains (1991, p. 25).

Meaning is messy; it transcends what we started out *thinking* we knew. It engages us with our colleagues—students, teachers, administrators, university professors. It expands the possibilities for self-awareness. It holds the promise of reform that changes how and what children learn in schools. We invite the reader to work the edges of the definition for educational research—and bring teachers to the center of the dialogue.

## REFERENCES

Atkin, J. M. (1989). Can educational research keep pace with education reform? *Phi Delta Kappan*, November, 200–205.

Cochran-Smith, M., & Lytle, S. L. (1993). *Inside outside: Teacher research and knowledge*. New York: Teachers College Press.

Eisner, E. W. (1994, April). *Yes, but is it research?* Symposium presentation at the annual meeting of the American Educational Research Association, New Orleans, LA.

Kincheloe, J. L. (1991). *Teachers as researchers: Qualitative inquiry as a path to empowerment*. London: The Falmer Press.

# Author Index

## A

Agar, M. H., 166
Agee, J., 77
Ahlgrem, A., *117–118*
Allport, 4
Altwerger, B., *83, 84*
Apple, M., 7
Argyris, C., 2
Ashton-Warner, S., 173
Asoko, H., *114*
Atkin, J. M., 193–194
Atwell, N., 2
Avery, C. S., 77
Ayers, W., 8

## B

Barth, R. S., 107, 133, 138
Battista, M., *114*
Beane, J. A., *68,* 68
Bertani, A. A., *133*
Bettelheim, B., *26*
Bickel, W. E., *63*
Biklen, S. K., *71, 72*
Bissex, G. L., *57, 169*

Bizar, M., *61*
Bogdan, R. C., *71, 72*
Boles, K., *148*
Boomer, G., 104
Bowen, B., 145
Brandes, D., *97*
Bredo, E., *168*
Bristow, P. S., *138*
Brodhagen, B. L., *68,* 69
Brodine, J. S., *13*
Brown, A., *84*
Brown, D. S., 146
Bruner, J., 174, 177
Buber, M., 135
Bullock, R. H., *57, 169*
Burnaford, G., *68*

## C

Calkins, L., 20
Cantor, N., 4
Caplan, P. J., *52*
Carr. J. F., *68*
Carr, W., 48
Clandinin, D. J., *49, 174, 176, 177*
Clark, C. M., 70

# SUBJECT INDEX